WOMEN WHO **KILL** MEN

Law in the American West

SERIES EDITOR   John R. Wunder, University of Nebraska–Lincoln

WOMEN WHO **KILL** MEN

California Courts, Gender, and the Press

GORDON MORRIS BAKKEN & BRENDA FARRINGTON

UNIVERSITY OF NEBRASKA PRESS   LINCOLN & LONDON

© 2009 by the Board of Regents of
the University of Nebraska

A portion of chapter 1 has been previously
published in "The Limits of Patriarchy: The
'Unwritten Law' in California Legal History,"
in *California History: A Topical Approach*,
ed. Gordon Morris Bakken. Copyright ©
2003 by Harlan Davidson, Inc. Reprinted by
permission.

Library of Congress Cataloging-
in-Publication Data

Bakken, Gordon Morris. Women who kill
men: California courts, gender, and the press /
Gordon Morris Bakken and Brenda Farrington.
      p. cm. — (Law in the American West)
Includes bibliographical references and index.
ISBN 978-0-8032-1361-6 (cloth : alk. paper)
1. Trials (Murder)—California. 2. Women—
California—Legal status, laws, etc.—History.
3. Sex discrimination in criminal justice
administration—California—History.
4. Women murderers—California—Social
aspects. I. Farrington, Brenda. II. Title.
KF221.M8B36 2009
345.794'02523—dc22
2009014060

Set in Sabon by Kim Essman.

To
Our Mentors:
John Phillip Reid
New York University Law School
and
David Ibsen
Fullerton College

CONTENTS

ACKNOWLEDGMENTS

We owe a great deal to Keith Pacholl of the University of West Georgia. Keith read the entire manuscript and made invaluable suggestions. Karen Lystra of California State University, Fullerton, read the manuscript with an eye to the meaning of love letters in trials and American culture. Her insights were critical and incorporated into the manuscript.

We thank our three outside readers for their significant suggestions. Clare McKanna Jr. made a variety of insightful comments, and his suggested changes are now in the text. Our anonymous readers made extensive suggestions for changes to bring the manuscript together as a book. We worked for months putting the suggestions into the text and making important distinctions for certain cases. The two readers substantially focused our work and arbitrated a real difference of opinion between the authors. As she has in the past, Professor Farrington clearly saw the holes her coauthor had failed to visualize.

We thank one of the inspirational leaders in education, Ronald Heusser of Santiago High School in Garden Grove, California. On Saturday, February 9, 2008, Santiago High School lost a good friend and colleague, Ronald Vincent Heusser. Heusser opened the school in 1961 as a boys' physical education teacher and the athletic director, and served in various positions throughout his tenure at Santiago, most notably as the ASB activities director and the girls' basketball coach. He was instrumental in Brenda's leadership role at the high school and a regular coach encouraging her along the way in higher education. "Coach H" truly lived every day of his life with passion and purpose—to make a difference in the lives of young people. He officially retired in 1996, although he continued to dedicate himself wholeheartedly to the students of Santiago High School throughout his retirement. On February 16 we joined a thousand mourners celebrating the life of a man who had influenced many, including the authors of this book.

We thank our many students whom we have engaged in discourse regarding this project. In particular, we thank Heather Allen; Mary Brisseau; Amy Green; Ryan Aaron Hernandez; Megan Leahy; Terence "Bob" Przeklasa; Richard Robledo; Heidi Sherman; Albert Ybarra; Martin Chavez; Lori Branson; Shannon Gerlach; Stephen Gomez; Maria Manzotti; Shawn Nelsen; Jennifer Pinera; Rene Radillo; Linda Schmidt; Stephen Tipton, USMC; Kimberly Hamquist; Neda Gahvavehchi; Kevin Hare; Michael Hascher; Anne Herrick; Quyen Huynh; Mattison Laventure; Fernando Maciel, USMC; Benjamin Pham; Ferdus Serhal; Sirin Sirirat; Michael Whitesell; Richard Madrid, USN; Lonnie Wilson, USASF; Tiffany Dalpe; Marcus Flores, USMC; Samuel Lee; Michelle Maxon; Andres Mejia; Michelle Oropeza; Gary Smith; Steven Thomas; Julie Frances Abutal; Barbara Brady; Jennifer Mizzell; Charles Sedey; Dale Sawyers, USN; Michael Seager; Karen Rosa; Ryan Woods; Brenda Bitgood; Michelle Bean; Lori Iacovelli; Scott Kesilis; Neal Lynch; Carolyn Stull, USN; Timothy Finch; Larry Natividad; Elaine Nelson; Miguel Garcia; Thomas Bojorquez; Thomas DeMartino; Jennifer C. Pinera; Norma Esparza; Dean Cole; Charlene

Riggins; Christopher Small; Michael Woods; Susan Meier; Melissa Miller; Austin Yuen; Riley Alegre; Adrian Donaldson; George Stantis; Huong Pham; Nancy Diep; Catherine Bilachone; Jamie Haugh; Andrew Newkirk; Michael Vencill; Robert Tardiff; Patrick Brown; Richard McFarlane; Scott Behen; Robert Miller; Caroline Owen; Jaime Dietz-Velez; Diana Pena-Bisnett; Eduardo Barrios; Lamon Starks, USMC; Kenneth McMullen, USN; and Jeffrey Kvech.

Finally, we thank Elizabeth Demers, who thought so much of this project that she issued an advance contract. After she moved on to another press, Heather Lundine took the wheel and steered this manuscript into book form. We thank Heather for her patience with us.

We take responsibility for any errors of fact that reside in these pages and the interpretations of events and their meanings.

WOMEN WHO **KILL** MEN

INTRODUCTION

The Feminine Side of Women on Trial

This study of women on trial for homicide examines newspaper coverage of these proceedings and the constructions of their attorneys in California cases, 1870–1958. Our focus is on the representations of women, case by case, in the newspapers and in trial-court settings, and the rhetoric of attorneys. We make comparisons over time and place to ferret out the nuances of gender, femininity, and the law. We cover almost a century of cases in a single state, giving this work a unique legal focus.[1] We explore trial tactics as well as public relations with the press. In our nineteenth-century cases, we ask whether the all-male juries exhibited the anxiety so frequently ascribed to men in the era.[2] We pay particular attention to how law-enforcement personnel, prosecutors, and defense attorneys portrayed women caught up in the criminal-justice system. In terms of the law, we look at evidence offered at trial, judicial rulings on its admissibility, and the interpretations of the prosecution and the defense. In the mid-twentieth century, the role of the police and their relationship with the press emerged as a factor in the construction of gender, accusation, evidence, and trial strategy. Clearly, media were selective in the cases they covered, and police, lawyers, and judges learned how to manipulate the media. Newspapermen needed to sell copy. Lawyers wanted to advertise their wares and promote their client's interests. Judges knew they stood for election periodically and needed name recognition. All these concerns involved the construction of gender and justice in particular settings. In the end no simple theory covering gender, class, or race explains the behavior of people involved in murder trials. Often it is the law rather than the constructions that determine the verdict.

A focus on women who kill men is not new. Robert Ireland wrote pioneering articles in the late twentieth century about the "unwritten law" of the nineteenth century.[3] His 1992 article on women defendants scrutinizes the relationship of sexual dishonor and violence, femininity and insanity, and rage and law.[4] Based on a study of cases in 1843–96, Ireland found the invention of the unwritten law that exonerated men and women killers who avenged sexual dishonor. Ireland's trials exhibited an ideology arguing that men had a duty to protect women from "slimy, snake-like libertines" and punish "Eve-like women who too readily embraced those libertines."[5] At trial defense attorneys portrayed their female clients as "weak and hysterical, whose hysteria rendered them legally insane," and prosecutors painted them as "inherently licentious and the purveyors of social evil."[6] Theorists tied female insanity, in turn, to menstrual dysfunction and "an inherent condition of emotional instability."[7] Nineteenth-century physicians termed the problem dysmenorrhea, today known as postmenstrual syndrome, or PMS.[8] Popular paperbacks persisted in keeping the issue alive in a broad national setting.[9] Scholarly work focused on seduction litigation gave history another nuanced view of marriage, seduction, and violence.[10] In the twentieth century a new unwritten law emerged, which provided women the right to use deadly force to resist an abusive husband. The defense couched this unwritten law in terms of self-defense precipitated by wife beating.[11] As an example of the effects of this unwritten law's application, in Cook County, Illinois, juries convicted only 16 of 103 women who had killed men, and 9 of these defendants were African American.[12] Christopher Waldrep, reflecting on the work of Richard Hamm on honor and homicide in the South, concludes, "By the end of the nineteenth century, Americans widely understood that an unwritten law existed off the books allowing men to slay the seducers of 'their' women."[13] Looking at a national trend in historical interest in single cases, Waldrep further notes, "The appearance of so many historical crime stories from major, well-established, elite scholars writing for the top publishers, authors that used to write very different books, brings new gravitas to this line of inquiry."[14] Our inquiry goes beyond the single crime story to look at several women from different classes and social situations. Further, we focus on the construction of gender and ask different questions of the print evidence in each of the cases.

Historians have also explored race, violence, and immigrant status. Clare V. McKanna Jr. found that cultural conflict, transient populations, western boomtown attitudes, and the easy availability of firearms and alcohol created a climate of violence in Douglas County, Nebraska; Las Animas County, Colorado; and Gila County, Arizona.[15] McKanna also ascertained that American Indians were the least likely to receive justice in the American court system.[16] Kevin J. Mullen detected violence patterns inherent in immigrant communities that traveled to the urban West.[17] The relationship of crime, the police, and ethnic communities had a profound impact on Mexican American communities in Los Angeles.[18] In Chicago African American women who killed were not afforded use of the unwritten law because juries considered that defense "subversive and dangerous."[19] Anne M. Butler's work on women of various races in penitentiaries extends inquiry beyond the conclusion of a criminal proceeding and examines violence in prison.[20] David Peterson del Mar focuses on violence against women, particularly wife beating. His outstanding studies use a wide variety of primary sources for Oregon, Washington, and British Columbia. Wife beating was the "white noise" in society until the violence escalated into savage acts or death.[21] In some cases we address the significance of race and immigrant or ethnic status. However, most of our cases involve white women killing white men.

Our study is part of a broader interest in California criminal-justice history. Stanford law professor Lawrence M. Friedman and University of Maryland law professor Robert Percival's *Roots of Justice* remains the most important study of the system. In addition to providing an overview of the criminal-justice system and criminal statistics, the authors consider the problems of criminal evidence and the jury system. Termed "a giant cardhouse of rules," California law gave the jury great power but erected a complicated rulebook "to make sure that jurymen eat nothing but the safest, softest Pablum of evidence." The rules in law books had "exceptions, and exceptions to exceptions; and these in turn have exceptions."[22] Long trials with skilled defense attorneys put judges at risk of making errors that were grounds for appeal. The two most frequent grounds asserted on appeal reflected errors in the charge to the jury or on evidence. Evidence error questioned whether the judge permitted evidence testimony or physical evidence deemed "incompetent, irrelevant and immaterial."[23] Lawyers in the nineteenth century in particular made their reputations as attorneys in court performing before a judge, jury, and audience composed of members of the bar, the press, and the public.[24]

In twentieth-century Los Angeles, Earl Andrus Rogers won over seventy murder trials before Los Angeles juries, took advantage of ballistics and medical forensic science in trial, popularized the use of blackboards and charts, and created novel defenses such as "alcoholic insanity."[25] One of those cases details the successful defense of Gabrielle Dardley, who shot Leonard Topp, a bartender, on January 1, 1915.[26] Two days later Dardley "was unable to recall any incidents relative to the shooting."[27] Two weeks hence conflicting testimony claimed Topp beat Dardley before or after the fatal shot rang out.[28] By the time Dardley stood trial, the defendant admitted the killing but asserted a reason, "something betwixt emotion insanity and the unwritten law."[29] Trial testimony painted Topp as a sadistic opportunist who beat Gabrielle Dardley frequently and extorted money from her. Dardley asserted that during Topp's last attack the gun secured in her muff discharged accidentally or, in the alternative version, in self-defense.[30] Rogers, a skilled defense attorney, created numerous defenses painting Dardley as the victim. The jury further noted that the accidental killing saved society and this bride-to-be from a monster. As the cases unfold in the mid-twentieth century, lawyers on both sides of the aisle became increasingly talented in trying the case in the press and in court. Lawyers constructed legal narratives that "mirrored the accepted version of woman's role in society" and "what a society considers important public values."[31] Newspapers frequently printed a lawyer's speech and slanted it for the reading public's insatiable consumption.[32]

Crime news riveted 1770s America with crime pamphlets reporting on murders, murder trials, and anything shocking in nature.[33] By the early nineteenth century, lengthy pamphlets shaped by journalists, printers, and attorneys eclipsed scintillating tales of violence carrying a moral message molded by the clergy. The prurient subject matter focused on victims, the act of murder, and the dreaded discovery of homicide, mangled bodies, and the twisted motives of monsters afoot in society.[34] By the 1830s journalists turned to erotic themes as the murder of Helen Jewett in New York fed the lust for such entertainment. Helen Jewett practiced the world's oldest profession. The perpetrator hacked her to death in her bed with a hatchet. All of this "deepened the connections between titillating eroticism and titillating horror."[35] The five-day trial of the man charged in the case, Richard P. Robinson, also know as Frank Rivers, drew a flood of newspaper coverage. In the end, each of the five lawyers involved in the case created a theater spectacle. Their speeches contained powerful emotions, a logical train of reason, rhetorical flourishes, and direct engagement with their audiences, the jury, and the press.[36] The trial judge, also caught up in the drama, delivered a spirited monologue in the form of jury instructions. The jury deliberated only fifteen minutes to arrive at a verdict, but the newspapers provided readers far more than a quarter hour of riveting reading on the closing arguments and the verdict.

Journalistic interest in murder, crime, and sensationalism was not solely an American idiosyncrasy. English journalists also frequently ventured into the sensational. "Storylines featuring crime and bad behavior, often accompanied by scaremongering rhetoric, were a major feature of the Victorian press."[37] Regardless of the form or substance of this crime news, wrongdoing and its perpetrators sold well on both sides of the Atlantic. The alleged "criminal conversation" suit (a nineteenth-century cause of action for adultery and a substitute for the duel to satisfy sexual dishonor) involving Henry Ward Beecher, pastor of Brooklyn's Plymouth Church, Elizabeth Tilton, and Theodore Tilton similarly spilled gallons of journalistic ink. Further, the lawsuit and the audience, including Victoria Woodhull, Susan B. Anthony, and Elizabeth Cady Stanton, painted a feminist and suffragist border on the scandal. It became an irresistible mystery for the curious reading public, and it increased newspaper circulation in 1874–75.[38] Further, in that Beecher was a clerical celebrity, the press recounted stories that were "shocking and entertaining revelations of family disintegration and clerical shenanigans."[39] The *San Francisco Chronicle* sent a female reporter to New York in 1875 on the heels of the 1870 Laura Fair trial in San Francisco, which generated record newspaper sales.[40] In addition to twenty-nine days of testimony, numerous letters were admitted into evidence, giving readers and attorneys plenty of nuanced language to dispute.[41] In the end lawyers appealed to the jury to render the only verdict that would save civilization from the cultural crisis the case revealed. Thus the lawyers indulged in storytelling just like their witnesses.[42]

Robert A. Ferguson's *Trial in American Life* (2007) studies "high-profile" trials and calls them "a distinct phenomenon at the nexus of the legal system and public life."[43] Such trials are episodic but aid our interpretation of history and culture.

In these trials "participants turn into celebrities through prolonged exposure and speculation about their integrity in conflict."[44] In cases such as that of Mary Surratt, charged with conspiring to assassinate President Lincoln, the nature of her womanhood was at stake. Both the defense and the prosecution questioned her place in American culture's domestic sphere.[45] Although Ferguson's observations are apt for the trials he studied and most of the works cited in this introduction, not all our trials are high profile. Further, questions of gender and image extended beyond the coverage of high-profile cases. Although Laura Fair's trial was clearly high profile, other trials made varying impressions in the public sphere.

Moving west to Chicago and decades in time to the 1890s, we find that the arrest and trial of Adolph Luetgert for the murder of his wife, Louise, in 1897 generated similar newspaper coverage. Journalists printed all kinds of sensational stories because the police never located Louise's body. The public, aided by the press, speculated that Adolph, a sausage-plant owner, simply disposed of Louise's body by running it through the grinder and into the matrix of German sausage. Lawyers concocted tales about Louise's family involving insanity and strange disappearances. In the end the newspapers prospered, some of Adolph's attorneys became wealthy, and the Luetgert sausage business filed for bankruptcy.[46]

In Virginia after 1865, the press focused on northern violence and the virtues of southern honor. When covering local murder trials, journalists often cited regional standards of law and custom in the text or subtext of news. Murder gave writers the perfect venue "to explore the interplay of society, law, and the press."[47] One trial of national interest to the press in the 1930s involved Edith Maxwell, accused of killing her father. Importantly, by the 1930s the New South entrepreneurs and politicians steered the public away from old-fashioned honor. Equally significant was the changing role of women in the region. Women joined reform organizations, entered professions, and participated in politics.[48] Maxwell gained national celebrity status, and the National Woman's Party appropriated her as a victim of hillbilly culture.[49] Her first all-male jury convicted her of first-degree murder, but the Virginia Supreme Court ordered a new trial. The second all-male jury also convicted Maxwell, this time of second-degree murder, making her a "feminist martyr."[50] Hollywood produced two movies based on her trial, and Chicago's *Actual Detective Stories* magazine began running her saga in 1937. The press made "people care, setting the agenda through relentless, sensational, one-sided coverage."[51] Thus Maxwell's story meant more than the trial in the hands of a media eager for sensation and sales. Eastern papers campaigned for Edith Maxwell's acquittal, and southern newspapers championed the rule of law and justice in the South.

Rocky Mountain newspapers supported similar values when covering crime stories. Editors thought it their duty to fight injustice and elevate the moral tone of their communities by promoting the rule of law.[52] Many of these editors eschewed the post-1865 trend of the "penny press," yellow journalism that sensationalized crime stories to target a mass market.[53] Rather they advocated law and order to build up their communities and reviled wife-beating husbands as enemy deviants.[54]

One area where the law of evidence and journalistic interest merged involved love letters. Prosecutors often offered love letters as evidence because love letters were private expressions of deeply held emotion intended only for the eyes of the author's beloved. Prosecutors culled love letters in most cases and included passages touching on motive or the violation of cultural norms. They did so to influence juries filled with individuals who believed in the veracity of love letters. Newspapers, although they edited out explicit sexual content, printed the letters because their voyeuristic readers viewed love letters as expressing sexuality as well as the tender emotions associated with romantic prose.[55]

Enemy deviants of their time and place, women convicted of crime in Illinois, for example, were "whores and thieves of the worst kind."[56] Women who poisoned their men were deemed "horrific" because they "represented a perversion of woman's domestic image as loving spouse and nurturing homemaker."[57] Women who killed often presented "themselves as the long-suffering victims of their husbands' abuse, alcoholism, or marital infidelities."[58] One battered woman in 1888 poured kerosene over a man whom the judge termed "a brutal worthless fellow" and torched him. She entered a plea bargain of manslaughter, but after sentencing, the judge and her neighbors petitioned the governor to pardon her. She claimed temporary insanity, and the governor concurred.[59] Another abused woman who "accidentally" killed her husband with a shotgun blast while he slept won exoneration from a Chicago coroner's jury in 1936. A "score of women neighbors" applauded the verdict when issued.[60] The press noted with approval both the verdict and the acclaim of the audience of women. In fact, between 1913 and 1925 not a single white woman was convicted of manslaughter in forty-three prosecutions, and only 5 of 208 white women were convicted of murder in Chicago. For African American women defendants, 18 of 92 were convicted of murder. Race mattered.[61]

In the American West race also mattered. African Americans were quickly identified as enemy deviants and too often rushed to judgment and the gallows.[62] Anne M. Butler found this particularly evident in the lives of African American women. She asserts, "Race and class imperative deepened the formal response of society and burdened women of color with more frequent arrest and longer penitentiary time."[63] Kali N. Gross determined that "systemic biases in the courts, in policing practices, and in the minds of everyday citizens" played a "fundamental role" in the perception of African American women involved in crime or violence.[64] Again race clearly mattered.

Finally, in addition to newspaper coverage of women killers, fiction writers identified a reading public hungry for Gothic horror. In nineteenth-century ink, women were fallen angels as convicted criminals and monstrosities when murderous in fiction.[65] Twentieth-century noir fiction made crime entertaining and instructive for readers.[66] Movies moved women's violence to a larger audience albeit "cinema lag[ged] behind society."[67] Some of our cases inspired screenplays thus adding another dimension to the representations of women in trouble with the law. One of the most studied, stylized, and commercialized trials of the nineteenth century was that of Lizzie Borden. Tiffany Johnson Bilder's analysis of the evidence resonates with our account of many trials.[68] She found that the illustrations of Borden sketched during the trial depicted "muscular passivity as an assurance of emotional passivity and femininity."[69] Borden's demeanor during the trial manipulated the "politics of visibility and invisibility," portraying "her good breeding."[70] In terms of the political economy of consumption, Lizzie's home environment suggested "the notion of a woman driven mad by her interior surroundings," much like Charlotte Perkins Gilman's "Yellow Wallpaper," a fictional account of a woman's decline into insanity.[71] This narrative of feminine "breakdown" generated jury sympathy.[72] Borden's jury put steadfast faith in her outward appearance of femininity and "good breeding" equated with internal innocence and moral virtue. As one reporter of the trial observed, "She makes an exceedingly favorable impression."[73] Lizzie was dressed in middle-class fashion, carried flowers in the courtroom, and coded herself as feminine and aligned with nineteenth-century female domesticity. In Massachusetts in 1892 it was enough for an acquittal. The trial and the popular and scholarly attention that endures until today must be explained in terms of gender.[74]

As we move from the nineteenth century into the twentieth century, we note a decline in misogynistic language in the press and an increase in women both sitting on juries and constructing with their attorneys new images within a criminal-justice system slowly providing more procedural protection to the criminally accused. Our analytic narrative is not the familiar one of *Law and Order* or the fantastic one of the departed *L.A. Law*. Rather it is our attempt to tease out the nuanced nature of gender and law in California culture.

In the process we explore a variety of legal strategies. Love letters frequently appear in trials or in the media. As noted previously, attorneys often turned to such letters for evidence of a motive. In the Laura Fair case, attorneys on both sides made very different inferences from the evidence. The prosecution saw a heartless, degraded, and infamous woman in the letters. The defense found the despicable decedent to be a perfect example of male deceit, a man who deserved killing.

Love letters surfaced in the cases of Lastencia Abarta, Emma Le Doux, Aurelia Scheck, Madalynne Obenchain, Beulah Louise Overell, and Lana Turner. In the Turner case, the letters were not evidence for either side but were splashed about in newsprint to discredit Turner, who was not on trial but the subject of a civil suit. Defense attorneys often painted their clients as victims. Men promised marriage and reneged in the Laura Fair, Lastencia Abarta, and Marie Leonard Bailey cases. Men drove women mad, and lawyers offered the insanity defense, substantiated by expert testimony, in the cases of Laura Fair, Lastencia Abarta, Katie Cook, Beatrice Mallette, Betty Flay Hardaker, and Betty Ferreri.

Men also battered women. Clara Wellman, Nettie Platz, Claire Toler, Alice Haggerty, Gabrielle Dardley, Bertha Talkington, Erma Blanda, and Betty Ferreri all claimed self-defense. Angela Maria De Vita, Blanche Lescault, Marjorie Ferguson, Rose Miceli, and Cheryl Crane proclaimed self-defense as part of defending another person in the course of a homicide.[75]

Some men, it seemed, deserved killing. Katie Cook killed her husband, Tom, "a very immoral man."[76] Clara A. Wellman cut down her wife-beating husband, and the grand jury thanked her for ridding the community of the monstrous menace. Angela Maria De Vita used deadly force to stop threats against her husband and children. Gabrielle Dardley and Betty Ferreri claimed to perform the same service to humankind that forced other women to resort to deadly force.

Some women lamented that the shooting was unintentional. Lastencia Abarta, Marie Bailey, and Rosa Tarlazzi pulled the trigger accidentally; Laura Fair, Marie Bailey, and Effie Reynolds had no memory of the shooting. Rosa Tarlazzi was so intoxicated that she remembered nothing of the tragedy.

In addition to love-crossed killers, the police and the prosecutors often found greed to be a motive for committing murder. The police believed that Aurelia Scheck craved a $500 life-insurance policy. Gertrude Gibbons lusted for a $3,200 policy. Louise Peete and Juanita "The Duchess" Spinelli made killing a career. Peete left a long trail of victims on her way to the gas chamber; Spinelli served as the ringleader of a criminal gang.

Finally, we explore the press's interest in the audience for these trials.[77] Large crowds pushed their way into the courtroom and filled the streets to catch a glimpse of the women on trial. Laura Fair, Louise Peete, and Madalynne Obenchain drew substantial throngs. Women's rights advocates attended Laura Fair's trial. Emma Le Doux drew "the morbid curiosity of many women."[78] When Aurelia Scheck appeared, "women almost frenzied with curiosity, fought like demons to get into court."[79] Madalynne Obenchain attracted a "row of sob sisters."[80] Dolly Oesterreich found herself in court so often, the crowds grew with each failed prosecution. Although women in the audience claimed to be there to see justice done, newspaper commentary on female attendees was usually misogynistic until the 1940s.

We have chosen only a few of the many cases of the period 1870–1958 in hopes that we can illuminate the nuanced relationships of law and gender. In terms of periodization, we see nineteenth-century values and practices enduring until World War I and call this period the long nineteenth century. The 1920s and 1930s were distinct decades with distinct values and events. We consider the 1940s and 1950s a cultural and economic whole with World War II, postwar conservatism connected with the back-to-the-home movement, and the Cold War of the 1950s unifying the period. In the process of our discussion, we hope to provide insight into the changing public image of women involved in murder trials in the context of their times.

CHAPTER ONE

Mirror, Mirror on the Wall, Who Is the Sanest of Them All?

The Insanity Defense in Court and in the Press

Postbellum California put the gold rush, the Mexican War, and the Civil War experiences behind to build a new image of maturing economic life, bucolic agricultural enterprise, and cultural sophistication. California in the nineteenth century boasted two major cities, Los Angeles and San Francisco. In southern California, cultural elites labored to erase and at the same time capitalize on the romanticized Spanish past to create social, economic, and political power.[1] A potent means to this end was media, particularly the *Los Angeles Times* newspaper. Harrison Gray Otis and his talented journalists, including Charles Fletcher Lummis, Harry Carr, Robert J. Burdette, and John Steven McGroarty, worked indefatigably to produce a particular image. This image included the Spanish mission myth, an obsession with the Mediterranean-like climate, political conservatism, and a rabid "thinly veiled radicalism, put to the service of boosterism and oligarchy."[2] In the *San Francisco Chronicle*, Michael H. and Charles de Young tantalized readers with a different kind of journalism: "commercial and sensational."[3] Their innovations encouraged a new interest-group discourse and "helped powerfully to shape emerging class identities."[4] Thus journalism played a powerful role in defining postbellum California. In the second half of the nineteenth century journalistic images drenched in Victorian values and rhetoric found their way into legal proceedings.[5]

Women also took center stage, stepping into the male-dominated public sphere where female participation in politics often proved unwelcome. Americans esteemed Queen Victoria from afar, not necessarily for her ability to lead the British Empire, but for the high moral standards she exemplified. The American version of Victorian mores embraced an ideology of true womanhood that defined a "lady" as pious, pure, submissive, and domestic.[6] The "long nineteenth century" refers to the tenacity of these Victoria-inspired morals, which persisted well into the twentieth century despite challenges by women chafing under this narrow definition of "lady." Nineteenth- and early twentieth-century women venturing beyond the confines of the private, domestic sphere met with approval when engaged in causes that posed no threat to the social order such as charity work.[7] Women's suffrage, on the other hand, belied the private sphere and was perceived by many Americans as distinctly unfeminine.

Defying Victorianism, Laura de Force Gordon advanced women's rights by embracing a public role during the late nineteenth century. Gordon grew up in the spiritualist movement, which included a protofeminist program advocating radical individualism and a "woman's special gift to know justice."[8] She collaborated with Clara Shortridge Foltz to win the right for women to enter the state's Hastings Law School, practice law, and engage in any lawful employment.[9] Gordon served in the suffrage movement and achieved public notoriety when the California State Woman Suffrage Society held its first meeting at Dashaway Hall in San Francisco.[10] Foltz and Gordon spearheaded a lobbying campaign at the California Constitutional Convention of 1878 that resulted in provisions giving women access to "any lawful occupation" and California higher education.[11] Contrary to the cherished ideal of women as homemakers, women entered the workforce in increasing numbers year after year. Women spoke together in public and argued that women's work deserved respect and thus the privilege of full citizenship.[12] By 1908 members of the Woman's Branch of the Citizens' League of Justice attended trials to "encourage justice by [their] presence."[13] Thus California women became visible as part of the public city, in the workforce in public, and in courts as both attorneys and spectators for justice. In 1917 they even joined juries.

This public image of women in California dramatically challenged the antebellum place for women in the legal system. As Michael Grossberg has demonstrated, American courts proved increasingly "a masculine place."[14] Yet public discourse focused on the "language of law and the expectation that important rights were defined legally."[15] The law of marriage evolved in the long nineteenth century as men and women "became users of law as they pursued dreams and ambitions: of love, of wealth, of security, of an end to misery, of happiness."[16] Unwritten law excused homicide when betrayal sufficed as a motive in 1859, 1867, and 1869–70 cases involving "the trials of men who had murdered their wives' lovers."[17] Women's rights activists thought the verdicts "demonstrated the corruption of male-only juries."[18] California tried its first sensational homicide case in 1870, but unlike justifiable homicide as a defense for men accused of murdering their wives' lovers, the gender roles in this instance proved quite different. This time a woman, Laura Fair, had pulled the trigger.

Laura Fair

On November 3, 1870, aboard the ferry *El Capitan*, Laura D. Fair shot Alexander P. Crittenden, a San Francisco lawyer and her lover of seven years, in the presence of his wife and son. She then dropped the pistol and walked into the ferry's saloon. There Crittenden's son, Parker, and Capt. William H. Kentzel confronted her. She readily confessed to the killing, thus beginning a legal proceeding that consumed months of reporters' inquiries, generated pages of newsprint, and excited the public nationwide. Two counties vied for jurisdiction to capture the spotlight, notoriety, and publicity. The defense and the prosecution contended over the nature of women in making their cases. The defense maintained that Laura Fair suffered maniacal spells due to delayed menstruation. In short her "female complaint" led to a mental problem, thus an irresistible impulse to kill. For the defense Fair personified the typical woman victimized by male duplicity. For the prosecution she constituted an immoral seductress, a money-hungry opportunist, and an exploiter of male weakness. For thirty days lawyers portrayed their images of women to packed courtrooms that included famous suffragists. Newspapers splashed this lurid clash of Victorian values and the images of women reformers across their pages for a news-hungry populace.[19]

The counties of San Francisco and Alameda jousted for jurisdiction of the case. On the day of the shooting, Fair and Crittenden traveled on the Oakland–San Francisco ferry; the boundary lines of both counties extended into the bay. Alameda County took "time by the forlock and subpoenaed witnesses to appear before a grand jury in San Leandro." If an indictment followed, a bench warrant would spirit Laura Fair out of San Francisco and into the Alameda jail. While the East Bay authorities proceeded, the state surveyor investigated the issue.[20] When the state surveyor reported that the crime had occurred in San Francisco waters, Alameda County demurred.[21]

As the trial opened, the newspapers informed their readers of Laura Fair's lurid past. Despite the disclaimer—"We are not in the habit, in California, of burdening our memories for a very long time with even the most sensational events"—journalists revealed how Laura had driven her husband, Col. William B. Fair, to bankruptcy and suicide. Undaunted, she married again and divorced. Then she ensnared Crittenden and wantonly killed him.[22]

District attorney Harry Byrne opened for the prosecution in Judge Samuel H. Dwinelle's court with an outline of Fair's purchase of the murder weapon, her conveyance to the scene of the crime, and her premeditated murder of A. P. Crittenden. The prosecution summoned several witnesses who placed Laura Fair on the ferry with the murder weapon in hand. One testified that Fair had "one of her spells" and requested "some drops that her physician usually gave her." Further, "she only kept on repeating that she was ruined and her daughter was ruined; she was talking at random."[23] The defense cited an unsolicited statement from Parker Crittenden, A.P.'s son, that he did "not remember that she said [his] father had been to her room that day" or that "she said he promised to marry her and that they would go to Indiana." However, Parker recalled, "she did say something about publishing certain letters, and that he had ruined her and her child." Upon further questioning Parker testified, "She said nothing about his promising to marry her"; however, Parker "knew that they were acquainted and intimate to a certain extent." Nevertheless, he "did not know of any intimacy until within two years."[24] Mrs. Laura P. Sanchez, A.P.'s daughter, remembered a November 1869 meeting at her home between Laura Fair and A.P. and revealed her father's declaration, "You women have unsexed yourselves; I utterly despise and abhor you." Laura Sanchez explained that she did not know why he "used the word 'women,'" remarking, "He put it in the plural. I don't know why, and asked no questions."[25] Such a comment uttered in court and repeated in print reflected a Victorian anxiety regarding irreverent women who failed to adhere to social expectations.

Defense attorney Elisha Cook strenuously cross-examined prosecution witnesses to the point where the prosecution deemed his behavior "disgraceful." Cook retorted that applying the term "disgraceful" to the conduct of a member of the bar was improper. Further, Cook condemned "clap-trap" speeches "intended only to influence the jury." The spectators greeted Cook's exchange with "applause," prompting the irritated judge to order a deputy sheriff to arrest the next person who applauded.[26] Such trials could rival theater as entertainment for nineteenth-century San Franciscans.[27]

The prosecution closed on the fourth day of the trial, and the defense outlined its case. When Fair and Crittenden met in 1863, A.P. had lied about his marital status and aggressively pursued Fair. His ardency generated a prodigious trail of love letters. After Laura Fair ascertained that he was married, Crittenden averred that he had never loved his wife and was about to obtain a divorce so that he could marry Fair. Weary of his unfulfilled promises, Fair sought refuge in Havana. His letters pursued her. She then fled to New York only to receive more letters from Crittenden. A trip to Virginia failed to halt the love letters. Upon arrival in Louisiana, Fair discovered more letters from her persistent lover. There he joined her "in person . . . and accompanied her upon a visit to the watering places of the South even as late as 1869." Three times Crittenden claimed he was going to Indiana to obtain a divorce, but Laura, tired of his excuses, married a man named Snyder. Crittenden refused to acquiesce and ultimately convinced Fair to divorce Snyder. Once that divorce was in place, Laura and A.P. "were again as friendly as ever."[28] Perhaps their relationship seemed friendly because a pragmatic Mrs. Crittenden knew about her husband's philandering and that Fair was in an adjoining room in Oakland the day before they boarded the ferry.

According to the defense, Laura Fair was insane at the time of the killing; in fact, she had absolutely no recollection of pulling the trigger. The defense declared, "For twelve months prior to the commission of the act, Mrs. Fair was insane; . . . from that time, down to the present day, she has never menstruated without becoming a perfect maniac and furious." At the time of the shooting, Laura suffered "from retarded menstruation for two or three days past." Medical authorities recognized this condition "universally as insanity in females."[29] Thus Elisha Cook raised insanity and the nature of women's medical science as part of the defense.

Another defense strategy emphasized Crittenden's tireless pursuit of Laura as evidenced by his prolific, passionate correspondence. The prosecution, however, objected to the admission of a love letter as evidence, deeming it "irrelevant and incompetent." Prosecutor Alexander Campbell argued that the defense was attempting to insinuate "principles introduced for the first time in a Court of Justice." He censured the defense tactic because "a man may form an illicit connection with a woman and maintain it throughout a number of years," and when he shows "an inclination to return to his family and the paths of morality [it] is to be considered a cause of insanity in his paramour, and is an excuse for murder." Campbell called the defense's strategy "a monstrous doctrine" that was "against the law and against morality" because "it strikes at the marital relation and uproots civilization." Campbell pontificated to the jury in the form of an objection addressed to the judge's ruling on the admission of documentary evidence. Nineteenth-century attorneys relentlessly configured cases to deflect the attention of the jury.[30]

Defense attorney Cook reminded prosecutor Campbell that Campbell had also used the same argument to seek the admission of similar letters as evidence in a recent case and that it was for the jury to determine whether the letters affected Fair's state of mind. Campbell immediately retorted that in the earlier case his client had been a father whose knowledge of the seduction of his daughter drove him to insane violence. After extensive argument, much of it revealing the nature of the contents of the letters before the jury, the judge ruled the letter inadmissible.[31]

On the sixth day of the trial, the defense put police officers and reporters on the stand to establish Laura Fair's condition when she had arrived at the city jail. Her condition in court continued to deteriorate. She was "very pale and appeared quite weak," her eyelids "drooped languidly," and the "muscles of her throat moved often," clearly indicating "suppressed emotion, and [that] is a part of hysteria." Police officer Lawrence Sellinger noted, "She raved, and tried to get out of the cell; to me she seemed to be out of her head." Reporter Benjamin Naphtaly saw her struggling against restraints and "talking in an incoherent manner." The court adjourned at noon, and when the doors reopened at two, the crowd "rushed for the lobby. They pushed, struggled and howled in their anxiety to secure places from which they might gain a view of the prisoner." Unfortunately for the anxious horde, the court adjourned early because of Laura's weakened physical condition.[32]

Day seven of the trial produced more wrangling over letters, but now the debate centered on Laura's letters to A. P. Crittenden. Importantly, Dr. B. F. Lyford, Laura's physician, testified concerning his treatment of the defendant for insomnia and "retarded menstruation." Referring to the day of the shooting, he told the jury that Laura "was an unquestionable victim of that most dreadful condition of both mind and body—insomnia, as was also her system at that unfortunate period suffering not only from scanty and painful, but retarded menstruation." He reflected, "At times her mind was unsettled by the intense action of the nervous system and it seemed impossible to get medicines to reach the case. Doctors readily recognize this condition, and those who have seen females under such circumstances understand the peculiar excitement and irritability she labored under." For Laura Fair "retarded menstruation may produce mania" and therefore result in "any insane act." That insane act "may break out at any time, even immediately after a period of apparent sanity." Lyford gave an example of Laura crushing a glass in her mouth when he had administered medicine. However, prosecutor Campbell's cross-examination discredited Lyford because

MIRROR, MIRROR ON THE WALL

the doctor could not recall the time or place of much of his education and experience.[33]

The defense next called Dr. Trask to the stand to further establish the medical-mental state of Laura Fair and buoy up the insanity defense. Widely respected in the community, Trask proved a more credible witness than Lyford.[34] He testified, "Protracted loss of sleep will result in great cerebral excitement and a disturbed condition of the brain." Laura's physical condition "was bad and her mental condition considerably disturbed." Importantly, Trask had studied Laura's condition after the killing. He found "mental disturbance and great nervous excitement, incoherence of speech and vehemence in conversation on minor subjects . . . in every one of her menstrual periods." He concluded that Laura suffered from hysterical mania. Citing the medical literature, Trask maintained, "Cases of murder are not uncommon in persons afflicted with hysteria" associated with menstrual problems. In fact, "Dr. Mosley records the case of a woman who murdered her three children" and another of a "woman killing her husband, cutting him up and pickling him the same night to eat."[35] The science of the times substantiated Trask's observations, while newspaper accounts of his expert testimony fed the public's ravenous curiosity.

The defendant then took the stand. Fair testified that she had not purchased a gun to kill Mr. Crittenden; she always carried a gun at his insistence and had done so for years. Fair maintained that Crittenden was her "only friend and protector [she] had in the world." Then she broke down in tears and blurted out, "Mr. Campbell insulted me in Court the other day; if he [Crittenden] had been alive he would have made Mr. Campbell apologize on his bended knees." At this point several spectators burst into applause. Judge Dwinelle hammered the audience to order and dispatched officers into the crowd to locate the miscreants. One of those discovered was Emily Pitt Stevens, a prominent women's rights advocate. The judge fined her twenty-five dollars. Fair told the court that she would pay Stevens's fine, and Stevens graciously thanked her.[36]

For days Campbell cross-examined the defendant on her pervious marriages, her relationship with Crittenden, the circumstances of the killing, and her general character. Under questioning Fair offered radical statements regarding love and marriage. Campbell played heavily on her concept of marriage as free love because he knew the public would find it threatening to Victorian values and civilization itself. The press duly reported the prosecution's questions and answers daily to a captivated audience.[37]

The eleventh day of trial garnered little press notice, as it focused on the court reading the bundles of love letters. While legal minds pondered the admissibility of the letters, the "jurors [were] pictures of despair" languishing in their chairs listening to the drone of the clerk of court numbering documents.[38] Counsel reached agreement by the second day of the ordeal, permitting the reading of the letters into the record in closing arguments.[39] The letters now became public fodder as the newspapers started printing their contents day after day.[40]

On the thirteenth day of trial, Dr. Trask retook the stand. He testified that Laura Fair suffered from a prolapsed womb and hardening of the cervix. Compounding these maladies, she experienced a menstrual disorder that caused acute attacks of hysteria affecting her mental condition. Trask provided examples of this hysteria, citing statements that Fair had made in jail. Alexander Campbell objected. The testimony as well as the banter of counsel continued. When Trask answered one of Campbell's somewhat convoluted questions after the clerk reread it to the witness, Campbell declared, "What is an irregularity of a mental function but a mental derangement?" Cook quipped, "I am glad, Judge Campbell, if we have found something in this case which you understand." Campbell retorted, "But I cannot understand that question." Cook replied, "I am not responsible for your obtuseness." Trask then admitted, "The question is not very clear to me." Campbell reframed his inquiry: "Do you think hysteria is a cause of mania?"[41] The morning session produced Trask's consistent testimony, and the theatrics of counsel kept the jury and spectators entertained.

The afternoon session included more expert testimony. Dr. J. C. Tucker offered, "Mrs. Fair at the time she committed the act was in a disorderly condition." Dr. Charles T. Deane of San Francisco Female Hospital confirmed that "retarded menstruation usually affects the mind." Further, "hysterical women are apt to have an attack at any time, but more apt at the proper period of menstruation, as the womb sympathizes to a certain extent with the nervous system."[42] The doctors concurred that Fair suffered emotional insanity at the time of the killing.[43] Thus, the defense rested.

The prosecution chose to include testimony from James Evard on Fair's unchaste reputation, thus setting off a key legal challenge. Cook exploded with explicit objections to the whole line of inquiry. Judge Dwinelle overruled those objections. Evard "only knew by hearsay," but her reputation "was slack-loose." He did remember a "rather vulgar remark" of J. M. DePass, but he did not want to "repeat it as there [were] ladies present." Judge Dwinelle immediately gave the ladies in the spectator section five minutes to leave. "All eyes turned to where the dozen and a half strong-minded females sat with straightened necks and advanced chins," but only one woman left the courtroom. H. L. Roby was the next witness with the same result. William Campbell had known Laura Fair in Virginia City and heard "her general reputation for chastity . . . spoken of as bad." Joseph F. Atubil lived in Virginia City, and there he heard the "general reputation she bore for chastity in Virginia City, from hearsay only, it was not good." John A. M'Quaid, an attorney and formerly from Virginia City, had "conversed with a sufficient number of persons on the subject to form an opinion as to her general reputation for chastity." John Gillig had known Fair in Virginia City and "did not know what was her general reputation for chastity."[44]

A second day of chastity witnesses told their stories before a crowded courtroom. The "usual number of briefless attorneys, the score of reporters and the double row of strong-minded females who are anxious to see 'fair play' for Mrs. Fair" filled the audience. Also in the spectator's section were the "hole rif raf" of San Francisco. John E. Doyle remembered that Laura's reputation for chastity in Virginia City "was bad." He did admit that he had "no recollection of the time, place or what was said." J. M. Estudillo knew her reputation "was not very good." Lloyd Tevis, president of Wells Fargo, law partner of James Ben Ali Haggin, the "grand khan of the Kern," and San Francisco powerbroker, recalled that he had learned of Laura's reputation in San Francisco and from numerous lawyers and judges.[45] Cook's objections continued.

To rebut these witnesses, Cook placed Laura Fair on the stand. His questions allowed her to restate the key elements of the defense case, particularly her marriage to Snyder. Following that brief episode before the jury, Cook asked the court's permission to testify "as to the conversation he had had with Snyder." Judge Dwinelle suspended the rule barring counsel from testifying and arguing the case. Cook was so ill that he testified from his chair, but he devastated Snyder's previous testimony.[46]

The next day the court was adjourned. Cook writhed in bed while Judge Dwinelle ordered the courtroom floor inspected to prevent a collapse due to the weight of spectators day after day. To fill a column the *San Francisco Chronicle* reprinted a letter to the editor from one of the "woman suffragists" who was "a constant attendant" at the trial and an excerpt from Emily Pitt Steven's *Pioneer* newspaper. The letter stated, "Denied the privilege of acting as jurors, which they deem eminently proper when one of their own sex is on trial for life, as a matter of principle have they gone, and feeling it to be a solemn duty to sit by and listen for themselves as to the justice meted out to her." The women felt that "the atmosphere of judicial life would be purified by the presence and cooperation of women." The *Pioneer*, "the Woman's Rights organ in San Francisco," added that women spectators "would tend to protect [Laura Fair] from insult on the part of the counsel which would seek her conviction." The *Chronicle* opined, "These women are out of place in the Courtroom as spectators." Further, "they virtually assume that all men are prejudiced against women; that the judge is necessarily antagonistic to the prisoner because she is a woman"; and the jury had made up its collective mind because a woman was on trial. The *Chronicle* trumpeted that the women advocated all-women juries for women defendants because women had no part in making the laws. This was "the purest sophistical bosh." Lawyers attended the Fair trial to study talent. Newspapermen attended to perform their duty. With questionable motives, "an attendant mob of ill-favored, morbid creatures; and . . . the deputation of strong-minded petticoats" also attended. Thus the mob and the women "equally deserve[d] censure and contempt." Worse yet, suffrage women represented "insolen[ce] in the extreme, and characteristic[s] of that class of females who first outrage the acknowledged laws of modesty and decorum, and then raise their shrill voices to demand immunity from the 'persecution' of criticism." In supporting Laura Fair, these "strong-minded petticoats" condoned "a tacit indorsement of loose morality and an evidence of their belief in the monstrous theory that one woman is justified in acquiring the illicit love of another woman's husband, and thus bring disgrace on the man and misery to his family."[47] The *Chronicle* repeated the prosecution argument and continued its anti–woman suffrage line that it would maintain for decades.

The next day, an enormous crowd gathered outside the court, so the police admitted attorneys and the well dressed but turned away "the vulgar unwashed." The "strong-minded suffrage shriekers marched boldly up and demanded entrance. Much to their disappointment, they were not denied, and so lost an opportunity to raise their shrill voices in denunciation of a fresh evidence of man's tyranny," the *Chronicle* reported.[48] The women present in support of Laura Fair now constituted a critical part of the drama.[49]

With the crowd seated, Alexander Campbell opened for the prosecution. First, he attacked the insanity defense. He argued that the defense based its assertions on "doctrines and principles which we regard as wholly subversive of all social peace, harmony, order and decency, when the attempt is made under the guise of a plea of insanity to justify murder." Even more certainly, the "new system of free love" must not be "engrafted on our jurisprudence" because it would allow "the wife of four husbands" to "shoot him [Crittenden] down because he pays some decent respect to his earthly wife." With his list of crimes against Victorianism fixed in the jurors mind, Campbell next went after the defense expert witnesses. He read an article "which claimed that medical witnesses were not more competent to judge of insanity than others" and emphasized "the growing distrust with which such testimony [was] received in the Courts." If expert medical testimony had any credible weight, then "it should be taken at the period when [the witness] was properly disinterested, and when the condition of the patient was perfectly fresh, shortly after the commission of the alleged crime." Campbell then attacked Lyford's tortured testimony from the record.[50]

After eviscerating the medical experts, Campbell assailed Laura Fair. He rhetorically asked the jury, "Have you ever seen upon the stand a less shattered female witness? Have you ever seen one of more ready resources?" Then he turned her demeanor to his advantage, asking, "Have you ever seen one who could invent a lie more rapidly and more plausibly, and tell it with a better grace?" What she exhibited during her testimony, Campbell averred, was "that species of moral insanity which is not legal insanity at all, but which is simply moral pollution." At base Laura Fair's plea of insanity constituted fraud. For Campbell "it [was] the act of a great criminal who, having committed an enormous crime, [sought] to cover up that crime by the invention of an enormous lie."[51]

Campbell then started reading the love letters into the

record. He characterized the letters as products of a heartless, degraded, and infamous woman. He vehemently argued that Fair "kept Crittenden impoverished. She was willing to take everything from him that cost money." Campbell spent the morning and afternoon sessions attacking Laura Fair's moral character.[52]

Campbell's condemnation of Fair soon extended to her supporters. He informed the jurors and the reading public, "There are certain persons who dignify by the name of progress every vicious thought which vicious men and women put forward for the utter destruction and debasement of society." The worst of these are "so called strong-minded women, who have a mission to reclaim and subdue the brute man, to reduce him to absolute obedience and subjection; a class of women who are wiser than their generation." These are women "who never attend to their own business, but are always anxious to interfere in the business of others." Campbell thought these women threatened the very nature of American civilization. Laura Fair's advocates sought to emasculate men; their subversive movement must be crushed with a guilty verdict.[53]

On April 18, 1871, Leander Quint opened for the defense. He reminded the jurors of gender: "Bear in mind that the defendant is a woman." Next he noted her age and past: "Take into consideration her condition, her circumstances and her character so far as the evidence has developed it before you." He then spent the rest of the day reading Crittenden's love letters into the record.[54] Subsequently, Quint focused on the law of insanity and the testimony of the expert witnesses.[55]

Elisha Cook returned to the court from his sickbed to close for the defense. He spoke to the jurors, a packed courtroom including "Mrs. Laura De Force Gordon, the eloquent advocate of Woman's Suffrage," and San Francisco newspaper readers. In total it was a four-day closing argument with two days given over to reading additional letters into the record. Significantly, Cook objected to Judge Dwinelle's ruling that he should follow Quint, arguing that in a capital case prosecution and defense attorneys must speak alternatively. Noticing Quint's call for the jurors to consider Laura's gender and circumstances, Cook countered by reminding them that the decedent's unrelenting duplicity was the real reason for Crittenden's demise.[56]

With suffragist Laura De Force Gordon present, the *Chronicle* could not restrain itself. The editor splashed "Women in Court" across the front page, quoting a *Marysville (CA) Appeal* story. Women attending the Fair trial, according to the *Appeal*, "either desire to influence the course of the Judge or jury in the interests of the defendant or they do not. If they do, then their conduct is inexcusable. If they do not, then their presence in Court can have no effect, except so far as it disgusts the public and encourages Mrs. Fair in the belief that they indorse her shameless course." The *Chronicle* agreed, observing, "The representative, strong-minded women . . . have . . . been in attendance lest an indelicate word might escape them." These women "represent a small coterie of social mischief-makers who are only happy when they can meet in Convention and prate about their wrongs and their rights." Such anomalous women obviously reside outside San Francisco because "no true woman could listen to the details of the Fair trail and not feel the blush of shame."[57]

Cook's second-day arguments focused on the failure of the prosecution to establish that Fair's "reputation was bad for chastity." Crittenden had deceived her, no question. Cook attempted to rehabilitate Dr. Lyford's testimony by reminding the jurors of Dr. Trask's expert testimony.[58] The following day Cook resumed these themes. He accused Campbell of throwing "a slur upon the character of Mrs. Fair" with the suggestion of "prostitution." Cook characterized that as "entirely uncalled for." Regarding medical expert testimony, he reminded jurors of "cases where women ha[d] these menstrual difficulties [such] that insanity [was] produced. That is, momentary insanity—insanity for the time being." Fair shot Crittenden "under an irresistible impulse." Specifically, Dr. Deane testified regarding her mental state while she pulled the trigger. It was "the point of time when reason was dethroned." Deane called it "partial insanity," but it was sufficient defense in a murder case.[59] Cook closed the fourth day with "a masterly effort." Members of the bar crowded the courtroom, and "they evidently thought the show and the actors pretty good—at least it was worth the price of admission." Cook concluded with a call for a thorough consideration of all the expert testimony and the content of the love letters. Evidence wrapped in mercy could only result in a verdict of not guilty by reason of insanity.[60]

Harry Byrne closed for the prosecution with a blistering assault on both Fair's character and the defense's expert testimony. He warned the jury that a not-guilty verdict would signal the end of civilization and be an insult to the intelligence of their enlightened age. At the conclusion of Byrne's argument, Judge Dwinelle carefully instructed the jury, particularly on the law of insanity. The jurors retired for forty minutes and returned a verdict of guilty.[61]

The defense attorneys immediately filed a motion for a new trial. Judge Dwinelle denied the motion, so the defense petitioned the California Supreme Court. The *Chronicle* published a survey of journalistic opinion on the guilty verdict on April 28, 1871. The San Francisco papers praised the jury for rescuing civilization. The *Bulletin* declared, "Had the prisoner been acquitted on the plea made in her behalf that she was a wronged woman, momentarily crazed by a sense of injury, the verdict releasing her would have put a pistol into the hand of every designing woman who had courage or motive to use one." Such a verdict would have promoted "loose living." The jurors had preserved "the sanctions of pure wedded love, and maintain[ed] unimpaired the holy relations of the family institution." The jurors had also sent a message to the "higher circles" of San Francisco that tolerance of vice must cease. The *Examiner* reflected on the victim, musing, "No more can we understand how a man of the social standing of Mr. Crittenden could have penned the disgusting outbursts of passionate devotion which have been laid before the public in his letters."[62] The paper thought Crittenden's letters proved that he suffered from insanity.

Clearly, the press sensed a crisis of class as well as morals in San Francisco. The *Sacramento Union* declared, "[The court, jury, and prosecution] ought to teach the people, who have each a direct personal interest in the punishment of this greatest of all crimes, the necessity of having murderers tried by juries selected with as much regard to the welfare of the State and the security of the lives of quiet citizens as to the acquittal of a murderer." The *San Francisco Call* focused on the insanity defense, terming it "trumped up." The editor wrote, "The people have felt for years that this plea has too long been used and abused to shield murderers from punishment." The *New York Standard* agreed, siding with the McNaughten rule of knowing the distinction between right and wrong. The editor penned, "It behooves juries as well as judges to consider well these hair splitting theories of insanity. Once let the idea prevail that the commission of a horrid and desperate crime is *per se* evidence of insanity, and there is an end to human safety." Press opinion clearly contested the insanity defense and reflected class concerns about morality.[63]

Before the California Supreme Court, Fair's attorneys contested three basic points. First, Cook and Quint argued that juror Beach was incompetent because he had stated that he thought Fair guilty prior to the verdict. Second, they asserted that the admission of evidence regarding chastity, over objection, constituted error. Cook and Quint maintained that they had never opened the door to such evidence; thus Fair's chastity was irrelevant. Finally, the court had erred in not directing counsel to close alternatively as prescribed by legislation. Alexander Campbell, for the state, disagreed. Regarding juror Beach, a statute precluded the granting of a new trial on the ground stated, and even if it did, the evidence offered was vague and uncertain. Because Fair represented herself as "a respectable widow," her chastity was fair game. On the third point, Campbell weakly argued that the defense had acquiesced to Judge Dwinelle's construction of the statute.[64]

Chief Justice William T. Wallace found the first objection unconvincing, albeit a single case could be construed otherwise. To eliminate uncertainty, the court overruled the case that allowed a defendant to object to the competency of a juror after verdict. Regarding the evidence admitted on Fair's chastity, Wallace held that chastity involved "a trait of character not in the slightest degree involved in the alleged commission of the crime." Counsel had failed to offer evidence on the issue, so the prosecution could not. The lower court had erred in its ruling on this matter. Finally, Wallace reviewed the legislative history of the statute commencing with the 1850 version, its reenactment in 1851, its repeal in 1851, its amendment in 1854, and its meaning in 1871. He concluded that the statute provided the right to close to the criminally accused, not the prosecution. Thus Wallace reversed the judgment in Fair's trial and remanded the case for a new trial. Justice Joseph B. Crockett wrote a concurring opinion emphasizing that the prosecution's attack on Fair's chastity was an error. He admonished prosecutors, "In the absence of all proof on her part tending to show that her alleged mental aberration was in any degree produced by a sense of shame or mortification occasioned by any damage to her good name, it was not competent for the prosecution to prove that her reputation for chastity was bad."[65]

Fair returned to the trial court in 1872 without extensive press coverage and the throng of spectators threatening the foundation of the courtroom. After eight days of jury selection and two days of trial, the jury retired to consider her fate. On September 30, 1872, after three days of deliberation, the jurors returned a verdict of not guilty by reason of insanity.[66] The newspapers generally decried the verdict, but civilization did not collapse. A San Francisco jury listened to the same evidence of insanity and found it compelling, not to save a woman from hanging but to abide by the law and the evidence.

It is clear that Laura Fair's insanity defense generated a heated debate for the public and the legal community. The inherited English law, the McNaughten rule, dating back to 1843, asked the jury to consider whether a person because of mental disease did not know if what he or she was doing was wrong.[67] An alternative test involved the notion of irresistible impulse; the jury should ask whether the defendant because of mental disease could control his actions. More narrowly, the jury must ask whether the defendant committed the criminal act because mental disease overcame the will to resist. In 1871 the New Hampshire Supreme Court devised a rule asking the jury to weigh rationality along with the other evidence offered to prove or disprove sanity.[68] Thus the jury determined if a particular defendant according to a particular set of facts was legally insane. Counsel raised the irresistible-impulse insanity defense in the case of Anthony Fischer, accused of the attempted murder of Charles J. Beerstecher, a railroad commissioner and prominent member of the California Constitutional Convention of 1878–79. Fischer's attorney, E. S. Salomon, offered to prove that his client exhibited no motive for the act, enjoyed a prior good relationship with Beerstecher, but had a "severe mental malady which rendered him irresponsible for his acts," a long history of suicidal behavior, the absence of a "logical mind and a self-abnegating spirit," and no memory, "an entire blank," of the event.[69] In the far more sensational trial of Adolph B. Spreckels, defense counsel claimed insanity.[70] "The counsel, however, soared away on the wings of his eloquence on the presumptions of law and the questions of reasonable doubt" and after talking an hour and a half said, "The grounds of defense are—first, insanity; second, self-defense." He then drew a comparison between "irresistible impulse and moral inclination to commit a crime." The offer of proof included a buggy accident resulting in a brain concussion, two operations, a painful abscess behind the ear, and *San Francisco Chronicle* articles attacking his father that destroyed "the intellectual poise of a young man who had suffered" greatly.[71] In this particular case the defendant was accused of shooting the editor of the *San Francisco Chronicle* because the newspaper's scathing attacks on the lad's father had triggered irresistible impulse. Today the libel suit is the preferred remedy.[72]

The public contested the insanity defense as well. An editorial in the *New York Times* was emblematic of popular sentiment in the nineteenth century. Commenting on the not-guilty verdict in the Spreckles trial, the writer declared, "The result of the protracted trial was a genuine surprise to the community." Many expected a hung jury due to the money expended by the Spreckles family on the defense. The *Times* observed, "The better element revolts against the verdict, which virtually declares that a newspaper daring to criticize the management of a monopoly does so at the risk of the proprietor's life."[73] The editorial focused on the verdict rather than the particular defense, but a plea of not guilty by reason of insanity was the only defense offered by attorneys.

Defense counsel from 1870 to 1958 possessed a quiver of factual arrows to aim at the prosecution and expert witnesses to support these contentions. In the trials that follow, attorneys set up insanity, accident, self-defense, and the "unwritten law" to free their clients from criminal penalties. In the course of doing so, they also established gender images intertwined with these legal defenses.

Lastencia Abarta

The *Los Angeles Evening Express* of March 16, 1881, announced the terrible news. Eighteen-year-old Lastencia Abarta, "a half-Basque, half-Mexican beauty," according to the press, had shot Francisco "Chico" Forster, the forty-year-old son of

Don Juan Forster on the streets of Los Angeles.[74] She fired a single shot from a distance of ten feet, and the ball entered his right eye. Disarmed by a bystander, Lastencia joined her sister, Hortensia, and calmly walked "to Judge Trafford's old Court room, corner of Temple and New High streets, for the purpose of giving herself up. Throughout the ordeal, Lastencia seemed perfectly cool and collected."[75] She committed the murder at four o'clock in the afternoon, and a coroner's inquest convened one hour later. Witnesses described the scene, but their testimony regarding Lastencia proved far more descriptive.

Lastencia Abarta personified civic responsibility. Louis Goodfriend testified that after the shooting he told her "to go up to the Sheriff's office. She remained composed." She said, "No, I am going to Judge Trafford's." As they turned to depart, one of the sisters addressed the deceased: "You are not going to fool another woman again." Frank H. Burke, the man who had disarmed Abarta, agreed that she willingly went to the law. He testified, "We got into Judge Trafford's office. I asked him if he was Judge Trafford and gave him the pistol that I took away from the tallest of the two women." Lastencia Abarta remarked to him as they marched to the judge's office, "Why didn't you let me have another shot at him?" She also "made the same remark, when she went into Judge Trafford's office." There was no struggle, no attempt to deflect the obvious.[76]

Nick Covarrubias put another spin on the affray. The previous evening he had met with Chico Forster and questioned him concerning Lastencia's demand that Chico marry her. According to Covarrubias, Forster "had never promised to marry her." In fact, Covarrubias asked him directly, "Chico, have you promised this girl that you would marry her?" He replied, "No, Nick, I never did."[77]

The coroner's jury reported the expected verdict. Chico Forster had died at the hand of Lastencia Abarta.

The trial occupied the last days of April 1881.[78] Facing an all-male jury, Abarta appeared "neatly attired in black and with a modestly self-possessed manner." When the trial opened, mostly "young men whose speech betrayed their Mexican descent" filled the courtroom.[79] The prosecution successfully ushered all facts surrounding the crime into evidence. Counsel even produced the gunsmith, John Leiver, who sold the defendant the pistol about one hour before the killing. On cross-examination Leiver revealed that he had shown Abarta how to load and fire the weapon.

The defense then presented its case. Col. John F. Godfrey told the jury that "at the time of the shooting, the mind of the defendant was incapable of judging between right and wrong." Not surprisingly, Abarta's counsel argued the insanity defense. However, there was much more to the story. Forster had promised to marry the defendant, and believing marriage to be certain, Abarta succumbed to his seduction. Thus ruined when Forster refused to marry her, Abarta had purchased the gun to kill herself. However, convinced that they were going to Judge John Trafford's office to be married, she accompanied Forster there. When the couple alighted from the carriage, the gun went off accidentally. According to her attorney, "From that time until she found herself in Trafford's office she remembers nothing of what occurred. It will also be shown that the defendant is subject to hysteria at certain times of the month and is then subject to great physical and mental perturbation."[80] Thus, Abarta's attorney offered a veritable defense smorgasbord, something for every juror! Or was this just good lawyering?

Abarta took the stand in her own defense. She recounted a love story punctuated by Forster's numerous promises of marriage and entreaties for sex prior to ceremony. After she had resisted repeatedly, Forster insisted and she acquiesced. "I loved Mr. Forster," she testified, "and was afraid he would not marry me if I did not consent and went to bed with him." Further, she had a note from Forster that read, "Come quick, I am waiting for you, don't be afraid, I am going to marry you." She produced the note in open court. Abarta also testified that prior to the seduction Forster told her, "It would be just the same to-morrow, we are just the same as if we are married." Her sister witnessed a similar commitment the day of the shooting: "My sister asked him if he was going to marry me; he said, 'Oh, yes, of course, I have promised her, I am going to marry her.'"[81]

But when they arrived at the church, Forster "told the driver to drive to Ducommon Street." Abarta blanked out at this time. She testified, "All I remember was seeing Mr. Forster standing on the sidewalk and hearing a shot." She concluded by telling the jury, "I have always suffered from hysteria at certain times of the month."[82] The true victim had testified!

During cross-examination, Abarta "maintained her composure unruffled, even under the somewhat embarrassing questions put to her" by the prosecution.[83] Her memory sustained her.

Then came the battle of the experts. Dr. Joseph Kurtz "made a decided impression on the jury" and held firm during cross-examination in his opinion "that any virtuous woman when deprived of her virtue would go mad undoubtedly."

The courtroom spectators greeted this opinion with "decided marks of applause" from "the concourse without the bar." Dr. N. P. Richardson had treated Abarta for dysmenorrhea "accompanied by hysterical spasms." Dr. K. D. Wise had also treated her for dysmenorrhea. Further, Wise noted, "At times she suffered under mental aberration, due to the physical troubles from which she suffered; at the time of the shooting undoubtedly her nerves were entirely unstrung, and she was irresponsible for the act." Wise also defined an insane impulse for the jury. He concluded that Abarta did not know that "her offense" was "against God and man at the time of her slaying Forster; at the time her brain was undoubtedly congested with blood." Dr. Henry Worthington testified that he, too, had treated Abarta for "dismenorrhea" and deemed his patient's behavior the day in question as "irrational and insane." Worthington noted, "Uterine diseases tended to disease the mind." He asserted, "When a medical expert testified of his own personal knowledge, his opinion was more entitled to weight than that of an equally capable physician who had not that personal knowledge." Asked whether he had seen another case like Abarta's, Worthington testified in the affirmative, noting "a case of homicidal mania produced by dismenorrhea."[84]

This defense was not new. In 1865 lawyers had produced experts on temporary insanity and premenstrual syndrome in *People v. Harris*. On January 30, 1865, Mary Harris had pumped two .32 rounds from her four-barreled Sharps into the back of Adoiram J. Burroughs on the second floor of the Treasury Building in Washington DC. Harris proclaimed that he had promised to marry her but instead ruined her and then married another. Her lawyer, Joseph H. Bradley Sr., produced experts who told the jury that "severe congestive dysmenorrhea due to irritability of the uterus . . . always affects the nervous system."[85] The prosecution had countered with "common-sense" medical experts, but the jury bought the uterine connection and the judge sent Harris to a psychiatric hospital. The PMS defense was hardly precedent, but medical journals addressed the Harris case seriously.[86]

The prosecution also produced experts at Abarta's trial. Dr. W. W. Ross testified on the difference between hysteria and mania, asserting, "A hysterical person is never afflicted by homicidal mania." Ross had "treated a great many cases of dismenorrhea"; he declared, "It may, in time, affect the mind, and in various ways," but "the period at which the patient suffers must differ . . . it lasts, sometimes, all week." Ross thought Abarta suffered from the disease and that "insanity might result, but not in one so young." Further, "a person cannot be sane, then insane so as to commit homicide, then sane again, previously not, having manifested insane symptoms." On cross-examination, Ross defined "irresistible impulse" as "a disease of the mind"; he drew "a distinction between mental and moral insanity" and concluded that Abarta was not "insane or suffering from dementia of any kind" and "knew right and wrong."[87] Ross also admitted that he had never treated a patient with such symptoms.

Dr. Joseph Hannon, the county physician, testified next. He had seen one hundred persons "charged with insanity." He opined, "Insanity in women does not generally depend on sexual diseases." He had encountered "a few cases of insanity due to uterine trouble, almost all occurring at the change of life," but he had never seen "insanity arising from dismenorrhea." With this testimony, the court adjourned at 10:50 p.m.[88]

All assembled the following morning at 9:00 a.m. The *Los Angeles Evening Express* declared, "The fair protagonist in the drama, of which it may be, to-day's proceedings form the last act, attended by her sister, gracefully sought her accustomed seat."[89] The cross-examination of Dr. Hannon took center stage.

Hannon admitted believing in the "same teaching as Drs. Kurtz, Wise, and Worthington." He differed with Worthington on some points, but not on others. "His principal difference with Dr. Worthington [was] as to transitory mania, emotional insanity." Hannon admitted that he did not "know that in Mexican families girls are brought up to never be alone with men" and that "such a girl would be more apt to be excited when alone with a man for the first time than a girl brought up in the American way would." He also admitted that "emotional insanity [was] recognized by medical writers all over the world," but he was "not prepared to say that a great proportion" believed in the mental state.[90] Defense counsel then produced a copy of *Ray on Insanity* and obtained Hannon's admission of the authority of that text recognizing emotional insanity. The prosecution concluded its case, and the defense told Judge Ygnacio Sepulveda they were ready to address the jury with their closing arguments.

Theodore Lynill opened for the prosecution, reviewing the evidence as well as reminding the jury of their duty under the law. He also "elaborated the usual argument against transitory insanity."[91]

Attorney J. E. Stevenson strutted upon the stage and delivered the defense's first soliloquy. He emphasized the defendant's youth and her inexperience at the hands of a duplicitous suitor. The *Evening Express* offered, "The orator detailed in an eloquent manner the steps by which Forster accomplished his purpose, and the gradual approaches of that despair that seized upon her in consequence . . . rapidly culminated in insanity." He closed asserting, "Forster met his just deserts and the jury should show by their verdict that it thinks so." At the conclusion, "the speech was followed by applause, suppressed by the Sheriff."[92]

Col. John F. Godfrey, for the defense, emphasized insanity and accidental shooting, "a chance shot." Then "the gentleman closed with an eloquent appeal to the sympathy of the jury, sympathy the outgrowth of a full and conscientious consideration of the evidence." He "painted a glowing picture of the woman wronged as the girl has been wronged, and the horror attending her future as contrasted with that of her seducer." "The speech was followed by applause, and one passage was applauded by one of the jurymen."[93]

G. Wiley Wells, for the defense, informed the jury of its duty to society and reiterated how Forster had used his "arts" to ruin Abarta. Wells asserted that he would be happy to call Lastencia Abarta "sister." Some members of the audience "burst into applause—which was not checked." Finally, he argued that Abarta did no wrong in killing Forster. "Mr. Wells's speech throughout was delivered with evident feeling, and its close was the signal for great applause."[94]

Prosecuting attorney Stephen Mallory White, later U.S. Senator White, delivered the final oration, calling upon the jury to adhere to its oath and "carry out the will of the blind goddess whom it legally represent[ed]."[95]

Judge Sepulveda's instructions took thirty minutes; afterward the jury deliberated. "Their verdict might almost be read upon their faces," the *Evening Express* reported.[96]

The jury was back fifty-four minutes later with a verdict of "NOT GUILTY on the ground of insanity." The crowd responded immediately. "A cheer, loud and long, went up from the assembled crowd, a demonstration which passed unreproved of justice." Her "friends crowded about the lady and shook her hand." The jury had "stood two for conviction to ten for acquittal" on the first ballot, but inevitably carried out the will of the blind goddess.[97] In the process the press initially drawn to the story by the social status of the deceased discovered that the feminine was on trial, and the jury saw a proper woman wronged by wanton man.

Katie Cook

On December 18, 1899, the trial of Katie Cook opened in Santa Ana, California, for the murder of her husband, shot through the brain while he slept. The *Los Angeles Times*, December 19, 1899, reported, "Since the tragedy Mrs. Cook has been suffering greatly from nervous prostration, but has so far recovered now as to sit composedly in the prisoner's dock between her father and mother." She admitted the killing, explaining that when she could no longer stand her husband's infidelity, "she took the law into her own hands, sending a bullet through his brain." The *Times* concluded, "Public sympathy is strongly with Mrs. Cook."[98]

The trial began on December 19 with a jury seated by noon and the prosecution putting in its case. W. W. Barton, the Cooks' hired man, testified to hearing a shot, then discovering Katie Cook with a smoking gun in her hand shouting accusations at Mabel Moody, the hired girl, "of taking her husband." Barton also testified that the night before he had heard "some one walk into Miss Moody's room, and afterward heard two voices, those of a man and woman." On the fatal day he went into Moody's room and noticed "by the pillows and the appearance of the bed that it had been occupied by more than one person." Other witnesses testified regarding a few material facts, but when Katie Cook's father, Henry Pope, testified about "an alleged deed to the valuable peat land farm of the deceased from Mrs. Cook to her husband," the ears of the packed crowd perked up. Pope said he could not find the paper. J. A. Turner's testimony as notary public proved that "such a deed had been acknowledged." The defense objected, "making a strong fight to not permit this evidence . . . as it [would] tend to strengthen the theory that Mrs. Cook had another motive than that of injured feeling for killing her husband."[99]

The next day an overflow crowd appeared along with the principals. The *Los Angeles Times* reported, "Mrs. Cook still retains that stolid indifference which has characterized her conduct since the beginning of her trial." She sat with her father, mother, and brother "calmly until adjournment." Only when Mabel Moody took the stand did "her face" assume "a crimson hue."[100] Moody served as a defense witness, the prosecution having rested with the admission of the testimony regarding the acknowledgment of the deed to the Cook ranch.

Mabel Moody testified regarding Katie Cook's condition two weeks prior to the homicide. Moody said, "She seemed depressed, absent-minded and weak, and the greater portion of her time was spent lying on a couch, crying hysterically." When asked whether Cook knew right from wrong, the district attorney objected, resulting in a "heated debate" that lasted "more than an hour, during which many authorities were cited."[101] The court admitted the testimony that Cook, in Moody's opinion, did not know right from wrong.

The day's last witness was J. H. Paty, a butcher, who had also observed Katie Cook's "steady decline." According to Paty, "She had become daft for some reason."[102] Other experts on insanity would be heard later.

The defense's parade of twenty-six witnesses on December 21 heavily tarnished the deceased's reputation in the audience's mind. The *Los Angeles Times* noted, "For many years Tom Cook has been known here by many people as a very immoral man, but until today the full import of his hellish disposition was not realized." In fact, those who criticized Katie Cook "for taking the law into her own hands" recoiled at the shocking news of Tom's sin and Katie's chastity. One young girl testified that Tom had forced her and Katie "to sit and listen while he read them over twenty pages of a vulgar poetical effusion, declaring he would kill them both if they did not listen to it." The testimony of jailer Graham's wife revealed that Katie's "mind seemed gone" the day after the killing. Further, Katie appeared "very thin in flesh, extremely nervous and hysterical," and had refused "sufficient nourishment to keep her alive."[103]

On December 22 the *Los Angeles Times* noted, "The court, jury and the great crowd of spectators were apparently moved when Mrs. Cook took the stand." Her testimony was worth the wait. She told of "the unspeakable life led by her husband." He "brought young girls to their home, and . . . accomplished their ruin." She "entreated him to live different" and "begged him to send the girls away." He "compelled one German servant girl to appear in the 'all-together' before himself and Mrs. Cook." Tom Cook forced "another young girl and herself to sit and listen to the reading of page after page of the vilest poetry known to the tenderloin district." Finally, he "openly boasted to her of his degradation, and what he would do with her if she betrayed him." The abuse culminated when Tom Cook moved his mistress, Mabel Moody, into the Cooks' home.

When Tom started addressing Mabel with dirty language while trimming his mistress's fingernails, Katie "implored him to come and live with her, be true to her, and to forsake his wicked ways," but "he pushed her away—and then she knew no more." Until she found herself in the county jail, "her mind had been a blank." At this point "she burst into tears, sobbing bitterly for some minutes, during which many handkerchiefs throughout the courtroom brushed away tears."[104]

After cross-examination, the defense put four physicians on the stand to testify that Katie Cook was insane at the time she killed her husband. Two other witnesses testified that she had taken a hard fall and hit her head three years prior to the shooting. The defense offered this testimony to counter the prosecution's claim that Cook had killed with deliberation and malice.

The closing arguments proved predictable. The defense's Jud Rush of Los Angeles delivered "one of the best addresses before a jury that ha[d] ever been heard in the county." Victor Montgomery of Santa Ana and prosecuting attorney Jackson added their versions, but defense attorney Lecomte Davis of Los Angeles drew a clear picture of the "depravity of the murdered man . . . while . . . the misery of the trusting wife [was] pathetic." District attorney Williams closed and the judge gave the jury "a brief but vigorous charge."[105]

The jury was out fifteen minutes. Katie Cook rose and faced

the jury. The foreman read the verdict of "not guilty." The *Los Angeles Times* reported, "Mrs. Cook fell into the arms of her mother, and the great crowd of spectators arose as one person, filling the corridors with deafening applause. Such a scene probably never was witnessed in the courtroom before." Two items of equal significance deserve underscoring. First, the verdict was not guilty, rather than not guilty by reason of insanity. Second, "one juryman remarked after the adjournment of court that he was sorry the jury could not have awarded a medal to Mrs. Cook." The jury spoke clearly: Tom Cook deserved killing.[106]

To find historical meaning and significance in these three California cases, we need to return to Hendrik Hartog's article on the more-established East.[107] Hartog's three subjects are the 1859 Sickles-Key trial, the 1867 Cole-Hiscock trial, and 1869–70 McFarland-Richardson trial, all involving a husband killing the lover of his wife under various circumstances. Hartog notes that these trials attracted major media attention: complete transcripts found print, separate pamphlets for prosecution and defense attorney arguments were published, and the attorneys, if not already famous prior to the trials, consequently achieved celebrity status. More importantly, Hartog's trials "tell us much about changing understandings of gender, contending visions of marriage, and the role of the mass media in American life."[108] His evidence also reveals a "profound disquiet about lost or changing rights and traditions, and the cases themselves were used by defense lawyers and by parts of the media to create a new legal understanding designed to restore male honor and property rights in women."[109] If there was similar male disquiet in California, the Fair, Abarta, and Cook juries should have decided accordingly, at least in the theoretical world of Victorian thought and male anxiety. They did not.

Hartog's observations on the history of the insanity defense warrant comment. A novel defense at the time, "the Sickles case is . . . one of the first occasions when the claim of temporary insanity was raised."[110] In the three cases he studies, the client's insanity proved "less a medical or psychological defect and more a legitimate and appropriate attribute of male identity." Further, "an expanded unwritten law became, in the defense attorneys' rendition, a reflection of a realistic understanding of the limits of husbandly rationality and restraint." In arguments to the jury, "it was the 'tumult' or 'transport of passions' created by knowledge of a wife's adultery that justified the taking of a human life."[111] All-male juries found these arguments credible.

Feminists, including Susan B. Anthony and Elizabeth Cady Stanton, vehemently decried the insanity defense. "To woman's rights activists, the success of the defense demonstrated the corruption of male-only juries. Others thought the verdicts revealed the need for reform of the law of adultery."[112] Hartog observes that these successful defense arguments used "the rhetoric of law reform usually identified with liberal (woman's rights) law reformers." The thrust of the argument declared that "the jury, not the law, was the best representative of enlightened moral sentiment. And the jury, in acquitting, would be establishing new, better law." Finally, "by rejecting existing law, the jury would establish a new legal right for husbands, one that was appropriate for a modern, democratic society."[113]

For Hartog the text of trials provided meaning. "The intense language of male honor in these trials came into being because traditional conceptions of male honor and of the rights and expectations of husbands had changed." These traditional conceptions "had been challenged by competing ideologies of companionate marriage and of contractual freedom within marriage."[114] What we now must ask is why these California cases took a similar linguistic turn, yet did so to exonerate women, not men.[115] Was it just good lawyering in the East and good lawyering in the West? Lawyers continue to offer as many arguments, rhetorical twists, and visual displays as possible to win.

Perhaps the West was simply different, and these California cases reflect that difference.[116] The concept of marriage as partnership has been deeply imbedded in California law since 1849.[117] Women litigated their property rights to maintain them in the Hispanic period, and "ironically, despite legal obstructions, the tradition of married women independently owning land continued in this increasingly inhospitable environment."[118] Community property and sole-trader laws in California allowed women to conduct business for years, and feminists in the West "recognized the common-law badge of inferiority" and worked to lift it across the region.[119] In fact, by 1890 the gender imbalance in California no longer existed, and thus women expanded the reach of their reform campaigns.[120] Perhaps the all-male juries in the West were simply more accustomed to women exerting their rights than their eastern counterparts were.

Perhaps as historians we are too enamored of journalistic flair. True, the trials contained fashion reports; cosmetic evaluations of complexion; assessment of feminine beauty; courtroom antics worthy of *Perry Mason*, *L.A. Law*, or *Boston Legal*; and bedroom adventures worthy of daytime television.

However, with the trials and appeals concluded, we are simply left with the law. The constructions of gender as well as the nature of unwritten law can be teased from the historical documents.[121] On appeal the insanity defense exonerated Laura Fair, a woman who had murdered her duplicitous lover. Chico Forster violated Lastencia Abarta, his betrothed, and abandoned her, thus destroying the young girl's chance for marriage to a respectable man. Tom Cook ripped every fiber of the Victorian tapestry. He ruined servant girls, local adolescents, and the minds of innocents. Who, then, could stop these violators of the unwritten law? Wives and lovers with the strong arm of the unwritten law, doing what they could not remember, and defended by lawyers who knew enough to use every possible defense argument, however preposterous. Sometimes a jury remembered a slogan about ill-fitting gloves and dismissed the rest of the evidence.[122] Not as interpretatively interesting, granted, yet it is a fact of legal and historical analysis.

CHAPTER TWO

Good Riddance

Justifiable Homicides of Enemy Deviants

California's nineteenth century featured several cases in which women, like Katie Cook, found themselves driven to rid their households, if not civilization, of enemy deviants. In 1901, for example, Clara A. Wellman shot her husband through the heart with a rifle, ending three years of terror. Clara Wellman, like Katie Cook, terminated a community terrorist, this time in the San Jacinto Mountains in California's inland empire.

Clara had married Frank P. Wellman, a quarter century her senior, at age thirteen. Frank worked as a rancher and "was a decent fellow when sober."[1] By the time she was nineteen and the mother of three-year-old Mary, Clara had endured endless physical abuse from her drunken husband. Clara desperately wanted a separation, but Frank ultimately refused and threatened to kill her, their child, Clara's family, and anyone else who got in his way.

In this ranch community tucked away in the San Jacinto Mountains, Frank Wellman had earned an unsavory reputation. "He terrorized the mountain ranchers and their families by riding by and firing a revolver viciously at their homes."[2]

Frank, like T. J. "Tom" Cook, was an enemy deviant in the community. He was considered "a very immoral man," whose presence in Orange County threatened the safety of every woman. Cook's attorney skillfully painted the portrait of the "depravity of the murdered man . . . while the misery of the trusting wife [was] pathetic."[3] So too Frank Wellman "had been a desperado for years in the locality." Worse yet, he "had been abusing the baby all the morning, choking it until it grew black in the face." According to Clara, when the baby started to cry, "he started to come in, at the same time calling the baby the vilest of names, threatening again to shoot my —— head off and baby's also." Reacting to the threat, Clara "ran into the room where the rifle was"; she recalled, "When I saw him trying to get his knife out of his belt . . . I grabbed up the .22 rifle lying on the bed, and pointed it at him, pulled the trigger."[4] Clara's aim proved true.

Frank L. Trimmin, a neighbor, corroborated Clara Wellman's tale of woe. The sheriff and the coroner from Riverside County arrived at the scene, formed a coroner's jury, held a hearing, and declared that Clara had shot Frank in self-defense. The *Los Angeles Times* concluded, "Public opinion exonerates Mrs. Wellman of all blame in view of the dead man's past character. Mrs. Wellman is a fine shot with a rifle, having handled firearms all her married life."[5]

In 1910 Angela Maria De Vita cut down Abele Bove, a boarder in the De Vita home, in defense of her husband and family. After braving long-term harassment and threats of death to her family, De Vita drew a .38 caliber revolver and fired five holes into Bove's body. "He got what he deserved," she told the desk officer in the police station.[6] In jail De Vita displayed confidence, assured of "acquittal in her trial in Superior

Court," a procedural necessity because of her confession.[7] At her trial the prosecution brought "little evidence," and the press declared that De Vita's attorney would invoke the "higher law."[8] With De Vita on the stand, a story of terror and intimidation emerged. "Deputy District Attorney Keys paid but little attention to her cross-examination." The press observed, "The strength of the testimony tending to free the woman was so strong" that the prosecution made no effort "to exculpate Bove in any way."[9] The jury took only three minutes to deliver a verdict of not guilty. De Vita clearly stepped out of a Victorian female role into a male role, using deadly force to protect her family.

A 1913 Los Angeles coroner's jury found Lea Delmon's killing of her husband justifiable because he had tried to sell her into prostitution. "Without hesitation the jurors vindicated Mrs. Lea Delmon, whose tragic story was reenacted before a sordid crowd that thronged in the undertaking parlor where the inquest was held." The press concluded, "The wife who shoots her husband when he would force her into a life of shame commits a justifiable homicide."[10]

An Acton, California, coroner's jury was out for three minutes and returned a verdict of justifiable homicide in the case of Nettie Platz. Her husband's brother had attacked her in retaliation for criticism by her husband. Platz's husband testified that he had told his wife of his brother's violent tendencies and instructed her to kill him if attacked. Other witnesses confirmed the veracity of his testimony. Platz displayed bite marks on her back inflicted during the tussle. The unwritten law or simple self-defense was sufficient for coroner Nance's jury in 1921.[11]

The cases of Clara Wellman, Angela Maria De Vita, Lea

Delmon, and Nettie Platz reflect the long nineteenth century's consistent desire to protect women from enemy deviants, even when these women were bound to their assailant. The law, forearmed with Victorian values, affirmed the rights of these women with verdicts of justifiable homicide when a male threatened to destroy the family, the center of Western civilization. However, some women accused of murder seemed to possess traits that deviated from Victorian mores. The defendants that follow, Emma Le Doux, Aurelia Scheck, and Gertrude Gibbons, were examples of such female deviants.

Emma Le Doux

On March 24, 1906, a railroad worker discovered the body of Albert McVicar in a trunk at the Stockton Southern Pacific Railroad station. Police immediately suspected his estranged wife when they ascertained that she had arranged for the trunk's shipment. The next day Stockton's sheriff sought Emma Le Doux in connection with the death of her husband.[12] The sheriff successfully located the suspect, and with Le Doux in tow, the Stockton district attorney took charge of the investigation. Journalists soon dubbed Emma Le Doux "the Trunk Murderess."[13]

Medical scientists arrived at varying conclusions regarding the cause of McVicar's death. One autopsy surgeon thought that he died of blows, thus was beaten to death. The coroner's assistant thought McVicar's demise resulted from poisoning. Coroner H. E. Southworth agreed, reasoning that someone administered "knock-out drops" and then crushed McVicar's body by inserting it into the trunk, but admitted that chemical tests might offer an alternate cause of death.[14] Those tests revealed knockout drops and morphine in the victim's system.

However, investigators found that Emma Le Doux had purchased cyanide of potassium at a local drug store.

Although the tests failed to reveal any traces of cyanide, the coroner's jury concluded that McVicar's death resulted from morphine, chloral hydrate, and injuries sustained when the perpetrator crammed his body into the trunk.[15] In the trunk McVicar lacked sufficient "oxygen to sustain what life there was present" and expired at the hand of Emma Le Doux.[16] In an interview with the press that morning, Le Doux admitted that she had concocted a story for the police, explaining, "[I did so] until I could see my attorney and have him secure a certain piece of evidence which is my whole case and which might have been destroyed if I had not protected myself in this way." Thereby, "the real facts which establish my innocence were protected from them."[17]

The criminal proceedings moved slowly. Le Doux entered a plea of not guilty in April.[18] In June a jury formed, and "it became evident [that] morning that the defense [would] be largely technical."[19] The prosecution focused on bigamy, a lover's quarrel, and love letters, not unlike the parade of love letters in the Laura Fair case.[20]

The defense claimed that the prosecution had failed to make its case. First, no direct evidence proved that Le Doux had poisoned McVicar. Second, they could not place Le Doux at the scene of his death. Finally, McVicar obviously committed suicide by ingesting drugs, jumping into the trunk, and expiring at his own hand.[21]

Nevertheless, the jury believed the prosecution narrative, found Emma Le Doux guilty of first-degree murder, and condemned her to death. Her attorneys promised a motion for a new trial and an appeal. Le Doux took the verdict in stride, made light of the jury's decision, and returned to her jail cell with an air of nonchalance that startled the judge. Thus Emma Le Doux, the Stockton "Trunk Murderess," challenged gender stereotypes and confounded journalists because of her aplomb.

The press reported on Le Doux's unusual composure throughout the trial. In fact, she "seemed to smile as they discussed the case with her counsel and friends who were with her through the trial. Despite the verdict, she shook the hands of her attorneys in genuine gratitude for their hard work on her behalf, and seemed to have no fear for the future."[22] The press concluded this phase of coverage with contradictory images of Le Doux. First, journalists found her behavior uncharacteristic of a woman. She possessed "remarkable composure" for a woman.[23] She exhibited the nerve "of the strongest man."[24] Yet the artwork depicting her at the moment of judgment portrays her as feminine, in fact fashionable in her hat.[25] The press also noted that "a remarkable feature of the case was the morbid curiosity of many women who thronged the courtroom from the commencement of the trial" to its conclusion.[26]

The *San Jose Mercury News* editorial titled "Woman and Capital Punishment" offered an equal opportunity view of the death penalty. There was "no moral or logical reason why a woman should be exempt from the extreme penalty of the law in the case of capital crime." The law made no gender statement regarding the penalty. Only "natural chivalry" in man could oppose hanging for a woman. Yet times had changed. The paper wondered whether "the pressure of woman for political and business equality had had, or is likely to have any influence upon public sentiment and opinion in the case of capital crimes perpetrated by women." Equality in access to employment and suffrage "should raise a feeling in favor of holding [women] to equal responsibilities." It was merely a "logical conclusion."[27] The editorial reflected many sexist images of chivalry, nature, and inequality.

Le Doux's attorney, C. H. Fairall, raised a legal challenge in his motion for a new trial, going to the heart of patriarchy and misogyny. One juror after being sworn declared, "I will hang the ——."[28] The juror further announced, "I believe that the woman is guilty and she ought to have her neck broken."[29] Under such circumstances Le Doux's trial jury lacked fairness and impartiality. At the hearing Le Doux appeared before a crowded courtroom. "The majority of spectators were women." She seemed to the reporter to be "dressed as though for a shopping tour."[30] The judge ruled that the juror misconduct was insufficient for a new trial and sentenced Le Doux to hang.[31] Her attorney filed a bill of exceptions with the California Supreme Court, and Le Doux departed for the Stockton city jail.[32]

In 1909 Le Doux, though still incarcerated in the Stockton jail, possessed the same nerve and conviction of exoneration in a new trial. The press observed, "The jail appears to agree with her, as she has grown plumper, and is said to present a much better appearance than when she was arrested."[33] The image of woman on trial or at trials never seemed to slip by the journalistic pen.

On May 19, 1909, the California Supreme Court granted a new trial on the ground that juror prejudice had prevented Le Doux from receiving a fair trial. Charles H. Ferial argued and the court agreed that the disqualification of the sheriff calling the panel of jurors extended to his deputy. Further, the deputy went to Le Doux's mother's house, took the love letters introduced at trial, and did so without a warrant or permission. This search and seizure was unconstitutional. The court nevertheless properly admitted the letters into evidence. The trial judge's refusal to admit evidence that McVicar had pushed Le Doux into prostitution was error; the jury should have decided its weight as to motive. Finally, the trial judge erred by failing to grant a motion relating to the prosecution's expert witnesses.[34] The decision was thirteenth-page news.[35] District attorney George F. Monocle petitioned for a rehearing before the supreme court.[36] Monocle lost, and the new trial was set for February 2, 1910.[37] Before the trial date Le Doux entered a plea of guilty and won a visit with her mother before moving to San Quentin. "She was very cheerful when she entered her plea of guilty, though always insisting she never committed the murder. She hopes for an early parole after seven years."[38] Her deal to see her mother worked; however, Le Doux remained in jail until 1920, when she finally won parole.[39] A recidivist, she landed back in prison, and her 1934 parole board denied her request for parole.[40] Le Doux's annual trek before the parole board continued, because two prior paroles and violations returning her to incarceration weighed heavily against her.[41] Emma Le Doux, like other women convicted of murder, languished in the county facility for women.

Aurelia Scheck

In the early hours of June 14, 1906, Joel Scheck died of two gunshot wounds. Police arrived and heard Aurelia (called "Arilla" by the *Los Angeles Times* until the time of trial) Scheck's account of burglars, a scream in the night, and shots. Aurelia claimed that Joel died at the hands of unknown burglars, but the police doubted her veracity. After hours of interrogation, the police took Scheck and Earnest G. Stackpole into custody on suspicion of murder. "Captain Paul Flammer and Deputy District Attorney Fleming told the press that Stackpole was Arilla's paramour." The *Los Angeles Times* described Aurelia as "19 years old, but she appears somewhat older. She is fat and dark complexioned, with black eyes and hair. She is not pretty nor especially attractive in appearance."[42] Coroner Trout worked on the case all day and held an inquest the same day. The inquest jury failed to identify the killer of Joel Scheck, age twenty-two. The police, however, doggedly built their case against Scheck and Stackpole.

On June 16 Captain Flammer and deputy district attorney Fleming gave the pair a "severe sweating," resulting in a confession. Captain Flammer offered, "The case is a hard one, but we have been making rapid progress and expect to clear it up in good time." The police discovered a motive, a five-hundred-dollar life-insurance policy. The two planned to collect and marry, but "something miscarried." Police also found "blood-stained clothing belonging to Scheck" in Stackpole's room at the home of Aurelia Scheck's mother.[43]

The *Los Angeles Times* put another twist on the case, telling the public that Aurelia Scheck's confession confirmed police theory. Moreover, "Stackpole [was] believed to have first conceived the plan to murder Scheck." The paper claimed that the lovers conspired to murder the husband and make it look like suicide. That plan went awry when the second round found its mark in Scheck's brain. As of June 17 Aurelia Scheck was "on the verge of a complete nervous collapse." She was "constantly attended by nurses" and "hysterical the greater part of the time and [lay] on a bed . . . sobbing night and day."

Stackpole, on the other hand, had "become defiant." He denied everything, but the *Times* declared that he had "led the life of a degenerate and ha[d] a peculiar cunning."[44] The press tried the case and had already arrived at a verdict.

On June 18, Los Angeles witnessed the burial of Joel Scheck. The funeral story portrayed him as "humble and straightforward" and "loved and respected" in his workplace. The home funeral proceeded from the Scheck cottage to the cemetery. Along the way "the peculiar morbid curiosity" of the crowd compelled people to stand "on tiptoe" and "crane their necks to get a sight of the widow." Aurelia Scheck was like "a marble statue," not exhibiting any emotion. Her demeanor revealed "a disposition and nature seemingly without feeling, but when compared with the degenerate Stackpole, her faults [shrank] into insignificance."[45]

Unlike the situation for the press and the public, things were far less certain in the district attorney's office. Formal charges against the alleged perpetrators were delayed by "a slight hitch in the development of the evidence." Capt. Paul Flammer told the press that the police now believed every word that Scheck uttered. Further, the confession improved her countenance. As the *Los Angeles Times* reported, "After her confession she appeared calmer, and now answers all our questions and explains how it all occurred, her relations with Stackpole, when and where the murder was planned and discussed other details." This new woman obtained privileges. "Mrs. Scheck is accorded every courtesy by the police. She is allowed to see members of her family every day, and it was a special favor that she was allowed to go to the funeral of the man she helped to murder."[46] Police favors multiplied as the arraignment approached.

Scheck insisted that she not be dragged into court with Stackpole. The district attorney complied. "As the police ha[d] need of her testimony, her request was granted; Stackpole was arraigned alone." Stackpole appeared without a lawyer and asked that one be appointed for him, "an impossible request in the justice court." Later in the day he negotiated with Hugh J. Crawford to serve as defense counsel. The *Times* then shifted its characterization of Scheck. "The woman over whose exceedingly dubious charms the killing occurred, was allowed to wait in the jail below shedding crocodile tears while Stackpole was facing the music alone." The story speculated, "It is probable that the woman will escape with her most unworthy life as a reward for having turned traitor against her husband's slayer."[47] Scheck—a marble statue and a traitor, hysterical, stony calm, fat and slow witted—she was characterized many ways, none of them positive in print.

Stackpole, on the other hand, proved less complicated. An inquiry in Twin Bridges, Montana, revealed his long criminal career, including a conviction for highway robbery in California, a pardon springing him early; burglary in Silver Star, Montana, with no conviction; robbery and a conviction in Salt Lake City; and drifting from New Mexico to California.[48] Despite his record the *Times*, in words echoing the journalistic treatment of women throughout the long nineteenth century, noted, "Stackpole could almost plead insanity and prove it by the fact that he was enamored of Mrs. Scheck. She is a big, fat, dumpy, dull-looking, unattractive woman."[49]

Stackpole emerged from his preliminary hearing "on the verge of utter collapse." Scheck looked him in the eye, and he acknowledged, "I must get a lawyer." Scheck "turned from him in court with frightened horror as though he were a snake.

Her attitude had shaken him with fear and apprehension. He realized he had nothing to hope for from her."[50]

The proceedings proved irresistible to the press. "Women, almost frenzied with curiosity, fought like demons to get into court. . . . They were wild to see the fascinating fat lady—Mrs. Scheck—whose charms are alleged to have driven Stackpole to murder her inconvenient husband—Joel Scheck." What they saw was "a miserable quivering wreck on the verge of absolute collapse." Stackpole's attorney called C. W. Dowling, the defendant's barber, who testified that he had cut Stackpole while shaving him the day before the murder. Accordingly, the bloodstained handkerchief that police believed was soaked with Joel Scheck's blood could, in fact, have been the product of the slip of the razor.[51]

The trial started on August 10 after "three special venires" passed through the jury selection process to secure "twelve men of impartial and unbiased mind." The prosecution brought witnesses to identify Joel Scheck, to tell of "Mrs. Aurelia Scheck's" explanation of the crime, and to determine the cause of death. Dr. G. W. Campbell, in response to a question from defense attorney R. C. Nolman, testified that the wounds could have been self-inflicted.[52] The defense immediately created an alternative narrative of causation.

On August 13, Aurelia Scheck took the stand and recounted numerous plans to kill her husband. These plots included poison, throwing him off a high cliff, and shooting him. She "testified slowly and deliberately, seemingly unconscious of the enormity of her offense." Stackpole listened in "calm insouciance." The *Times* imputed some understanding of this testimony, telling the public, "He realized, however, what the babblings of this weak woman meant for him." Even more

66   GOOD RIDDANCE

damaging to Stackpole was Scheck's account of letters from Arizona. "Murder was their theme," she claimed. Stackpole promised to marry her when she was a widow. In his letters he referred "again and again . . . to his returning and slaying the man who stood in his path." Stackpole, inspired by a story about two Mexicans holding up a man, hatched the story of the crime. Scheck's testimony about the murder weapon created "one of the curious points of the case." The bullet wounds were those of a .38 caliber weapon, but Scheck's pistol was a .32 caliber. She recalled the murder scene and the killing. After the murder, she and Stackpole met several times, and he told her "to amend her story to suit the situation." Stackpole instructed her to tell the story his way or "he would put the whole blame on her."[53] The defense spun a story making Scheck the victim of a scheming older man skilled in his criminal ways.

The next day belonged to Stackpole's attorney. It also was "ladies day" as "fully one-half of those present in court [were] women." When the testimony turned to Scheck's intimate relationship with Stackpole, "the women in court used their fans a little more vigorously." Stackpole's defense focused on the coaching of Scheck by the district attorney and police officers. However, Scheck denied any promise of a reward for telling the truth. Further, her attorneys, Horace H. Appel and Paul Ussher, told her to tell the truth in the hope that she would not be brought to trial. When the interrogatories turned to the Stackpole letters, she claimed memory loss regarding particulars. The *Times* reported that "'I can't remember' became a stock phrase, and with parrotlike pertinacity Scheck kept repeating it when confronted with a question she considered a possible pitfall." When questions focused on Scheck's sexual relations with men other than her husband, her attorney successfully objected to every one.[54] Stackpole's attorney failed to break Scheck's image as a youthful, inexperienced victim.

The *Times* saw a different case evolving. The paper offered, "The highly sensational story by the wife of the murdered Joel Scheck may have impressed the jury, as being true or false, but at least it could have little force when a man's life is at stake standing alone."[55] After all, the press portrayed Scheck as a dimwitted, pathetic woman. In terms of class Scheck represented a commoner in the Victorian world.

The trial continued with the prosecution offering testimony to corroborate the details of Scheck's narrative of the circumstances. First, police officer H. B. Wallace told of finding Joel Scheck's .32 caliber revolver in the bedroom. The testimony rebutted the defense suicide notion, but interestingly "the revolver with which the killing was done ha[d] mysteriously disappeared." The next witness, George Williams, testified that he had overheard Stackpole say, "I'll get rid of him." Defense questioning substantially destroyed his credibility. Other witnesses contributed minor points to the prosecution.[56]

August 16 proved to be a more exciting day in the trial because love letters moved center stage. In a scene reminiscent of the Laura Fair case, the jury learned of 160 letters. The *Times* noted, "Mrs. Scheck burned the letters she received, in accordance with a common understanding existing between them and by what strange and fatal chance Stackpole elected to keep this bundle of love letters is almost past comprehension." Fifteen letters were offered into evidence. Three of Stackpole's letters "contain[ed] no incriminating sentences, but burn[ed] with a fiery lust that indicated the strength of the passion that the woman had raised in his breast." The prosecution told the jury that they had obtained access to Stackpole's safe-deposit box and seized the letters. District attorney Fleming read the flaming fifteen into the record, and "the women in the crowded courtroom sat up and craned their necks so as not to lose a word of the slangy, lustful and murderous allusions couched in coarse and sometimes indecent language." The paper reported on the content of the letters and then explained to readers the significance of the words. The *Times* saw "the vanity of the woman in dilating upon the trousseaux she is preparing—on money furnished by her lover—unctuously smacking her lips over a good dinner. . . . [It] is a terrible commentary upon the cold blooded treachery of Mrs. Scheck." The prosecution closed, and the defense opened with witnesses including Myrtle Flowers, "a simple minded girl"; "no one seemed to know, not even the attorneys for the defense," why she took the stand.[57] It was not a good omen for the defense.

On August 17 Earnest G. Stackpole floundered on the witness stand. He repeated his story of leaving the Scheck home at 10:30 p.m., going to his room at the Blaine Hotel, hearing a fire engine, running to help the firefighters, returning to his room, and learning of Joel's murder. He denied all the material elements of the case and affirmed that the blood on his handkerchief resulted from a shaving mishap. He admitted being convicted of felonies in Utah in 1902 and in Alameda County in 1880. The defense produced May Irving, who testified that she saw a "short, heavy-set man run out and down the street" away from the Scheck home on the night of the crime. Finally, the defense went after the love letters, arguing that they "tended to show that Mrs. Scheck while faithless and disloyal to her husband, was also making a dupe of Stackpole."[58] The defense failed, and the jury convicted.[59]

What to do with Scheck now that Stackpole was headed for prison? A month later, with Scheck still jailed on the murder charge, the district attorney constructed a "creditable solution." He abided by the "almost invariable custom to release the prisoner that consents to turn State's evidence," but he decided to prosecute her for perjury. The *Los Angeles Times* applauded the decision but took space to comment on Scheck and women in general. Scheck was "flabby both mentally and physically. Like many weak, unattractive women, she [was] conceited and romantic." Even more certainly, "sudden attention from a man as clever as Stackpole completely turned her head." Universally, "there are other stupid women in this world who are as dangerous, at this very minute, as Mrs. Scheck. Only the clever man hasn't come along."[60] Deviant, dim-witted women, all too willing to exploit male weaknesses, populated this world. Mesmerizing, marginal women lurked with murder on their minds. Men must be alert to their deadly designs, so said the press.

A grand jury returned an indictment of perjury against Aurelia Scheck in October; however, the *Times* noted, "Mrs. Scheck has promise of pardon on the murder change, but is face to face with the indictment for perjury. With ordinary good fortune, there is no reason why she should ever serve one day in the State's prison for that offence. Indictments in this county have almost without exception failed to reach the mark."[61] The *Times* also observed that jail food gave Scheck "lines of plumpness."[62] Despite its savvy regarding the reality of the legalities, the *Times* could not resist the journalistic swipe at women.

The district attorney kept Scheck in jail on the murder charge pending the perjury trial.[63] In fact, despite an "agreement . . .

to the effect that her case on that accusation was to have been dismissed" in a court hearing, it did not happen because the district attorney did not appear. The fact of the murder charge made bail "impossible."[64] The defense attorneys awaited the perjury trial.

Scheck's attorney, Horace Appel, moved to set the indictment aside, and Judge Trask agreed. The judge acknowledged, "Admittedly she was a partner in one of the most cold-blooded murders ever perpetrated in the State of California, but that is not before the court. Here she is charged with perjury, and is entitled to the benefit of the law as much as any other defendant." The law favored Scheck because to prove a case of perjury the prosecution had the burden of bringing testimony indicating that "the statements made by Mrs. Scheck in the first instance were absolutely false." The prosecution offered no such testimony. Judge Trask also stated that he "doubted if a case ever could be made out" and discharged Scheck from custody.[65] Thus the law set her free.

Stackpole, on the other hand, remained a prisoner. His attorney moved for a new trial.[66] That motion lost, and the court sentenced Stackpole to life in prison.[67] However, his incarceration at San Quentin was delayed until April 4, 1907. Until then he remained in the county jail because of the pending appeal, but the judge later changed his mind when Stackpole and two other felons attempted a jailbreak.[68] Scheck, freed by law, disappeared from the headlines.

Gertrude Gibbons

On December 17, 1918, Frank G. Gibbons, a Pullman car conductor, expired at his home in Los Angeles after taking a dose of potassium cyanide. Police arrested his wife, Gertrude

Myron Gibbons. She claimed that she had purchased the drug for her husband, a long-time sufferer from tuberculosis. Captain of detectives George Home and district attorney Asa Keyes thought otherwise and arrested her for murder. They found a motive in a $3,200 insurance policy and the desire to get rid of an invalid. Gibbons's construction of the facts differed significantly from the investigators' version. She told journalists, "My home life has been most unhappy, and my husband had the most irascible disposition. He was a chronic sufferer from tuberculosis and for the last eight months made threats to commit suicide at the same time urging me to do the same. When he saw that I would not think of the plan, he urged me to assist him in doing away with himself." She finally gave in and acquired the poison. She declared, "If it is any crime to purchase poison for another to commit suicide then I am guilty."[69]

The next day the *Los Angeles Times* located the proprietress of the Miramar, where the Gibbonses lived, stricken with an ailment with "every appearance of strychnine poisoning." Was a "Borgia plot" afoot? The headline caught the attention of the reader, but in jail Gibbons maintained her innocence. The reporter observed, "She is calm and in complete possession of herself and her emotions. She discusses the past with the same grasp of details as she talks about the present situation and every ramification of the case." She told the journalist, "I have been unhappy in my life with Mr. Gibbons' constant nagging, continual jealousy all the time." Most significantly, she declared, "It was his own idea to commit suicide. Time and again after an unusually bad spell he would say it was the only way out of our difficulty, and he kept it up until it became a matter of no surprise to hear his probable death discussed." The reporter offered a description of Gibbons: "[She is] a woman [of] large frame and robust constitution. Her face is somewhat lined, but her carriage and walk, her talk and mannerisms speak of a woman still in the prime of life. Deep chested, well formed, she does not look the 45 years she claims." Gertrude devoted her time to caring for Frank and reading to him nightly, particularly psychology. Frank "hoped mental influence and psychology would help him where medical science had failed." In sum Gertrude expressed relief regarding his demise, stating, "[I'm] glad his body is liberated, that he's free."[70] She bought the cyanide and Frank had gratefully dispatched himself.

Detective Capt. George Home revealed part of Gertrude Gibbons's past and thereby raised a question relevant to motive. He disclosed that Gertrude never legally married Frank because she had neglected to divorce her first husband. Home told the press that her claim on the $3,200 insurance policy constituted fraud for two reasons. First, she was not Frank Gibbons's wife, and second, the death was not natural. Finally, he declared, "Our case is complete from every point of view."[71] The matter, although clear in detectives' minds, had to withstand the scrutiny of a jury.

In this case science defeated the detectives. Dr. Arthur R. Maas reported to the coroner, "I have made a chemical examination of the stomach contents in the case of Frank C. Gibbons and find no poison present. I have also made a chemical examination of the portion of the liver, some of the blood and additional stomach content and find no cyanide present." The autopsy surgeon, Dr. A. F. Wagner, concurred and added, "The cause of death was pulmonary hemorrhage caused by the tuberculosis. The autopsy findings did not indicate that any poison had been administered." Undeterred by this turn of events, district attorney Thomas Lee Woolwine believed that the police investigation created a clear case of murder despite scientific findings. Regarding those findings, he asserted, "It is my judgment that the examination, so far as the chemist is concerned, should take a wider range and that his conclusions should be fortified by the opinion of another in his profession, to all of which he is entirely agreed."[72] A second scientific opinion must resolve the question.

With the press waiting for the second laboratory result, attention turned to Gertrude Gibbons's past. A *Times* reporter caught up with Josiah Herrick and confirmed his marriage to her and their failure to obtain a divorce. Even if cleared of murder, "she may have to face a bigamy charge," the reporter speculated. Gibbons's attorney, Harrison Cassell, refused to speculate because he observed "a number of gaps in the case as outlined by the District Attorney and the police." In the meantime Dr. Lyman B. Stookey, the second chemist, discovered that Frank's body had been embalmed.[73]

On Christmas Eve, Carolyn Chapin Kurtz's face was splashed all over the newspapers, identifying her as the prosecution's star witness. In a tell-all story, Kurtz recalled that twice Gertrude Gibbons had confided in her about attempts to kill her husband. Hearing of these plots, Kurtz turned detective with her physician and traced the cyanide purchase that Gibbons admitted to police and press. Kurtz had gone to Detective Home with the story and that had resulted in Gibbons's arrest.[74]

The *Times* declared that the "Gibbons poison case bids fair to be unique in the annals of crime" in a section 2 front-page story splattered with pictures of all the leading men and women, now including city chemist Erwin Miller and Professor

Laird Stabler posing in their laboratories. District attorney Woolwine promised that "important new evidence" lurked around the corner.[75]

Woolwine's experts, Lyman B. Stookey and Robert E. Swain, chair of the chemistry department at Stanford, both found cyanide in Frank Gibbons's body. This ran directly contrary to coroner Hartwell's certification of death by natural causes based on the findings of the autopsy surgeon Wagner, Professor Arthur R. Maas, Professor Laird J. Stabler, and city chemist Erwin H. Miller. Woolwine believed his experts "regardless of other findings and reports."[76] The battle of the scientists fueled speculation and newspaper circulation.

The case moved on to the Los Angeles County Grand Jury. In another front-page story, the *Times* presented the position of the prosecution and the defense with three pictures of Frank Gibbons: in good health, as a tuberculosis victim, and shortly before death. Defense attorney Harrison Cassell and district attorney Woolwine took graphic positions opposite each other with a chemistry laboratory in the background featuring a large question mark centered in the laboratory. The story also portrayed a contest of colleges with "the science departments of California's three biggest universities pitted against each other." Swain represented Stanford University. Maas and Stabler taught at the University of Southern California. Professor Green of the University of California had not yet filed his report. Stookey was "also closely allied with U.S.C." as was the city chemist Miller. Since Maas's report found no cyanide in Frank's body, Gertrude "brightened wonderfully"; the *Times* reported, "[She] is entirely sure of her ultimate freedom. She now believes that Gibbons meant to kill himself, but that his long-standing disease providentially interfered."[77] All that psychology proved provident as the case unraveled.

The case went to the Los Angeles Grand Jury, where women took their seats for the first time. Judge Craig charged the grand jury regarding its duties and remarked, "Of the different steps marking the advance of women to full political equality with men, few, if any, are more important, not merely to the women themselves, but to the State, than their participation in the performance of the important duty of acting as grand jurors." Further, he expressed satisfaction "that this body [would] be more useful, more generally efficient, and more capable of rendering exact and equal justice because of the presence of women as members of it." That said, district attorney Woolwine started his parade of witnesses.[78]

Most of the two dozen witnesses provided testimony favorable to Gibbons. The grand jurors, including four women, adjourned for about thirty minutes and then announced their refusal to indict. Thus they set Gibbons free to pursue her goal of teaching the philosophy of happiness.[79] Even more astounding, "the compensation fund company in which Gibbons was insured, it was announced, [would] pay the insurance money to Mrs. Gibbons without waiting for the outcome of the case against her."[80] Out of jail, Gibbons decided "to sink her identity by taking another name and taking up work by which she hope[d] to make a living, by teaching philosophy."[81] Thus, incognito, Gertrude Gibbons faded away into the Los Angeles night along with the long nineteenth century.

In 1870 California's first sensational trial featured an oft-married woman, Laura Fair, accused of murdering her duplicitous lover, A. P. Crittenden. Crittenden, a member of the upper-class Victorian world, pursued Fair relentlessly, promised her marriage, and then reneged. The press, prosecution, and public put Fair on trial, condemning her as a threat to Victorian civilization. Apparently, A. P. Crittenden had suddenly experienced an epiphany and unexpectedly chose to renew his commitment to his wife. Fair, now the discarded mistress, wantonly sought revenge by shooting her lover in cold blood, then conveniently filed a plea of insanity. Although Fair was supported by women's rights advocates, civilized society deemed her a monstrous woman who advocated free love. The public refused to brook this unchaste anomaly to true womanhood and applauded when the jury convicted her of murder. However, error in the Fair trial resulted in a retrial in which the jury found the defendant not guilty by reason of insanity. Victorian civilization failed to crumble; on the contrary its cherished notion of "lady" clung well into the early twentieth century.

Although the insanity defense was anathema to most Californians during the Fair trial, the public enthusiastically approved the acquittal of Lastencia Abarta in 1881 by reason of insanity. Abarta, like Fair, found herself engaged to a devious man who proposed marriage but failed to keep his promise. Unlike Fair, eighteen-year-old Abarta exhibited the qualities of a nineteenth-century lady until a much older Chico Forster compromised her virtue by seducing her and then refusing to marry her. Despite Abarta's beauty, Forster's actions destroyed her prospects of marriage to any decent man. An expert defense witness testified that the loss of her virtue could drive any true woman mad. Thus, Chico Forster's demise proved a fitting end for his licentious, lascivious life.

Although appropriate, the insanity defense proved unnecessary in the 1899 trial of Katie Cook. Her husband, Tom, violated every precept of the sanctity of marriage and family. His debased character extended beyond their bedroom as he compromised the virtue of other Orange County women as well. The jury sympathized with the much-maligned Mrs. Cook and found her simply not guilty rather than not guilty by reason of insanity. Tom Cook, a lecherous enemy deviant, clearly threatened the virtue of any woman he encountered; thus he deserved killing.

Other women such as Clara Wellman, Angela Maria De Vita, Lea Delmon, and Nettie Platz resorted to murder to defend themselves and family members from enemy deviants in California's long nineteenth century. Juries judged these defendants' actions as justifiable homicide. However, murder defendants Emma Le Doux, Aurelia Scheck, and Gertrude Gibbons did not fit the mold of the nineteenth-century "lady" driven to defend herself. On the contrary their motives, at first glance, appeared grounded in greed.

Emma Le Doux, the Stockton "Trunk Murderess," stood trial in 1906 for the murder of her estranged husband, Albert McVicar. Of all the women defendants covered in the second chapter of this study, Le Doux was the only one ultimately convicted of murder. Le Doux clearly lacked the typical traits of a Victorian lady, but journalists admired her unusual composure and confidence, comparing her bravado to that of a man. Yet the press also referred to her feminine appearance as the jury announced its verdict. Despite Le Doux's nonchalance, her demeanor failed to prove prescient for a verdict of not guilty, even on appeal. Although she escaped the death penalty, Le Doux, a recidivist, never remained paroled for any length of time.

Portrayed in the media as dim-witted, fat, ugly, and lower class, Aurelia Scheck was no Victorian lady. Nevertheless, she managed to escape a murder conviction in her 1906 trial because of her youth and inexperience, like Lastencia Abarta's; those qualities, coupled with her willingness to turn state's evidence against her worldlier accomplice, Earnest Stackpole, facilitated her release. The press, incredulous that Stackpole had murdered Joel Scheck to gain Aurelia's hand and a five-hundred-dollar insurance policy, made consistently scathing remarks about his paramour throughout the trial. It is clear the public at large deemed this couple an insult to the mores of the long nineteenth century and perhaps even breathed a collective sigh of relief that Stackpole's life sentence would prevent the lovers from procreating.

Bigamist Gertrude Gibbons, accused of poisoning her husband, Frank, in 1918, never stood trial for murder. Instead, the grand jury, for the first time comprised of women as well as men, set her free. The prosecution cringed, convinced that she murdered Frank Gibbons because she had tired of caring for an invalid and wished to acquire a $3,200 insurance policy. Conflicting forensic evidence failed to convince the grand jury of Gibbons's guilt. Thus Gibbons changed her name and with plans to pursue a career teaching philosophy, disappeared from history.

Collectively, these cases reveal the reluctance of courts, the press, and the public to condemn middle- and upper-class women accused of murder during the long nineteenth century except in instances where women defendants threatened the Victorian social order such as in the first trial of Laura Fair and the trial and retrial of Emma Le Doux. Well versed in the Victorian standards of what it meant to be a lady, courts and the public at large deemed violent behavior in middle- and upper-class women as incongruous. Thus all-male juries consistently demonstrated that in order for these woman to commit murder, there must be a plausible reason such as a definitive case of insanity; male duplicity leading a young, inexperienced lady astray; or the presence of a male enemy deviant. Ever-protective of true women, the Victorian mind held that only women who were insane, deviant, or lower class could wantonly commit murder.

CHAPTER THREE

Toward the New Woman

Feminine Wiles on Trial

The Victorianism of the long nineteenth century gave way to the "new woman" of the 1920s. Fashion, although arguably frivolous, clearly documents this change. The stylish turn-of-the-century Victorian woman's hourglass figure required a tightly laced whalebone corset exerting twenty-five pounds of pressure per square inch on her ribcage. To prevent fainting fashionable Victorian ladies carried smelling salts out of necessity. By 1913 the fashion-conscious new woman strapped down her breasts, wore a girdle under a short hemline, and sheared off her Victorian tresses to a chin-length bob—the so-called flapper style. The new woman also wore makeup, whereas a respectable Victorian lady shunned "face paint," equating its use with prostitution. By 1921 women competed in one-piece bathing suits at the first Miss America beauty contest in Atlantic City. Never before had women's bodies been so publicly exposed.[1]

This radical shift in fashion, although adopted by only a small percentage of American women, nevertheless reflected dramatic political change in the 1920s.[2] California women won the right to vote in 1911 by state constitutional amendment and won the national franchise by constitutional amendment in 1920. They entered courtrooms as attorneys in the nineteenth century, and in 1917 they took their place in the jury box. As women entered the public sphere that men had largely dominated during the long nineteenth century, women's physical appearance became more masculine. Like men, new women even smoked and drank in public. Thus, the new woman of the 1920s pronounced the Victorianism of the long nineteenth century dead. That did not mean, however, that other Americans did not still try to live up to Victorian values of social responsibility and personal morality.[3]

While California women joined the political public sphere, "Freud" and "free love" entered the vernacular, thus contributing to the sexual revolution of the 1920s. The automobile fostered this sexual revolution, and Californians' love affair with motor-vehicle ownership soared, particularly in Los Angeles. The automobile altered courting patterns as many couples enjoyed sexual freedom in rumble seats because chaperones no longer safeguarded Victorian female purity.

California's new women happily participated in the liberated "jazz age" or "roaring twenties," as the 1920s were often called. Reflecting the decade's discovery of jazz, Hollywood produced the first talking movie, *The Jazz Singer*, in 1927. Movies gave women new images, with Theda Bara symbolizing the "vamp" and Clara Bow the ideal "It" girl. Nevertheless, Hollywood popularized "the happy ending," and for most women this meant marriage to the handsome hero. Both men and women harbored the "material dreams" portrayed in film and aspired to live out the fantasies.[4] Earlier William Fox's *Fool There Was* (1915) warned moviegoers of the fallen woman who goes unpunished for her parasitical acts.[5] The messages were mixed. For some California women these dreams and aspirations landed them in court and charged with murder.

Marie Bailey

Just before Christmas 1920, on a lonely foothill road in Pasadena, California, former stage actress Marie Leonard Bailey fired a single shot that ended the life of Clarence Hogan, a salesman from Oakland. On that fateful day Marie, armed with a revolver, took a scenic drive with her paramour, Clarence. Bailey later told police that she "had tried to make a man of Hogan but had failed and disgusted with living, made careful plans to kill herself." According to Bailey, she revealed her "plans" to Hogan while in the automobile. Perhaps using reverse psychology to break through his fiancée's melancholy, Hogan taunted her, "Well, why don't you kill yourself then?" Enraged, Bailey turned the weapon on him and fired a shot that penetrated his lungs and heart. However, once Bailey's parents retained the Pasadena law firm of Tichnor and Carter, her account of the shooting dramatically differed from her initial statement to police.[6]

Bailey stood silent at her arraignment and remained equally taciturn at her preliminary hearing.[7] The *Los Angeles Times* described her silence as the "mute impassiveness of a sphinx," as her "young face was expressionless . . . she said not a word to her attorneys, Tichnor and Carter." The witnesses recounted the events on the day in question, and the county autopsy surgeon revealed the cause of death. A reporter observed, "It was intimated by the line of questions asked by the defense counsel that something regarding the acquaintanceship of Hogan and Mrs. Bailey will have an important bearing on the defense in a trial before a jury."[8]

Bailey's attorneys spun their version of the case via the press before the formal proceedings commenced. On May 17, 1921, defense attorney George Carter declared, "The shooting was accidental and during her trial Mrs. Bailey will endeavor to prove this to the jury. She was very despondent at the time of the tragedy and was planning at that time to divorce her husband and marry Hogan." Hogan bore the responsibility for Bailey's mental state. "When she became convinced that Hogan was not the kind of man she thought he was she resolved to commit suicide, but in trying to prevent her act Hogan received the fatal wound."[9] No longer taunting her, the deceased now tried to prevent his fiancée's demise, according to the defense attorneys' version of the shooting.

On March 25 the trial began. Bailey, "with the faintest of color in her pale cheeks, listened to the testimony given by the prosecution in Judge McCormick's court with what appeared an impersonal interest." The prosecution pursued a charge of murder in the first degree, while the defense argued "accident and misfortune" under the penal code as an exculpating defense.[10]

The key to that defense was Marie Bailey. Taking the witness stand on May 26, 1921, "little Marie Bailey . . . by baring her soul regarding her relations with Clarence Hogan" completed her testimony. Her account of the events focused on the unintentional discharge of the weapon. "Mrs. Bailey—she is only 21—declared she did not intentionally shoot Mr. Hogan." She remembered finding "her father's revolver in the automobile," and "it felt cold and sinister to the touch." She recalled that Hogan complained about his financial affairs and blamed her for his situation. According to Bailey, Hogan said, "If only you would go and meet some of those people that I knew, I would not have to be embarrassed." He implored her "to send her photographs to these people." Bailey testified that Hogan's suggestion that she become a prostitute to alleviate his financial difficulties drove her to suicide. A reporter noted, "This purported ulterior suggestion to a woman who loved him, and according to the testimony, with whom he was living, apparently paralyzed the mind of Mrs. Bailey." In a stupor Bailey asserted that her "hand touched the revolver. She drew it into her lap under a lap robe. She worked it around so that the weapon pointed at her." Then, according to Bailey, "there was a bang. Hours afterward, it seemed to me, I heard Mr. Hogan saying 'I am shot.'" Bailey failed to recall exactly what happened the day of the shooting, but she clearly remembered that Hogan "took the revolver from her father's house and stuck it between the cushions and the side of the machine."[11]

The jury deliberated five hours and returned a verdict of manslaughter carrying a sentence of one to ten years. "The serious attitude of the jury as they entered the courtroom and their evasion of Mrs. Bailey's glances foretold the outcome and she paled slightly. When the verdict was read, the smile left her face and her cheerfulness departed. She said she had no comment to make on the verdict."[12] Bailey's admissions in the first police interrogation and the testimony of crime-scene witnesses weighed heavily in the verdict, as did her age and the circumstance of a failed marriage and a tragic romance.[13]

Press coverage of the trial included frequent pictures of Bailey that varied from early shots reminiscent of the Laura Fair trial to very flattering portraits of a young, attractive woman.

Perhaps those photographs and, more likely, her age and circumstances drew the sympathy of the jury and resulted in the conviction for a lesser included offense. Marie Bailey's trial verdict illustrated the clear national trend that "domestic homicide, the killing of relatives and sexual intimates, appear[ed] to be discounted in perceived seriousness and punishability, certainly as compared to homicides by and against strangers."[14] Louise Peete was clearly the other kind of killer.

Louise Peete

Louise Peete murdered men for profit, but in 1921 a Los Angeles jury proved impervious to her wiles.[15] Born into a privileged New Orleans family that provided her an expensive private education, she nonetheless married Henry Bosley, a traveling salesman, in 1903. Bosley discovered his bride in bed with a New Orleans oilman, and inconsolable, he committed suicide.[16] She then turned her attention to Joe Appel, another oilman, whom she shot in cold blood. The Waco, Texas, grand jury believed the southern belle's story of a Yankee trying to force himself on her and ordered her release.[17] She moved to Dallas in 1913, married Harry Faurote, who apparently hanged himself because of her sexual promiscuity. In 1915 in Denver, she won Richard Peete's heart, settled down in a small house, and bore a child, but in 1920 left Richard for Los Angeles. She quickly wooed Jacob Denton, a millionaire, on the pretext of serving as his live-in companion. Upon moving into his Wilshire Boulevard mansion, Peete murdered Denton.[18] She told neighbors a variety of stories regarding his business trips to explain his extended absence.

When the police finally started investigating Denton's protracted disappearance upon the insistence of his attorney, they discovered a body buried in the mansion's basement. Peete, now living in Denver with her husband, concocted wild stories to cover her complicity in the murder such as Denton having a double and his quarreling with a Spanish woman.[19] By October the police had ripped the mansion apart searching for clues.[20] Determined to solve the crime, officers stopped a train carrying Louise Peete and her family in the Cajon Pass and whisked them away for hours of interrogation.[21]

Peete's attorney, O. N. Hilton of Ontario, called for a grand-jury indictment of the deputy district attorneys who "kidnapped" his client.[22] The proceeding proved unnecessary because the district attorney admitted that he had no right to hold Peete, her husband, and their little girl, Betty.[23] Nevertheless, the grand jury indicted Peete for murder.[24] Jury selection started in January, and with a jury seated, the trial began.[25]

The trial moved to the scene of the crime and the cramped space where Peete allegedly dragged Denton's lifeless body. The defense persistently hammered away on the question of whether Louise Peete possessed the physical strength to accomplish such a feat.[26] Public defender Aggler tried to create reasonable doubt; however, Oda Aument, Denton's "nimble-witted and attractive niece," repudiated virtually every story that Peete told about Denton's whereabouts and financial affairs.[27] Then a surprise witness, the Denton's Japanese gardener, testified that he had loaned Peete the shovel found in the basement.[28] The case commanded more than just the attention of the judge and the jury. Thousands stood on Buena Vista Street daily just to catch a glimpse of Louise Peete walking from the county jail to the Hall of Justice.[29]

Finally, the defendant took the stand in her own defense, proclaiming, "I didn't kill Denton and I don't know who did."[30]

Unconvinced of Peete's innocence, the all-male jury convicted her of first-degree murder and sentenced her to life in prison. While incarcerated, she refused to respond to her husband's letters, so Richard Peete killed himself.

A model prisoner, Peete received parole eighteen years later. She briefly resided with her probation officer, Emily Latham, who conveniently died of a stroke, enabling Peete to appropriate a .32 caliber Smith and Wesson revolver. She subsequently moved in with Margaret and Arthur Logan, the couple who raised Betty while her mother was in prison.[31] In May 1944 Peete, now going by the name Lou Ann Lee, married Lee Borden Judson, a former railroad official, advertising executive, and newspaper reporter. On December 20, 1944, police arrested Peete for the shooting death of Margaret Logan. The disclosure to Judson that his bride was, in fact, the notorious Louise Peete led to his suicide.[32]

Louise Peete, now sixty-three, stood trial for the murder of Margaret Logan. Her public defenders, William B. Neely and Ellery E. Cuff, relied on reasonable doubt.[33] The prosecution targeted greed as a motive because Peete had appropriated several of the Logans' assets.[34] Prosecutors presented physical evidence in the form of a .32 caliber revolver belonging to Emily Latham and Margaret Logan's property now in the possession of Peete.[35] The court allowed evidence of Peete's prior homicide of Denton; however, the nonsequestered jurors undoubtedly read the oft-recounted scintillating stories of the misdeeds of the accused in the newspapers.

On May 28, 1945, after three hours of deliberations, the jury of eleven women and one man arrived at the verdict of guilty of first-degree murder. The jury foreman, Ed Malley, told the press that he and his fellow jurors voted unanimously

for a guilty charge, and the second ballot polled 11–1 for the
death penalty. The third ballot confirmed the death penalty.[36]
In 1947 Louise Peete died in California's gas chamber.[37] The
jury, after five weeks of hearing testimony, mostly incriminating, and with clear physical evidence providing motive and
opportunity to commit the crime, confidently concluded that
Louise Peete, a female enemy deviant, deserved to die.

Madalynne Obenchain

John Belton Kennedy, a prominent insurance broker, met his
end in 1921 outside his Beverly Glen cottage. The Los Angeles County Sheriff's Department identified Arthur C. Burch
and his "attractive companion," Madalynne Obenchain, as
suspects. "Shrouded in mystery and tangled in complicating
circumstances for many hours, as new clues were rapidly uncovered," the evidence pointed to Burch, the boyfriend, as
the perpetrator. Authorities initially lacked a motive for the
slaying, but "*Times* men" played detective and accordingly
contaminated the crime scene. Reporters discovered the spent
shotgun shells. "One lay at the side of the road, about thirty
feet from the cottage. The other was lying against a wire fence,
about thirty feet farther south, indicating that the slayer made
his escape along the west side of the road, ejecting shells as he
ran." The *Times* men also gathered evidence of automobile
tire-tread design.[38] Although the story appeared on page 11,
five columns wide, and continued on page 15, the *Los Angeles Times* provided avid crime readers with photographs of
Obenchain and Kennedy and details of the crime scene. Journalists had morphed into detectives for the prosecution.

The next day Madalynne Donna Connor Obenchain, held
in custody as a material witness, conducted an interview from

the county jail. The coverage in the *Times* included a picture on page 12 of Ralph Obenchain, the "discarded husband" and source of her current wealth. She told reporters that Arthur Burch was only a college friend, "never a suitor of [hers] in any sense," and that she saw him only occasionally in Los Angeles. Even more titillating, Madalynne revealed that she and Burch had encountered "the bad luck omen of the three black cats on [their] previous stop at the glen" that they tried to undo by retrieving a "lucky penny." She added, "Two men, each about my height or a trifle higher, say five feet eight or nine, brushed very close to me and were gone without saying a word."[39] Evil omens, phantoms of the night, and mysterious shotgun blasts kept an anxious public riveted on the murder mystery.

Los Angeles Times reporters continued their police work. The most "sensational" front-page development in the case featured newspaper personnel finding clues to the possible getaway roadster. Most importantly, *Times* men "in investigating the scene where the car was supposed to have been hidden on the night of the murder" found that the right rear tread was "unusual" because it left the "imprint of little squares." The forensic team of "two *Times* reporters, Chet Dean, a taxi cab driver, and a resident of the canyon" surveyed the crime scene. Later they uncovered a Dodge roadster with unusual tire treads in Parson Brothers Auto Livery. The manager of Parson Brothers, Lynn Keith, identified Burch as the person who had rented the vehicle. The *Times* announced, "The tires from the roadster and plaster paris casts of the imprints on the Beverley Glen road will be used as principal exhibits if Burch is brought to trial." Photographs of the vehicle, tires, Burch on his way to jail, and Obenchain escorted by Undersheriff

Biscailuz to the district attorney's office graced every page of the August 9 edition.[40] Even more titillating was the discovery of almost one hundred love letters in Kennedy's safe-deposit box. "Most of these letters were written by Mrs. Obenchain during a period extending over many years. They told of her profound love for him, contained pleas for a reciprocal love and revealed all the heartaches, the joys, the happiness, the disappointments of their love affair." To ensure that readers understood the relevance of the letters, the *Times* published one of Kennedy's more pensive missives. He penned, "Do not think me cold, ungrateful. Ah—no—'tis only that I wander in the dark, an[d], oh—Madalynne, I cannot see the light— I know it lives, but the darkness is smothering, smothering me. If only I can lift the black mantle away and up from my shoulders and step out into the glorious day."[41] The shotgun blasts cut short the life of Kennedy and his poetic broodings while wandering in the dark. The public remained fixated on the man and the mystery.

The next day district attorney Woolwine announced that his office had obtained enough evidence for a grand-jury hearing. On August 9 Woolwine met with Obenchain, and "after the star-chamber conference progressed for three hours," Woolwine sent for Burch. The *Times* reported, "[Burch is] the man who, from a hotel window opposite Mr. Kennedy's office, kept a ceaseless vigil for two weeks on the movements of the broker, and around whom, through the finding of an automobile he is said to have used on the night of the murder, has been woven a long chain of circumstantial evidence."[42] In other words Burch stalked Kennedy and killed him, presumably to avenge his rejection of Obenchain.

In the same edition the *Times* ran an interview with Emma

Smart, Obenchain's mother. Smart revealed that Kennedy's obsession with her daughter included a special-delivery letter delivered the day of her marriage to Ralph Obenchain. Smart declared, "None of us likes to speak of this phase of Belton's connection with Madalynne, but if, as is apparent, it is Mr. Kennedy's [Belton's father's] intention to show that Madalynne was pursuing Belton and that Belton had refused to have anything to do with her, there will be evidence produced that will startle even the father himself."[43]

To ensure that the public knew the depth of this tortured romance, the *Times* printed the contents of more love letters straight from the hands of the district attorney's office. Obenchain's letter of February 29, 1920, told Kennedy that she was happy back in Illinois. Regardless, she wrote, "You, nor any one else could not hold my love, doing as you have done. I give you credit for being clever enough to know this and can arrive at only one conclusion—consequently it probably will be the simplest way out—for you to play the part of a gentleman and return my letters as long as I really want them." Rather than play the part of the gentleman, Kennedy stashed the letters in his safe-deposit box. One of Belton Kennedy's letters to Marie Obenchain, dated March 4, 1918, spoke of love in classic terms, and she penned a similar letter to him in 1919.[44] The public devoured the love letters even though this pretrial publicity might prove prejudicial for would-be jurors.

Beyond the Kennedy-Obenchain tales of love, attorney Ralph Obenchain, the discarded husband, spoke from Chicago: "She is the one woman in the world for me." Despite the divorce, Ralph said, "Our friendship has never ceased." The *Times* preferred to criticize Madalynne's character, noting that she had inherited fifty thousand dollars from her father's estate and spent the entire sum with unabated abandon.[45]

The grand jury indicted both Madalynne Obenchain and Arthur Burch. Held without bail, Obenchain collapsed when taken to jail, but Burch "retained the remarkable composure and self-assurance that characterized him." The *Times* proudly took credit for these indictments because of "evidence furnished by the *Times*." The evidence included the spent shotgun shells, the perpetrators' automobile, and the witnesses identified by the reporters.[46]

The *Times* also waxed eloquent in an editorial pitting "sentiment versus sense" and blaming movies for the choices made by the cast of characters in this real-life drama. The directors of the Chicago insurance company fired Ralph Obenchain for leaving his job to defend Madalynne. The editorial offered, "This rush of the knight always happens in the movies, where the voice of passion is eloquent and that of duty dumb; but when the movie characters walk off the scene into real life they make a sorry mess of theirs." The author deemed duty more imperative than sentimentality. Ralph Obenchain, the protagonist, was "an idealist, physically courageous but lacking in poise and virile common sense." He erred in marrying "a pretty woman who crave[d] admiration." The writer proclaimed, "Beauty is the joy of the gods, and their eternal torment." Ralph sinned against civilization by granting Madalynne an easy divorce. If Ralph had understood his gender role, "he would have told Madalynne that life is something else beside kisses, billet doux and violets, that they had both assumed responsibilities toward society that were not to be cast aside like a last year's gown." Ralph lacked "a little of the caveman spirit." He further violated cultural code by neglecting to father a child because "pretty wives who are not mothers are the object of amorous attack." Madalynne Obenchain possessed "a pretty face and a fickle heart, too shallow to know the dangerous nature of the passions she awakened [in] Burch." Arthur C. Burch, although noble, proved "an anachronism, a Don Quixote, born four centuries too late." Belton Kennedy, "devoid of honor," failed to marry Madalynne Obenchain and "paid a penalty for his foolish passion for married women that none, not even a husband or brother, had a legal right to exact." After eviscerating the principals, the editorial stated, "The *Times* says all these things without a desire to prejudice the case of any of the accused. They may be innocent of the crimes alleged, but it is a newspaper privilege to fairly discuss the pros and cons of the case, as it has developed."[47] The *Times* viewed the trial as fodder for a debate on cultural roles. Culturally, "women and heterosexual regularity represented civilization, which the American man resisted in the interest of his autonomy."[48] Further, these cultural images and debates sustained Victorian values in the twentieth century.[49] Others, like Reverend Briegleb, found different messages.

Rev. Gustav A. Briegleb, president of the Ministerial Union, preached the moral lessons of the case. Briegleb argued, "When the sinner enters upon a course of wrongdoing, the innocent suffer as well as the evildoer. There seems to be no escape from this inexorable law." Those who watched Arthur Burch's father, "the aged clergyman from Illinois, Rev. W. A. Burch," going to and from the jail to see his son felt his pain and his cry, "Oh, Absalom, Absalom; Absalom, would God I had died with thee." All could imagine the pain Arthur Burch endured. So too Ralph Obenchain because "God alone knows the deep sorrow which fills his life." All of this made clear "how infinite sin is in its extension." Ralph—"the real hero of the sordid tragedy, the perfect embodiment of that of which the great apostle to the Gentiles said, 'suffereth long and is kind, seeketh not her own, is not easily provoked, thinketh no evil, beareth all things, hopeth all things, endureth all things'"— embodied the law of love of the New Testament. Madalynne Obenchain, on the other hand, was a sinner, unless she had privately repented.[50] Briegleb never considered that Madalynne might be blameless in the whole affair. Clearly, the reverend constructed her as the devil in the shape of a woman.

While the press trashed "pretty" women and religious figures cast women as the source of sin and moral decay, the Los Angeles District Attorney's Office turned to the occult to explain the motive in the Kennedy murder. The sharp minds downtown identified "strong, weird emotions" summed up as "occult influence" and termed "mystic love of great power." While the district attorney's office gave the press titillating quotations, Madalynne Obenchain's attorneys, Paul W. Schenk and his partner, Richard Kittrelle, argued that insinuating that "relations between Mrs. Obenchain and Mr. Burch were not of the most proper kind" was "unfair." Further, Kittrelle stated, "It is not the duty or the province of the District Attorney's office to persecute as well as prosecute." Nevertheless, the chorus of condemnation from press and pulpit propelled huge crowds to gather so that "six deputy sheriffs were pressed into service to keep the sidewalk clear for Mrs. Obenchain when she walked to court." To capture the excitement for those unable to witness the spectacle firsthand, "a motion-picture camera . . . placed in position by an enterprising 'news film' man with a clean sweep of the entire distance

Mrs. Obenchain would have to walk" recorded every move outside the courtroom.[51]

At the preliminary hearing Obenchain entered the building, shielded by court personnel from photographers vying for the best angle. She wore "a large black hat, trimmed with white, and the same dark clothes in which she appeared at the previous arraignment." She walked over to the counsel table and sat down with her three attorneys, Richard Kittrelle, Ralph Obenchain, and Warren Williams. Madalynne and Arthur exchanged smiles as the preliminary hearing began.[52]

While the press awaited the festivities of the trial, they reported that Allie Gale Burch's divorce in Kansas had been "filed several months before the murder of Kennedy." Arthur had abandoned Allie and their son, presumably for Madalynne Obenchain. "Mrs. Burch is a daughter of Bishop William A. Quayle," the story noted.[53] Thus, the circle of the morality play closed. Another saintly woman, from the loins of a clergyman, stood on the periphery pointing a finger at her weak husband, beguiled by Madalynne Obenchain's unmatched beauty.

Once the trial began, Obenchain grabbed headlines because she decided to separate her defense from Burch's. Warren Williams joined her exclusive defense team. Ralph Obenchain experienced a legal parting of the ways with Paul W. Schenk and his partner, Richard Kittrelle. Despite this event, the *Times* reported, "a witness whose testimony may play an important part in the defense of Burch . . . has been found by the defense."[54] The trial mystery darkened.

Legal battles ensued over the denial of bail and the failure of the prosecution to provide the defense access to a transcript of the grand-jury proceedings.[55] While the attorneys argued points and authorities, investigators in Illinois combed for more evidence in support of their legal positions. In the meantime Dr. William A. Burch, Arthur's father, traveled west, and "Malcolm McLaren, the private detective acting as the chief investigator for the District Attorney's office," turned up witnesses who saw Obenchain and Burch "at spiritualistic séances."[56] While readers devoured more evidence on the occult angle, the legal stakes in Los Angeles suddenly escalated.

Ralph Obenchain retained Charles Erbstein, "the famous Chicago criminal lawyer," for Madalynne's defense team. "Mr. Erbstein, who has defended twenty-two women charged with murder, every one of whom was acquitted . . . may be relied upon to make a most determined fight for the acquittal of the Evanston beauty." Erbstein offered in a Chicago interview that "the case seemed to him one in which women jurors would be particularly fitted to pass."[57] District attorney Thomas Lee Woolwine attempted to block Erbstein's admission to the California bar, labeling Erbstein "a trickster, a jury fixer, and a suborner of perjury." Further, Woolwine reminded the public and the Los Angeles Bar Association in particular of previous Chicago lawyers permitted to try cases in California. Woolwine trumpeted, "Los Angeles County has, in the past, been treated to one exceedingly unhappy experience with a Chicago lawyer, who was accorded the same courtesy." That dastardly attorney was Clarence Darrow, "[on] whose guilt or innocence a jury was unable to agree, the county being put to the expense of trying Darrow twice on a charge of jury bribery in the MacNamara case." Put another way, the district attorney's office failed twice to convict Darrow, so the risk of grappling with another famous Chicago criminal defense attorney might prove equally "exceedingly unhappy."[58]

With the legal jousting proceeding apace, Los Angeles readers needed something to savor. Harry Carr's jailhouse interview with Madalynne Obenchain in late October more than whetted the appetites of a ravenous public. Carr compared Obenchain to Cleopatra, observing, "Egypt's queen was the greatest fascinator of men I ever heard of until this murder case came along. But as a matter of cold fact, Cleopatra was a piker compared with this woman." Burch, in contrast, possessed "rather faded, ineffective gray eyes . . . ineffective teeth, too; they have no shape and mean nothing." Carr marveled at Obenchain's statuesque presence, reflecting, "Nearly all women with this strange hold over men have been small." Moreover, Carr declared, "She is sentimental, rather inclined to be exotic, mystic and passionately sympathetic." Carr warned, "There is a kind of rough amateur among woman vamps, who listen to the troubles of men and gain the reputation of being sympathetic." Worse yet were "the finished artists . . . who tell their troubles to men and—so are sympathetic." Carr warned, "Boy, run when you meet the kind who tell you their troubles in a gentle, stricken voice! They are the unconscious aliens of the world."[59] Carr thus moved women like Madalynne Obenchain into the twilight zone of alien possession, not unlike a Wagnerian Valkyrie.

With Carr's overture delivered, the trial brought early sensations. Without warning, Burch's attorneys "made the statement that Burch is an insane person." For Burch "it was as though someone had reached into his body and pulled out his spine." Physically Burch's "skin went gray and ashen." The situation worsened; "as the attorney went on reading affidavit after affidavit from attorneys and physicians and even from his father, Burch seemed to sink lower and lower in his seat." In the end "he seemed to be dissolved into a pathetic little lump." While Burch sank, Obenchain "shook her head like a frightened child when a photographer asked her to pose for a picture." Women jurors in the courtroom watching the proceedings expressed "great indignation when the photographer took the picture anyhow." The *Times* reporter editorialized, "There are many women who object to hanging as a punishment for murder; but there are very few women who would intervene to save a photographer from being lynched for taking a picture of a woman who hasn't had a chance to fix up for the ordeal."[60] The misogyny expressed in print trivialized women seemingly without limit.

Harry Carr's story took a new slant for the afternoon session of court. Carr claimed that Obenchain made an "entrance." He wrote, "The door swung open and in stepped a smiling, confident, rather dazzling figure in blue with a low-cut neck and a diaphanous gown that showed the gleam of her skin under the texture." She had also donned "a little brown fur boa with a fascinating gleam of white flesh between the line of the blue gown and fur." With potential women jurors to impress, "her stricken, maimed walk had changed to an easy, graceful, swinging sweep." To Carr it meant that "pity had given way to charm." He credited Obenchain for instructing him in feminine wiles because he had "learned about women from her." Burch, in contrast, entered with a businesslike stroll. When Burch exited the courtroom, "the street was densely crowded with people—mostly women. Some had even taken station on the lawns of the Courthouse to get a good view of the hero of the day." Carr's hero was Burch. He imputed intent to the women in the crowd without fear or research; thus Arthur drew special ink. "Burch may get hanged or be put in an insane asylum, or a prison or something: but he has lived. Yes, brethren, he has lived."[61] Men lived, whereas women exhibited "the air of sweet deprecation." Carr's story dripped with stereotypical images and macho misogyny. He was repeating the nineteenth-century mantra that "men wanted women to become workless, desireless, smiling, delicate, and undemanding panders to men, with an inner structure of undeviating repression, the whole amounting to an antenna sensitive to every male need."[62] Victorianism died hard.

While Carr mesmerized readers, the Los Angeles Bar Association recommended the admission of Charles D. Erbstein. District attorney Woolwine strenuously objected. Meanwhile, the grand jury asked the Los Angeles County Bar Association to take action against Woolwine under a section providing for the removal of public officials for corruption in office or failure to perform duties according to the law.[63]

On November 7 Judge Sidney N. Reeve ruled that Arthur Burch was sane. Thus Charles Erbstein immediately moved to dismiss the indictment against Obenchain or to try her at once.[64]

A week later Ralph Obenchain visited Madalynne in jail armed with a marriage license and his "desire to rewed the woman to whom he gave a divorce because of her love for J. Belton Kennedy." Ralph and Madalynne had spoken "in low tones for more than an hour in a secluded corner of one of the visiting rooms" when miraculously Arthur Burch appeared. He had "slipped past the watchful eyes of the jailers and, falling on his knees before Mrs. Obenchain, pleaded with her" for her hand. With two men begging her to marry them, "Madalynne was half-reclining in a chair, facing her former husband. Mr. Obenchain was watching her intently, propping his head with one hand." Cleopatra's superior held audience for the thinker while "Burch was on his knees at the feet of Mrs. Obenchain." Jailer Cronin intervened to break up the triangle and leave the reading public breathlessly hanging. Overcome with curiosity, Undersheriff Biscailuz caught up with Ralph and asked whether he planned to rewed Madalynne. Ralph divulged that he had consulted a judge about conducting a ceremony in the jail.[65] Juicier than pulp fiction, this love triangle would have caused even Shakespeare to marvel!

The district attorney tried Burch first. Testimony placed Burch in a "death vigil" of Kennedy and linked him to Madalynne Obenchain. Although the prosecution had no murder weapon, Woolwine called R. J. Sanderson, a Pullman porter, who testified that he had seen Burch with a gun case when he arrived in Los Angeles.[66] District attorney Woolwine and his deputy, Asa Keyes, also read Obenchain's love letters to Belton Kennedy into the record. After the titillation of a honeymoon with love letters to and from another man, the jury visited the hotel room where Burch allegedly stalked Kennedy's daily movements.[67] The prosecution's case wound down without the introduction of Burch's alleged "confession" but with the usual parade of witnesses.[68]

The defense arsenal boasted "two important witnesses, whose testimony [was] expected to disrupt the State's case by proving that Burch was not in Beverly Glen at the time Mr. Kennedy was shot." According to the Los Angeles Times, these two unidentified witnesses "were closely guarded last night by the Firman detectives to prevent anyone from learning their stories in advance of their appearance on the witness stand." The defense also located three female eyewitnesses who adamantly concurred that Burch had arrived in Los Angeles without a shotgun case.[69] In contrast to the court's finding of sanity, Burch's genealogy on his mother's side supported "the defense contention that Burch [was] insane." The defense summoned Rev. William A. Burch, Arthur's father, to lay a foundation for the expert witness's testimony to follow on insanity. Reverend Burch held his own while fencing with district attorney Woolwine. Other defense witnesses, Mr. and Mrs. Abraham Kantor, told the jury that they had seen no car tucked away on the gravel road in Beverly Glen at the time of the murder.[70] This testimony struck at the heart of the case constructed by the *Times* men and adopted by the district attorney.

Ever mindful of circulation, the *Times* attempted to deflect the defense's attack on its detective work by going after its competition. Impugning the insightfulness of "boy-authors," the *Times* discredited journalists who, as a January 1, 1921, article claimed, had "discovered for us that Judge Reeve's eyes 'blaze with love' in the courtroom. Who, oh, who inspires that blaze of love?" Rhetorically inquiring, "Can it possibly be Dist.-Attny. Woolwine? Or the row of sob sisters at the press tables? Or the radiant film stars that go to see the show?" the editorial retorted, "Or little 11-year old boy authors who announce through their newspapers that attractive lady prisoners are innocent and maligned—his avowed opinion of both Mrs. Peete and Madalynne?"[71] Combining misogyny with venom sold newspapers, but the *Times* was not alone in attacking Madalynne Obenchain.

Deputy district attorney Asa Keyes opened his summation to the jury in the Burch case with an extended evisceration of Obenchain as a home wrecker, a conspirator, and an exploiter of male weakness. Keyes bellowed, "Oh, what a wreck Mada-lynne Obenchain has made! She has made a fool out of the man she swore she would love, cherish and honor. She has made a corpse of Belton Kennedy, the man she swore she loved. She has made a murderer of Arthur Burch and a murderess out of herself." Then he turned to the case against Burch.[72] The jury of ten women and two men must do justice by hanging Arthur Burch. Again, just as in Laura Fair's trial, the prosecution put civilization in the scales of justice and called on the jurors to save it from the clutches of enemy deviants.

After seventy-two hours Judge Reeve dismissed the dead-locked jury. Two women disagreed with the majority voting for conviction. One thought Burch insane, and the other found him innocent. District attorney Woolwine attacked juror Eva DeMott for her "knowing smiles in the most brazen way, not only with Ralph Obenchain, but with the defendant, Burch. She feverishly took down in shorthand all such testimony as seemed to favor the defense, while she took no account of, nor did she seem to take any interest in or to consider, testimony favoring the prosecution."[73] Perhaps Woolwine assumed that female jurors never read newspapers.

To further increase public exposure to the defense version of the case, Ralph Obenchain announced a new film, *A Man in a Million*, based on the Kennedy murder case. The Los Angeles Theater Owner Association unanimously banned the showing of the film. The secretary of the association told the press, "Theater owners feel there are enough wholesome stories to be filmed to make unnecessary the production of stories growing out of criminal or sensational situations or starring persons who have come into the public eye only through these mediums."[74] They refused to show films made "by newly created notorieties, based upon criminal situations and conditions inspired by notoriety."[75] The *Times* offered, "The Ralph Obenchains of this world seem to be rather productive of foolish wives. Encourage them in their foolish peccadilloes and in the fatal vogue for 'self-expression' which the ladies find so imperative just now."[76] Demonizing the "new woman" sometimes proved irresistible to newspapers.

The prosecution failed to secure a guilty verdict in Madalynne Obenchain's trial because a minority voted for acquittal.[77] A second trial proved equally adverse for the prosecution. Judge John Wesley Shenk ruled inadmissible all evidence concerning the movements of Arthur Burch after the time of the murder.[78] Meanwhile, Madalynne Obenchain's jailhouse stay made news. Inmates in the women's ward "were about evenly divided between those who thought Mrs. Obenchain ought to do her own housekeeping and that she primped too much and those that think she is 'too dear for anything' and that 'nothing is too good for her.'"[79] Obenchain struck up a friendship with Clara Phillips, accused of the claw-hammer murder of Alberta Meadows.[80] In the Los Angeles County Jail, Obenchain distributed candy to the African American female prisoners, and some white women took exception to the practice. A fistfight broke out, and "several complexions had been impaired and a blue eye turned to black before Matron Wallis could bring peace to the jail once more. Later, the matron stood guard while Clara and Mrs. Obenchain dined with the colored prisoners."[81] As Christmas neared, Obenchain's magnanimous behavior no longer mattered.

Judge Shenk, on motion by district attorney Woolwine, dismissed the indictments against Madalynne and Arthur, pending a "psychopathic" examination.[82] Woolwine admitted defeat or at least the futility of prosecution because in front of five juries over sixteen months, the prosecution had failed to win a conviction. A few days later Arthur Burch was set free "after standing trial three times for murder and once for insanity."[83] The accused left the criminal justice administration system but not the public eye.

Alma Whitaker's column, "The Last Word," noted Madalynne Obenchain among the other women who had killed men. Men, she wrote, "are infinitely more shocked when a woman commits murder than when a man does. But it doesn't seem to work out that way in practice." Media made the difference. When women "burst into print and public condemnation because of this alarming vogue for murder which our sex is evincing," the criticism was understandable. What was not understandable was men's attraction to these women, including marriage proposals.[84] When Madalynne Obenchain returned to the Los Angeles County Jail with the Women's Christian Temperance Union to play the organ, the *Times* noted the event and reprinted her file picture previously associated with "mystic love." The now Madalynne Conner was still a favorite among the inmates.[85] Burch resurfaced when a distraught John D. Kennedy attempted to kill him in 1927.[86] Burch bequeathed his estate to Madalynne Obenchain, now a Laguna resident in 1944, but she insisted that Arthur Burch's $1,472.21 should go to his son.[87]

Dolly Oesterreich

On August 22, 1922, Fred Oesterreich perished in Los Angeles, California. Police found Fred with a bullet in the head and two in the chest and his wife, Dolly, locked in a hall closet. Eight years later the police uncovered the cause of Fred's demise.[88]

The Oesterreichs' tale started in Milwaukee, Wisconsin, where Fred owned a successful garment factory and spent most of his time attending to his business. One day Dolly called the factory and asked Fred to send a repairman to fix her sewing machine. Otto Sanhuber, a seventeen-year-old handyman, appeared to service the machine. Dolly, clad only in stockings and a silk robe, invited Otto to service her instead.[89] For two decades thereafter, whether in Milwaukee or later in Los Angeles, Otto made his home in the Oesterreichs' attic.[90] Thus Otto progressed from Dolly's lover to her housekeeping slave.[91]

Yet during his sojourn in the Oesterreich attic, Otto thought of himself as Dolly's protector and that propelled him to homicide on August 22, 1922. Hearing Dolly scream one night as the couple entered their abode, Otto, thinking that Fred was beating Dolly, raced downstairs. Confronting Fred, who had not seen Otto in years, Otto managed to pump three .25 caliber bullets into him. Otto spirited Dolly into the closet, locked the door, and left the scene of the crime for the attic. Dolly disposed of Otto's two .25 caliber weapons, both through third parties.[92]

Initially the police thought burglars had perpetrated the deed.[93] They arrested James Casey, who was found with a .25 caliber weapon missing four rounds, exactly the number of shots fired in the Oesterreich home.[94] Days later the police wiretapped the telephone of an allegedly disgruntled employee of the Oesterreich firm.[95] Within days detectives abandoned that case.[96] Almost a year later police, acting on a tip, found the murder weapon in the La Brea tar pits and arrested Dolly Oesterreich.[97] Day after day new facts emerged regarding the events of August 22, 1922, and the .25 caliber automatic pistol.[98] The prosecution developed a theory on how Oesterreich had murdered alone.[99] The preliminary hearing evolved into a media event with both of the gun witnesses enabling multicolumn coverage.[100]

Despite the case's notoriety, Dolly Oesterreich lacked physical star power. Alma Whitaker, writing for the *Los Angeles Times*, thought she exhibited all the "attributes of a star murder defendant" in that she was rich, accused of killing her rich husband, was a "trifle over 40—a dangerous age," and the circumstantial evidence was "all Sherlock Holmesay."[101] Yet Dolly Oesterreich was "stolid, slightly numbed," and did not try to "vamp the judge—like Madelynne Obenchain did, or stare him out of countenance like Clara Phillips did, or wheedle him like Mrs. Peete did."[102] After citing the most famous women defendants of past Los Angeles homicides, Whitaker concluded, "Although she is such an exasperatingly uninteresting defendant, I found most of the women in court prejudiced in her favor." Perhaps Oesterreich's lack of physical beauty encouraged support from women spectators because "women [were] not strong for vamps and murderesses."[103] The press was still repeating the nineteenth-century prejudices against women in court and missing the point that women were not accepting the journalistic orientation.

The judge determined that sufficient evidence existed for a trial. Bail was set, but a long series of delays pushed the trial into 1925. At this point the district attorney moved for dismissal because "the evidence was not sufficient to justify a conviction, and that should a jury actually convict, the verdict probably would be reversed by the Court of Appeals."[104]

Dolly Oesterreich's narrative of innocence unraveled in 1930, and the police located Otto Sanhuber in San Francisco.

Sanhuber confessed to the murder, and the police arrested Oesterreich.[105] The press recounted the bizarre story of a man hiding in the attic, a boy-toy murderer. A kept man made headline news.[106] Otto asserted that he loved Dolly and suffered from the memory of killing Fred. He compared his years in the attic to living in a bat cave. The press immediately dubbed Sanhuber "Bat Man."[107] Oesterreich remained silent as the press retold Sanhuber's story of living in "his bat-like home in the attic."[108] The *Los Angeles Times* devoted daily coverage to Sanhuber's trial.[109] His attorney offered an insanity defense, while Oesterreich achieved bail on a fifty-thousand-dollar bond and traveled to Milwaukee to attend her mother's funeral.[110]

Sanhuber's attorney developed an alternative-killer theory arguing that Dolly Oesterreich had another lover who had killed her husband. He told the jury, "We will leave it to you, ladies and gentlemen, to decide whether it was Sanhuber, weakened mentally and physically by eleven years of love in a garret, or this other powerful lover who struggled with Oesterreich— himself a heavy figure—and finally murdered him."[111] The press reported on the jury visit to the "garret" and other trial sensations, naming Sanhuber the "garret ghost" and "mouse man."[112] Later on the witness stand Sanhuber repudiated his confession and implicated the neighbor who was a prosecution witness.[113] On July 1, 1930, the "Bat Man" case went to the jury; the jury found him guilty of manslaughter and sentenced him on July 3.[114] The law then released Otto Sanhuber on July 12, when a motion on the statute of limitations on manslaughter was heard and granted.[115]

Dolly Oesterreich's trial began in August, but the prosecution immediately experienced trouble getting Milwaukee witnesses to California.[116] Then more problems ensued: empanelling a jury proved difficult because several prospective jurors opposed the death penalty.[117] Finally, with a jury in place, the prosecution presented all the facts, while defense attorneys hacked away at accuracy and credibility.[118] The defense opened on August 19 with a motion for a directed verdict of acquittal. After the trial judge denied the motion, a parade of witnesses, including a tearful Dolly, now on friendly terms with her new husband, testified to a much different impression of the facts.[119] With closing arguments to the jury completed, the jurors deliberated. Hopelessly deadlocked after three days, they were dismissed by the judge.[120] After months of wrangling over a retrial, the trial judge dismissed the murder charge on a motion from the district attorney on the ground of insufficient evidence.[121] The case died in a one-column story on page 5 of the *Times*.

Nevertheless, the story inspired Hollywood. Screenplays including *The Bliss of Mrs. Bottom* (1968) and more recently *Man in the Attic* (1995), starring Neil Patrick Harris and Anne Archer, chronicled the bizarre, real-life story. University of Tennessee French, cinema, and women's studies professor Christine Holmlund argues that Hollywood finds women and homicide erotic.[122] The Oesterreich case certainly fit the profile, yet the jury set her free. Oesterreich's drama paralleled that of Gabrielle Dardley, who killed Leonard Topp, her lover and pimp, in a Los Angeles jewelry store. Her attorney painted her as the innocent victim of an unscrupulous man and successfully argued murder as self-defense.[123] A Los Angeles jury exonerated her, and she professed the desire to become a nurse and serve humanity, not unlike Nellie Madison a decade later. Hollywood saw a story, and *The Red Kimono* (1925) was the result. The cinema used her real name in the film. Gabrielle Dardley Melvin successfully sued and won a judgment for invasion of her privacy in *Melvin v. Reid* (1931).[124] The wronged woman of 1918 vindicated herself with an appellate court and set a precedent in California law.

From a legal standpoint Sanhuber's lawyers exploited their client's pathetic image and experience while Oesterreich's lawyers employed the strategy of delay. Regardless of the witnesses' testimony, Dolly Oesterreich's story from 1922 to 1930 managed to convince some jurors of reasonable doubt.

Marie Bailey, twenty-one and beautiful, stood trial for the "accidental" shooting of her betrothed, Clarence Hogan. Having divorced her husband, Marie turned to Hogan but soon discovered that Clarence was not the man of her dreams. Like Lea Delmon, Bailey claimed that Hogan planned to sell her into prostitution. Her earlier account, however, suggests that she murdered Clarence because he had taunted her. Lea Delmon killed an enemy deviant; however, the jury found Marie Bailey culpable for manslaughter, which carried a sentence of one to ten years.

Louise Peete, refined and elegant, murdered for profit. Incredibly, all four of her husbands committed suicide. A manipulator of male weakness, she excelled in feminine wiles. Clearly Peete was a serial killer, cold, calculating, and without a shred of remorse. Juries convicted her for the murders of Jacob Denton and Margaret Logan, the woman who raised Peete's daughter after the child's father committed suicide and while Peete languished in jail for eighteen years. A black-widow vamp and enemy deviant, Louise Peete received no mercy from the final jury, which sentenced her to die in California's gas chamber for the murder of Margaret Logan.

Madalynne Obenchain's physical beauty beguiled her ex-husband, Ralph, her college classmate Arthur Burch, and her lover, J. Belton Kennedy. The press and public concurred: Cleopatra was a "piker" by comparison; Obenchain was the consummate "It" girl. Five separate juries failed to convict the ravishing Mrs. Obenchain of murdering her lover Belton Kennedy, but when tried by the press and the pulpit, she was found guilty for making a fool of her husband, an adulterer of Belton Kennedy, and a murderer of Arthur Burch. In short Madalynne Obenchain's feminine wiles made her too danger-ous, a woman to avoid at all costs.

Dolly Oesterreich's seduction of seventeen-year-old Otto Sanhuber constituted an unseemly act if not molestation. Nev-ertheless, the attic boy fell madly in love with this much older vamp. Her husband died due to Otto's misunderstanding of an argument between Dolly and Fred, but the lascivious na-ture of her relationship with the "bat man" forced the lovers to conceal the crime. Through court delays and the statute of limitations, respectively, Dolly Oesterreich and Otto Sanhu-ber escaped murder convictions.

The cases detailed in this chapter reflect the public's am-bivalent attitudes toward the emergence of the new woman of the 1920s. Unlike the cases of the long nineteenth century, these four women were guilty to some degree, although Ma-rie Bailey and Louise Peete were the only defendants con-victed of murder. Madalynne Obenchain's role in the murder of Belton Kennedy remains unclear, but it is likely that Burch committed the murder to win Obenchain's love. Neverthe-less, the press and the pulpit, unlike jurors subjected to her beauty firsthand, day after day during the trials, found Obenchain culpable. Dolly Oesterreich's exploitation of her feminine wiles in the seduction of a boy, his reclusive life as her lover, and her adultery made her guilty of ignoring convention, at the very least. A woman capable of this kind of lecherous act flew in the face of societal mores even during the roaring 1920s. Covering up the murder of her husband made her an accessory and the reading public insatiable. Given these four female defendants, is it any wonder the 1920s spawned pulp fiction?

Even more certainly, the movies clearly alerted the viewing public to various types of women gone astray. Public women who behaved in ways that endangered the home were bad women. Being in the public sphere was not bad per se, but considering the marriage contract a mere financial transaction and flitting about as a social butterfly was bad. "She was bad when her meaning was limited to being an ornament. Worse yet was when she could not adjust her consumption to her income, her desire to her position."[125] Moviemakers were purveyors of the culturally sensational, but their work contained cultural messages just like those in the print media.

CHAPTER FOUR

The Haves and the Have Nots

Women on Trial during the Great Depression

The Great Depression of the 1930s endangered the material dreams of many Californians living outside the prosperity of Hollywood's movie industry and the corporate factories in the fields of California agribusiness. It was a period characterized by labor unrest with agricultural strikes in the Imperial Valley, the San Joaquin Valley, and other centers of corporate farming. Longshoremen successfully orchestrated a general strike in San Francisco in 1934, and the entire city shut down for days in support of their "boys." Corporate California organized to counter the gains of labor, yet New Deal programs brought socialism to a state that had initiated a general old-age pension system.[1] The 1930s also ushered in Hollywood's Golden Era of escapist motion pictures, providing millions the opportunity to forget their troubles and experience happiness in a darkened theater.

The film industry's short history reflected societal attitudes toward gender beginning with D. W. Griffith's *Birth of a Nation* (1915), a movie that extolled the virtues of white America while discrediting African American contributions to the nation. Further, the movie lauded revenge for rape.[2] Griffith reiterated the themes of defilement and retribution in *Broken*

Blossoms (1919) and *The Greatest Question* (1919). Victor Seastrom echoed similar themes in *The Wind* (1928), as did Alfred Hitchcock in *Blackmail* (1929).[3] However, *Blackmail* features a more liberated woman on the silver screen in the character Alice. Alice represents an emancipated woman empowered by the vote wanting social and sexual power. Unfortunately, she kills a man with a carving knife and is arrested, convicted, and incarcerated.[4] D. W. Griffith used Victorian sentimentality to convey a "fallen man" plot in *The Mothering Heart* (1913), in which a man swept away by success falls into the clutches of an "idle woman" who ruins the marriage, but a pious woman rescues the fool in the end.[5]

Films during the Great Depression depicted a variety of women ranging from Cecil B. DeMille's *Cleopatra* (1934) to John Ford's Ma Joad in the film version of John Steinbeck's *Grapes of Wrath* (1940).[6] *Cleopatra* tells the true story of a powerful woman brought down by passion, whereas fictional Ma Joad exudes a quiet strength and dignity despite the hardships faced by Dust Bowl refugees seeking employment in California. In clear contrast to Ma Joad was Lily (Jean Harlow) in the *Red Headed Woman* (1932). Lily works her way through bosses and up the status ladder, in the process destroying her marriage. She runs off with a new rich boyfriend and goes unpunished in Paris.[7] Nevertheless, the so-called Okies, like lower-class women defendants who stood trial for murder during the Great Depression, were often dismissed as marginal people. Regardless, journalists lumped concerns about disorderly women like Louise Peete together with feminists in the courtroom in good times and bad.[8]

In the print media the *Los Angeles Times* often portrayed women at the end of a rope or dying in the electric chair. A

February 22, 1930, story reviewed women legally executed in the United States on the eve of Eva Dugan's execution in Arizona. Dugan was the twenty-seventh female to die for her crime. "The first recorded instance of execution of a woman [in Pennsylvania] is that of Elizabeth Himby, who was hanged in West Chester, Pa. on September 3, 1808." Pennsylvania also hanged Elizabeth Moore on April 21, 1809, and Susana Cox on May 9, 1809, "for choking to death her newly born baby." Margaret Houghtaling swung on October 17, 1817, in Hudson, New York, for "strangling her child." Other New York women followed her to the gallows. Of national notice Mary Surratt died from the noose on July 9, 1865, for her part in the Lincoln assassination plot. Martha Melerhoffer perished in 1874 in New Jersey for killing her husband. Catherine Miller lost her life in Lycoming County, Pennsylvania, for conspiracy to murder her husband by poisoning. Roxana Druse died at the end of a rope in Herkimer, New York, for killing her husband. Elizabeth Potts hanged with her husband for a murder in Elko, Nevada, in 1888. Pennsylvania hanged Sarah J. Whiteling in 1889 for poisoning her husband and children. New York electrocuted Martha M. Place in 1899 for the murder of her stepdaughter. In 1909 Mary Farmer also died in Sing Sing, New York, for the murder of her neighbor Sarah Brennan. "In 1912 Virginia Christian, negro, [was] electrocuted in Virginia for killing her husband." In 1928 Ruth Snyder died in Sing Sing for conspiracy to kill her husband. The next year Ada Leboeuf hanged in Louisiana for the murder of her husband. "January 23, 1930, Silena Gilmore, negro, [was] electrocuted in Alabama for killing a white man."[9] The last story, as reported in the *Los Angeles Times*, carried no concluding comment. Clearly these women represented enemy deviants accused of murdering family members or involved in the assassination plot of a president of the United States. Perhaps the *Times* felt no explanation was necessary.

As the 1930s dawned, women accused of murder in California continued to make news. On January 11, 1930, Los Angeles police searched for "an unidentified woman who [was] said to have waited in a dark coupe in front of the barber shop of Mariano C. Mazzone." Inexplicably, Mazzone was very dead, but "the cash register in his place apparently had not been molested."[10] Police also searched for the perpetrator responsible for the death of Lucio Manuel Lapeda, found with his pockets inside out and a bullet hole in his right temple, and the beating death of Wolf Minsberg in his second-hand shop on North Main Street.[11] Meanwhile, Belle M. Lewis's preliminary hearing for "attempted murder, administering poison with intent to kill and mingling poison with food" resulted in a trial date.[12] Mary Hartman of Long Beach won a trip to the Patton State Hospital because she used arsenic to murder her husband and adult son and daughter.[13] On Valentine's Day in 1931 the *Los Angeles Times* reported that Julia Tapia would stand trial for shooting Manuel Quintana near Lancaster, California, after a drinking party and alleged battering.[14] Women defendants in the aforementioned cases were marginal women. These stories of lower-class women committing murder captured momentary media attention. Other cases involving middle-class women, such as Rosa Tarlazzi, in court for homicide drew far more print.

Rosa Tarlazzi

Frank Tarlazzi was shot during a "drinking party during which three people had been in a three-cornered argument among Tarlazzi, his wife and his mother, concerning rent the mother declared her son owed her." At the hospital he managed to recount the argument before he expired. "Mrs. Dorothy Tarlazzi, the widow, had been found standing over the body with a gun in her hand, according to the officers; she was arrested and assumed blame for the shooting." Detectives quickly unearthed an alternative story and filed "a complaint charging the mother, Mrs. Rosa Tarlazzi, 65, with having murdered her son." Underworld implications, in a time of prohibition, made the case interesting to the press. According to the prosecution's star witness, Ruth Biescar, mysterious voices on the telephone uttered, "The Mafia never forgets!" and, "Keep your mouth shut if you want to keep your friends." The police immediately arranged police protection for the witness.[15] At the coroner's inquest, "all witnesses excepting Miss Biescar stated they were too intoxicated at the time to remember who had fired the fatal shots." Biescar claimed that she was in the living room "when from the open doorway leading to a darkened bedroom there suddenly protruded the long-sleeved arm, in the hand of which a revolver was clutched." Then out came "another arm, this one sleeveless . . . and the hand clasped the wrist of the sleeved one." Biescar identified the sleeved arm as Rosa's.[16]

Rosa was arraigned based on the testimony and the police reliance on Biescar's identification of the sleeved arm. According to the *Los Angeles Times*, "Officers assert that Mrs. Rosa Tarlazzi was the only woman at the party wearing long sleeves and charged her with the murder."[17] The case went to trial despite the coroner's jury finding that "the shooting was accidental while the mother and daughter-in-law were struggling over possession of the gun." Officers continued to offer the motive of rent money even after the coroner's inquest.[18]

On March 3, 1931, Dorothy Tarlazzi testified that she could recall "little of what happened in the Tarlazzi home that night. At some point during the evening, she heard her mother-in law quarreling with Frank in the bedroom. A few minutes later she lapsed into a state of coma." She claimed, "They all had been drinking wine." The district attorney hoped to prove that Rosa hit Dorothy over the head with a "heavy water pitcher," thus causing the coma condition. Ruth Biescar, the only witness "sober enough to recall the scene of the killing refused to remove her dark glasses," and the judge adjourned court.

The trial went a full five days before the jury acquitted Rosa. The reporter speculated that the fact that Frank had made a dying declaration "exonerating his mother" was a major factor in the verdict.[19] Clearly the jury knew that a dying declaration, just as powerfully as love letters, conveys clear emotions as well as personal, objective observation. In law the dying declaration is admissible in evidence particularly when the person charged with the homicide is named in the declaration. The prosecution had misjudged its case. The coroner's jury found the killing accidental, a statement from a man about to step into eternity exonerated the accused, and a single witness claimed only that she saw a sleeved arm with a gun. In the quantum of criminal-law practice, the prosecution's case amounted to a feather on the scales of justice.

Rosa was a lower-middle-class working woman engaged in Italian drinking culture and part of a family tragedy. The critical point for the jury was the evidence. Juries do not make law; they give the court a verdict based on the evidence. Here insufficient evidence compelled the verdict.

Bertha Talkington

For days in October 1934, Merced County, California, witnessed a spree of slaughter. Aristo Martinez, a Los Banos cotton picker, met his end at the hands of Francisco Murguia on Saturday, October 14. Clarence P. DeMoss of Turlock extinguished the life of Mabel DeMoss, his wife, on Sunday. On Monday evening masked highwaymen blasted away at Lamar "Bob" Talkington and his wife, Bertha, on a lonely stretch of highway between Pacheo Pass and Gustine. Bob died of wounds and Bertha survived. Police threw up a "net of officers" around Gustine to snare the evildoers.[20] The passing of time revealed a different interpretation of the Talkington crime.

At the coroner's inquest Bertha's story developed inconsistencies. Investigators also found friends of Bob's in Watsonville who insisted that Bob had declared, "If anything happens to me, she will be the one to do it."[21] Bob, a barber, talked to quite a few customers. Bertha testified at the inquest "without makeup and wearing somber clothing"; she "elaborated upon her story as first given, but seemed confused in certain places."[22] District attorney Stephen P. Gavin held her in jail as a material witness.[23] In custody law enforcement officials used a ruse to break her story.[24] Then they grilled her at the husband's funeral. Finally, she cracked and admitted killing him in self-defense.[25]

The prosecution saw cold-blooded murder and obtained a confession. Investigators turned up more interesting facts in Bertha's past. Her first husband, John May, expired in San Francisco in 1922 and their two daughters died mysteriously, one in the bathtub and the other in a fire.[26] Deputy district attorney Lorimer B. Harrell told the press that the "thin-faced bespectacled" widow's confession was no more credible than "her original fantastic story of a holdup and cold-blooded murder by bandits."[27] The prosecution speculated that Bertha killed Bob to acquire his insurance money and to marry someone else. Her daughter's death by fire had yielded eight hundred dollars in insurance money, and the deputy coroner of Sutter County, Hugh P. Jones, recalled that the burned girl had cried out repeatedly, "Mamma, why did you do it?"[28] Bertha Talkington faced trial for murder, and she retained E. H. Zion of Modesto as her defense attorney.[29] Meanwhile the prosecution worked on scientific evidence.[30]

The machinery of justice proceeded slowly, but on October 29 Clarence P. DeMoss entered a plea of not guilty by reason of insanity, and Francisco Murguia claimed self-defense. Bertha's preliminary hearing was delayed.[31] Prosecutors then chose to use a grand jury to avoid presenting its case in a preliminary hearing.[32] The arraignment went true to form with the "neatly dressed" widow entering a plea of not guilty and a trial date set.[33] DeMoss and Murguia were the public context of justice done as Bertha's case went to trial. She seemed a disorderly woman and entitled to no more than the male enemy deviants received.

The prosecution asked for the death penalty in the second week of December, which found Francisco Murguia in San Quentin State Prison on a second-degree murder conviction and Clarence DeMoss awaiting trial after Christmas.[34] Jury selection resulted in a seven-man and five-woman panel in the Talkington case.[35]

The first day of the trial produced immediate fireworks when the prosecution asked John Lentz Talkington of Redwood City, Bob's brother, whether Bertha had children. The defense objected because prosecution endeavored to put the deaths of the May children before the jury. The defense won a ruling after five minutes of oral argument.[36] After parading several witnesses and plenty of physical evidence before the jury, the prosecution struck at the self-defense claim with science.

Roger S. Greene, a chemist and ballistics expert with the state Division of Criminal Identification, testified that the bullet hole in the hat Bertha claimed she was wearing when Bob fired at her could only result if "the hat were off her head and folded."[37] In addition to science, the prosecution produced witnesses who confirmed Bertha's death threats against Bob and a jailhouse conversation indicating the self-defense story was a fabrication. In total the prosecution called twenty-six witnesses to the stand and introduced thirty-one exhibits.[38]

The defense placed Bertha Talkington on the stand, "sobbing several times" and recounting tales of a drunken husband who abused her and then grabbed a gun that discharged accidentally, killing him and wounding her. To illustrate the last point, Talkington "took off her coat and showed her left forearm where livid welts still showed where a small bullet had ploughed through the fleshy part of her forearm."[39] A wounded Bertha also wounded the defense when the prosecution started cross-examination. She admitted forging two letters introduced by the defense in which Bob Talkington took "the blame for their domestic discords and intimat[ed] suicide." After twelve hours of "grueling" questioning, Bertha Talkington was worn out and her story worn thin.[40]

Branding Bertha a mad dog, the prosecution asked for the death penalty, citing three motives for killing Bob: five thousand dollars in insurance money, her romance with an Aptos lumber-truck driver, and Bob's "domestic abuse."[41] The third motive demonstrated a prosecution admission against interest because spousal battering could justify a self-defense killing. Andrew R. Schottky, Talkington's other attorney, attacked the newspapers for what he termed "propaganda against this little woman." He called the prosecution theory of Bob's assassination in the back seat of the car preposterous.[42] Not uncharacteristically, the press tried the case in public, in print using most of the negative images of women spread across newspapers in the past. The jury found Bertha Talkington guilty, and the defense promised a motion for new trial based on alleged misconduct by the trial judge.[43] The lawyers wrangled with the judge about procedure, but ultimately the court dispatched Talkington to the women's penitentiary at Tehachapi.[44]

However, Talkington's lawyers won the last word. The Third District Court of Appeals found that the trial judge made a serious error because he commented on the evidence and gave blanket support to the prosecution's closing argument. Further, the judge committed improper coercions by threatening to hold the jury until it reached a verdict and strongly suggesting that jurors determine a verdict within two hours. Talkington received a new trial. The *Los Angeles Times* opined, "It is apparent that the judge in this case went considerably beyond the bounds of propriety."[45] Bertha Talkington's name now appeared on the developing criminal law in California as part of the appellate record.

The prosecution retried the case and lost. This time the prosecution admitted that Bertha suffered from domestic abuse perpetrated by the deceased, Bob Talkington. Acquitted in February 1936, Bertha remarried in August to a thirty-year-old man from Crescent City, California.[46] Bertha Talkington's domestic abuse was no different than Clara Wellman's, but time and place made a difference bringing her to trial in the first instance. Domestic abuse, whether physical or mental, in the case of Tom Cook was grounds for self-defense. As the Nellie Madison case illustrates, the defense had to be made early and sufficient evidence brought to the trier of fact.

Nellie Madison

Eric Madison lost his life in a hail of bullets in 1934. Police suspected his wife, Nellie Madison, of the homicide. The autopsy surgeon found four bullets had hit Eric, two of them fatal. Nellie Madison had unsuccessfully tried marriage four times. Her third husband, Los Angeles attorney William J. Brown, provided the press with plenty of personal detail, including the fact that his ex-wife was an expert pistol shot.[47] Police interrogation of Madison made front-page news with a three-column photograph of Burbank chief of police Elmer Adams and deputy sheriff Killion questioning her. She chose to remain silent. The *Los Angeles Times* reported, "The tall, attractive 39-year old woman . . . poised and apparently unworried . . . sat in a small room at the Burbank police station last night and refused to answer a single question put to her by four officers as to anything which had even the remotest connection with her movements over the past weekend." Perhaps exposure to her brother's occupation as a county sheriff in Montana gave Madison insight into the interrogation process. In any case, "when officers tried to get her to talk about more recent years, she returned to all such inquiries the unvarying response that she would not answer until after she had consulted an attorney."[48] Madison's calm under fire soon resulted in a moniker: the "enigma woman."[49]

On March 27, 1934, Madison's attorney Joseph Ryan announced at a press conference, "What she told me to my mind constitutes a perfect defense." The *Times* reported, "Whatever she may have told her attorney, Mrs. Madison to the outside world retained the stony silence which has characterized her attitude in discussing the facts of the strange case since her arrest." Captain Bright, the head of the sheriff's homicide squad, told the press that his case was "practically complete." Bright did note that he had sent deputy sheriff Killion and Burbank chief of police Adams to Cuddy's Camp near Lebec, where Nellie Madison was found after the homicide. Bright instructed the men to further search the premises for the murder weapon, a .32-20 revolver. The police identified a sales slip for the gun, but not the gun itself. The revolver the police possessed, the "Spanish .32-20," had been tested by "Police Ballistic Expert Moxley" and was "definitely not the weapon from which the fatal bullets were fired." Bright expected a self-defense claim but warned, "We will be ready with evidence that she and her husband had been quarreling and that he was on the verge of leaving her."[50] The *Los Angeles Times* ran this story on the front page with a three-column picture of Nellie Madison with her attorney Joseph Ryan. The murder mystery intrigued the public with plenty of witness testimony before the inquest and criminal trial.

As the inquest neared, Madison "continued her calm silence" and received a visitor, William J. Brown, her third husband. "After a talk of nearly half an hour, during which Mrs. Madison showed her first signs of emotion, the couple shook hands and Brown announced he will do whatever he can to help his former wife," the *Times* informed its readers. She also received word that her brother was on his way from Montana to lend his support.[51] This announcement made the front page with a two-column picture of Brown and Madison shaking hands. Readers had to await the trial for juicy details. Interestingly, the *Times* made Eric Madison a "motion-picture studio auditor" in several of the early stories, and by April he was a "film studio employee."[52] That characterization kept class in play in the paper, but Eric actually worked in a coffee shop on the studio premises.

The preliminary hearing revealed few new details. The prosecution led by deputy district attorney Paul Palmer offered enough evidence to have Madison bound over to superior court for trial, and the defense refused to offer any evidence. Madison "retired even further into the mantle of silence" and wore a "dark dress and hat, her face partially concealed behind a pair of smoked glasses." The testimony of several witnesses made it into print, as did a two-column photograph of Madison in her dark dress, hat, and smoke glasses.[53] She looked middle class, regardless of Eric Madison's employment status.

The jury-selection process also produced interesting tidbits for the newspapers' readership. The prosecuting attorneys questioned potential jurors on whether they "would be willing to return a verdict of murder in the first degree on circumstantial evidence alone. They wished to know too whether sympathy would be put aside in considering the verdict." The defense asked "whether the jurors would be willing to give Mrs. Madison's testimony the same credence as that of any other witness and whether they would take into consideration the fact that every murder must have a motive and lack of establishing such a motive might play an important part in their deliberations." The prosecution was more aggressive in its palaver with the press. Deputy district attorneys George Stahlman and Paul Palmer told journalists they would bring as evidence "the bed on which the State asserts a man was murdered—still bearing the bullet marks and on which the blankets are still riddled with slugs."[54]

Witness testimony made front-page news. Belle Bradley, "perhaps the most colorful witness," told the jury that she had heard "kind of a crack" and "four more similar noises." Then she "heard a woman scream." She "thought a man was killing a woman or was chasing her." A flock of peacocks flew into the rear of the building and made noises "just like a woman calling for help." Then there was "the sound of more shots" coming from the movie studio three hundred feet away. She also remembered that "a man from another apartment expressed the belief that the noise came from the floor below." Although a jumbled account of the day in question, the story featured a very flattering picture of Belle Bradley.[55] Bradley gave the trial an even more middle-class image.

However, the most shocking strategy pursued by the prosecution in its attempt to undercut the self-defense claim argued by the defense occurred when Judge Charles W. Fricke, who fancied himself a firearms expert, took the stand to testify. The prosecution called "Judge Fricke . . . because Monday he had timed with his watch the intervals spaced by Wilma Smith, another prosecution witness, between the time she said she heard two shots and then a series of four shots." Judge Fricke had no problem overruling an objection to him testifying or objections to his testimony. With the judge concluding the prosecution's case and allowing all his testimony over objection, the defense began its case with an attack on the ballistics evidence and testimony. Police ballistics expert Moxley told the jury that the bullets that killed Eric Madison "came from a Colt .32-30 caliber gun, and from no other gun, because this type leaves characteristic marking[s] which were plainly visible on the spent slugs." The defense questioned this testimony because even though Nellie Madison had purchased a Colt .32-20, the murder weapon was not in evidence. The *Times* ran a three-column picture on page 1 of deputy district attorney Stahlman, Spencer B. Moxley, and Judge Fricke examining a revolver.[56] Judicial neutrality in this trial appeared irrelevant.

If a trial judge testifying in a trial over which he presided was unusual, the defense argued a theory even stranger. "As a further and even more bizarre situation in a trial already shot full of the weird, unusual and sensational, the defense attorneys clearly established yesterday that they intended to dispute the assertion that the murdered man was Madison!" the *Times* reported. Defense witnesses "looked at post-mortem pictures of the murdered man taken in the County Morgue after the shooting and testified they could not identify the pictures as those of [Eric] Madison." Cecelia R. Durst, also a resident of the apartment house, testified that she heard the commotion, "and on opening" her door she "surprised and startled a strange woman who made a hurried exit by a rear stairway." Joseph Ryan and his brother, Frank Ryan, Madison's attorneys, added to the courtroom theatrics by calling Judge Fricke to the stand for the defense. Firearms expert Fricke testified that .32-20 shells produce "an acrid odor." If fired in a confined space such as the Madison apartment, the smoke "would cause a stinging sensation in the eyes, possibly producing tears, and also, possibly, headache." No prosecution witness testified regarding any such odor.[57] The prosecution would have to clear the air to make reasonable doubt disappear in the jury's mind.

The defense put Nellie on the witness stand to confirm that the dead man in her bed was not Eric. "After telling her story, she just as calmly stood up under an afternoon of cross-examination as withering as all the forces of the prosecution could make it." As the proceedings ended that day, Madison "was still on the witness stand, voice steady and face practically expressionless, still parrying the thrusts of" the prosecution. While "on the witness stand, she looked without expression at the morbid morgue pictures of [the victim's] bullet-riddled body and declared they were not, in her opinion, pictures of her husband."[58]

Although Nellie Madison was proving a hard witness to break, the prosecution recalled her as a rebuttal witness and inquired into an alleged shooting affray with her ex-husband, William J. Brown. She denied firing six shots at Brown when he had obtained a divorce. The prosecution then questioned William's brother, Charles, as a witness to disarming Nellie after the alleged shooting.[59] Whether the prosecution ever wondered how an expert shot like Nellie missed six times remains a mystery.

With all the evidence in, deputy district attorney Stahlman declared, "The manner and means of this crime were so abominable that the State demands and expects a verdict of murder in the first degree, without a recommendation for life imprisonment." He labeled Madison's defense as "fantastic" and characterized her as "cunning and smart." Madison was unmoved; "wearing the same black dress which ha[d] been her garb throughout the trial, [she] sat impassive and unstirring at the counsel table with her two attorneys, Joseph and Frank Ryan, during the prosecutor's bitter attack." Madison maintained "the same icy calm which she ha[d] shown since her ordeal began."[60] She was not acting out the middle-class demeanor of an innocent woman.

The attorneys took more than three hours to recount key facts and to dabble in literary and historical allusions. The key discrepancy in the testimony was the fact that not a single prosecution witness had testified regarding the smell of cartridge powder in the room. Counsel reminded the jury that "the defense [had] called Judge Fricke as an expert witness on ballistics and not a voice was raised to refute his qualifications." He had testified that "the smell of this smoke is acrid, easily perceptible in a close room and might even cause a headache." Therefore, "a whole group of tenants of that apartment house stood outside Mrs. Madison's apartment for ten minutes or more and not one of them testified they smelled a thing unusual." The prosecution characterized Madison as "the coldest, cruelest, most calculating woman ever to be brought into the local courts on a charge of murder," and like Lady Macbeth she could "not erase the evidence that point[ed] to her unquestionable guilt." To rebut the Shakespearean allusion, the defense portrayed the prosecutor as Robespierre "with an unseemly lust for blood." The defense admonished jurors not to allow "circumstantial evidence of the flimsiest character" to cloud their judgment.[61] The jury returned a verdict of guilty, and the firearms expert sentenced Nellie Madison to hang.[62]

The defense appealed, but the California Supreme Court affirmed the trial court. The justices found Judge Fricke's rulings and conduct to be within statutory bounds. Regarding the bloody bed, the court reiterated its position that unnecessary gore was not to be countenanced at trial, but the bed and bloody bedding were not beyond propriety.[63]

In June 1935 Nellie May Madison created another narrative of events and her life. On June 21, 1935, "in a desperate and sensational last-hour effort to save herself from being the first woman ever hanged in California, Mrs. Nellie Madison, so-called iron woman of local court history, . . . broke down and for the first time admitted the slaying of her husband." Madison made this confession to Lloyd Nix, former Los Angeles prosecutor, and his wife, Beatrice, also an attorney. Nix declared, "Mrs. Madison's statement to us, which I believe is unquestionably true, reads like a fairy story. It throws a completely different light on this whole murder case and should certainly result in her getting a new trial."[64]

The confession changed Nellie Madison to the more stereotypically "appropriate" image of the "wronged" woman. She killed Eric after discovering he had married her to steal her inheritance. Nellie discovered the perfidy a week before the tragedy when she caught Eric in bed with another woman. To conceal her shame, Nellie bought a gun and fired without the intent to kill. On the advice of her attorney Joseph Ryan, Nellie refrained from disclosing the true story.[65] The new defense team started for court and the governor's office.

Nix appealed to Governor Frank Merriam for a commutation of the death sentence. Nellie claimed Eric threw butcher knives at her on the night she shot him.[66] The public appeal of this story included the leak of the "Boy Scout deed" of A. R. O'Brien on a visit, accompanied by Warden Jim Holohan of San Quentin Prison, with Nellie at the Tehachapi State Prison for Women. O'Brien confessed, "When Warden Holohan had gotten out into the corridor I turned to Nellie Madison and said 'Do not say anything to anyone—just keep this to yourself. I happen to know that Gov. Merriam will not let you hang. Don't worry, as you have been worrying. Everything will come out right.'"[67]

The *Times* told O'Brien that it was his duty "to conduct the prisons of California as the punitive institutions they are." Further, "Mrs. Madison would have nothing to worry about if she had not murdered her husband." Crime brings punishment. "To say to Mrs. Madison or to any other criminal that the logical consequences of crime will not be imposed by the State is hardly the business of a State Penal official." O'Brien's act "could be interpreted as encouraging crime." Finally, "members of the State Prison Board unwilling to do their duty should step out."[68]

Governor Merriam soon commuted Madison's sentence to life in prison. Madison saw the action as an answer to her prayers to God for help and dedicated the rest of her life to nursing in the prison.[69] The *Times* blasted the governor's action, mincing no words. Since the governor gave no reason for the commutation of the death sentence, his reasons remained a mystery. The editorial offered, "When a real question of justification exists, justice may well be tempered with mercy. But if Mrs. Madison owes her life only to the accident of sex, the safety of society is the worse for her sparing." Danger lurked in the action because "in the eyes of the law and of common sense, there is absolutely no difference between a cold-blooded male killer and a cold-blooded female killer and any effort to create one is merely to encourage other itching feminine trigger-fingers." During the desperate time of the Great Depression, the specter of a female homicide crime wave proved chilling. "Considering the number of premeditated murders committed by women in California, it is no special credit to the State that we have never hanged one. If we had, such killings would have been notably fewer." The editorial concluded by asking "how soon she [would] be turned loose altogether."[70] The case soon lost public interest, but Madison relentlessly sought a way out of prison.

Nellie Madison used her pen to gain her freedom. She inundated two governors with letters and petitions, and Governor Culbert Olson commuted her sentence to time served in March 1943.[71] On trial and in prison, Madison remained the "enigma woman," dark and mysterious much like the noir fiction of her times.

Beatrice Mallette

Police arrested Beatrice Mallette for the murder of her husband on May 28, 1939. Lyle Mallette, a machinist, died of .38 caliber pistol wounds to the head. Beatrice told police that her husband committed suicide. Then she showed investigating officers the hiding place of the revolver and admitted she owned the pair of white gloves found in the residence. Neighbors told police that Beatrice had been an invalid for years.[72]

On June 2 a coroner's jury recommended that the district attorney bring murder charges. Beatrice Mallette testified at the hearing and told jurors, "I've been 17 years flat on my back and I'm not responsible for what I said first." Further, her husband returned home drunk on Sunday evening, asked for the revolver they had recently purchased, "fired one shot from it which went into the wall, then dropped the gun; . . . it fell to the floor, and discharged accidentally, the bullet striking him in the head." A neighbor testified that she saw Beatrice in her yard, wearing gloves, with the revolver in her hand, shouting, "My husband has been shot." Police investigators testified, "The fatal shot could have been fired only from the

1. Beulah faces the cameras. Beulah Louise Overell is shown as she faces a battery of newspaper photographers. The eighteen-year-old heiress, testifying in her own defense, denied that she had killed her wealthy parents, Mr. and Mrs. Walter Overell. (Herald Examiner Collection, Los Angeles Public Library)

2. Beulah Louise Overell and her sweetheart, George Gollum, center, surrounded only by their attorneys and deputies in this courtroom view during a recess. (Herald Examiner Collection, Los Angeles Public Library)

3. Spectators by the hundreds flocked to the courthouse. In this view the spectators' section is so crowded that some of them have to stand against the walls. (Herald Examiner Collection, Los Angeles Public Library)

4. Beulah Louise Overell, calm and stoic as she sits in the courtroom listening to courtroom questioning. (Herald Examiner Collection, Los Angeles Public Library)

5. Defendants sitting calmly in the courtroom as the selection of the jury continues. From left to right: attorney Otto Jacobs, George "Bud" Gollum, Beulah Louise Overell, and unidentified woman. (Herald Examiner Collection, Los Angeles Public Library)

6. Beulah Louise Overell and George Gollum on their way to the courtroom, where they heard a public reading of their torrid love letters. (Herald Examiner Collection, Los Angeles Public Library)

7. Beulah Louise Overell wearing a new dress to court. Deputy Reba Crank accompanies the heiress to the courtroom. (Herald Examiner Collection, Los Angeles Public Library)

8. George "Bud" Gollum (left) and his sweetheart, Beulah Louise Overell (next to him), are shown in the Orange County Courthouse, where their trial for the yacht-blast murder of her parents resumed that day. (Herald Examiner Collection, Los Angeles Public Library)

9. Lana Turner leaves Juvenile Hall after
a visit with Cheryl Crane. Turner and
Stephen Crane, Cheryl's father, paid her
a visit on Easter Sunday, arriving and
leaving in separate cars. (Herald Examiner
Collection, Los Angeles Public Library)

10. Motion-picture actress Lana Turner
and escort Johnny Stompanato arriving
at Los Angeles International Airport with
her daughter, Cheryl Crane, later to be
accused of killing him. (Herald Examiner
Collection, Los Angeles Public Library)

11. Actress Lana Turner testifying in
the murder trial of her daughter, Cheryl
Crane, whom she watched knife Johnny
Stompanato to death. Although she
testified for sixty-two minutes, when the
deputy district attorney showed her the
knife, she could not look at it. (Herald
Examiner Collection, Los Angeles Public
Library)

back."[73] Municipal judge William R. McKay conducted the preliminary hearing and bound Mallette over for trial in superior court. Her story slipped from page 3 to page 10 in the *Los Angeles Times*.[74]

Mallette lost another page when superior court judge Clarence L. Kincaid ordered a psychiatric examination by Dr. Benjamin Blank, the county jail physician. Her attorney Henry Hayes agreed to the examination.[75] On July 5 she entered a plea of not guilty by reason of insanity.[76] On August 7 superior court judge Arthur Crum declared her insane based on the testimony of "three alienists [psychologists]."[77] However, in November state alienists declared her sane and sent her to Los Angeles for trial. The *Times* reported she told the doctors that "she shot her husband, who she declared had often abused her, when she thought he again was going to attack her."[78] Her story was reported on page 10. When she returned to Los Angeles from the Mendocino State Hospital, Mallette earned page 16 coverage with a two-column picture opposite a Bullock's Wilshire sportswear advertisement.[79] She slipped back another page when superior court judge Clarence L. Kincaid set trial for January 9, 1940.[80]

At trial Mallette admitted shooting her abusive husband, buying the revolver for self-protection, and telling police that Lyle died of an accidental gunshot wound. The *Times* story appeared on page 3, a single column with a less than flattering picture adjacent to a three-column Robinson's department store advertisement telling readers, "Crepes and prints will bring fresh new color into your life."[81] The jury convicted and recommended life in prison. The insanity phase of the trial opened with more alienist testimony.[82] The jury heard two alienists testify that Mallette was sane and two opine that she was insane. The jury found her sane.[83] Judge Crum sentenced her to life in the Tehachapi Women's Prison.[84] Her attorney, Henry Haves, moved for a new trial. Judge Arthur Crum denied the motion, and Haves appealed to the California Court of Appeal.

On May 28, 1940, the three-judge panel unanimously reversed the decision based on prejudicial statements by the trial court judge.[85] Superior court judge Thomas L. Ambrose reviewed the trial court record and acquitted Mallette on the ground of insanity.[86] She next had to go before the County Lunacy Commission, which found her sane, and in December Mallette defeated the efforts of her mother to have her committed. A superior court jury, after a brief hearing, "decided that Mrs. Mallette is sane at the present time despite the contention of the mother that her daughter's actions indicate she needs further treatment in an institution."[87] The facts of the case and the procedure at trial were similar to the Laura Fair trial of the nineteenth century. However, newspaper coverage proved minimal because Beatrice and Lyle Mallette came from the ranks of lower-class, blue-collar Americans rather than those of high-profile, socially and professionally significant people. Beatrice Mallette slipped off into the marginal world she already inhabited.

Class issues were journalism issues. Journalists pushed middle-class and elite-class stories to the front pages and graced such stories with photographs. Expert writers took care to put issues of gender and image ahead of justice. Juries had the duty to evaluate evidence, not just image. Movies entertained Californians with very changed images of women. Fashion and dress of the 1920s were dramatically different from the garb of the long nineteenth century. Yet Victorian values permeated lawyers' language in court and editorial verbiage. The men defending or prosecuting women used the full quiver of Victorian missiles in courtroom combat. Journalists repeated their arguments and added culturally nuanced judgments of women in custody, in court, and in public images in newsprint. Disorderly women were punished, albeit not with the death penalty in most cases. Many of the themes of the Victorian past resonated on the pages of Depression-era newspapers narrating events in court with the feminine on trial.

CHAPTER FIVE

War Women of the 1940s

Evolutionary Women in Revolutionary Times

World War II pulled the United States out of the Great Depression, created new employment opportunities for women, and made the country a world power. Women went to work in defense industries, joined the armed services, and flew military aircraft as Women Airforce Service Pilots. They helped the country win World War II, but after the war the country they had served disbanded their military units and denied them military benefits. Yet women now knew they could weld, fire antiaircraft artillery, and fly seventy-eight types of military aircraft. America would not be the same as women entered peacetime civilian life. So too in California. The state benefited from wartime production, but the end of the war brought economic and social adjustments. The 1950s ushered in the Korean War and the Cold War. It was a decade of anxiety.

The media told women to go back to the home after World War II. Historian Elaine Tyler May persuasively argues that this emphasis on the family in the 1950s was an attempt to find security in anxious times.[1] The economic boom of the war years in housing and consumerism lasted into the late 1950s. Anxiety ebbed somewhat with the end of the Korean War in

1953, Stalin's death in the same year, the creation of peaceful coexistence with the Soviet Union, and the calming hand of the Eisenhower administration. Hollywood provided plenty of film entertainment centered on the middle-class family, the pleasures of wealth, and the dating rituals of teenagers and urban professionals.[2] Regardless of image and media message, violence in women's lives continued.

Women and violence preceded the attack on Pearl Harbor. In January 1940, San Diego police searched for Beatrice Mary Cox, a former prodigy student at San Diego Teachers' College. Cox was armed with the .22 rifle she had used to kill her mother.[3] In February police apprehended Betty Flay Hardaker in Palm Springs, and the district attorney charged her with beating her five-year-old daughter to death and leaving her child's battered body in a Montebello park wash station. A coroner's jury found her "of unsound mind."[4] On April 4, 1940, Lolita Davis chased three of her children down and bashed out their brains with a hammer in their Los Angeles home. Barton Davis told the court that his wife "thought herself possessed of a strange 'power' and . . . she believed demons were coming to torture her children." According to Barton, Lolita believed that "she was possessed of . . . a power and that she had used this power to kill [his] sister's little girl Patty, who died." Lolita avoided trial by killing herself. Eleven-year-old Chloe Davis told her story to Judge Fox to determine whether she could return to her father's care. Chloe disclosed how her mother hit her with the hammer, ignited her hair, and attempted to torch Chloe, and how the child survived the ordeal by "dodging around her." The court returned her to her father.[5] The violence would continue as other female defendants stood trial for murder.

Juanita Spinelli

Ethel Leta Juanita "The Duchess" Spinelli was the first woman to go to the gas chamber in California. She started down the path leading to that fate in 1940, when Sacramento police arrested Juanita and her gang of four for robbery. Her daughter Lorrain "Gypsy" Spinelli, Mike Simeone, Albert Ives, and Gordon Hawkins had indulged in a robbery and burglary spree. Armed with two revolvers and blackjacks, they robbed service stations and unsuspecting motorists.[6] During the enterprise they discussed another crime, murder.[7] Police interrogation revealed the plot and provided the press with images of the enemy deviants. Juanita Spinelli was "the brains" of the mob. Albert Ives served as "the trigger man." Gordon Hawkins functioned as "the driver." Lorrain "Gypsy" Spinelli posed as the "come on girl." Finally, Mike Simeone was "the case man." The bumbling group of felons plotted to murder Robert Sherrad because his obsession with murder threatened the viability of the gang. To eliminate him and avoid his homicidal tendency, the group decided to give him knockout drops prior to dumping his body into the river. The method of death turned out to be the idea of "Gypsy" Spinelli. Once they hatched the plot, the gang carried it out and pushed the limp Sherrad off the Freeport Bridge. After the police had full information about the homicide, they quickly recovered the body.[8] The gang lacked cohesion and the ability to remain silent when confronted by the police.

In addition to snuffing out Sherrad's life, gang members started confessing to other crimes, including murder. Juanita Spinelli recounted a narrative of fear. "Mrs. Spinelli showed the only emotion apparent in any of the group. At times, she whimpered. She was forced to stay with the gang." Yet Juanita was "almost belligerent in denying she was the head of the gang." She averred, "I'm telling the truth, I was forced to stay with them. Ives said he loved to kill and I was afraid he'd kill me." "Gypsy" gained a further image as a "typical gun moll." With the press milling about with police in the interrogation process, she "screamed she would 'kill' a cameraman who snapped her picture." "The Duchess," amid her fear narrative, admitted to giving a .38 caliber revolver to her men, as "they needed it," and making the "homemade blackjacks."[9] None of the confessions or alternative narratives drew any sympathy from police.

Sacramento district attorney Otis D. Babcock took the case to a special session of the grand jury. In addition to announcing the trip to the courthouse, the police revealed further details of their investigation. "The Duchess" had moved to California in 1937 "to escape the vengeance of Detroit's notorious 'Purple Gang.' She was suspected of being the 'finger woman' for killings in the Detroit laundry racket." Additionally, "the police said she [was] the widow of a bank bandit who was slain in Mexico ten years ago." Spinelli now possessed the public pedigree of a gang leader, with a touch of organized crime, and a mother in a criminal family that yielded a "gun moll."[10] Before the grand jury assembled, the press revealed the rap sheet of Juanita "The Duchess" Spinelli and her mob.

To make matters worse for any defense attorney, two members of the gang willingly escorted police to the scene of the crime. Albert "Al" Ives and Gordon Hawkins "talked freely while they showed State Highway Patrolman Harry Hendricks and detective P. O. Emerine how they tossed 18 year old Robert Sherrad, one time inmate of a state mental hospital and a member of their gang, to his death." They also described how they all went for a swim so that Robert was in swim trunks when they dumped his limp body in the river.[11] The case for the prosecution fell from the lips of the enemy deviants.

Another part of the prosecution package opened when the San Francisco district attorney identified a case of murder against Ives and Hawkins to their grand jury. The charge involved the holdup slaying of Leland S. Cash, a barbecue-stand operator. Ives confessed to the murder when interrogated by Sacramento police. San Francisco's district attorney believed a connection existed between "The Duchess" and this killing. Sacramento district attorney Babcock agreed, saying, "The Duchess and Simeone definitely were the leaders of the gang." Further, Babcock proclaimed, "I am going to seek the death penalty against all four of them—The Duchess, Simeone, Ives, and Hawkins."[12]

San Francisco police tirelessly pursued their case against "The Duchess." According to the *Sacramento Bee*, in a search of "the gang's former headquarters," the police "uncovered what they believe is evidence the duchess conducted a crime school for her youthful band of robbers and slayers." The evidence included "two pieces of eight inch steel, fashioned into needle sharp daggers, a knife with an eight inch disappearing blade and a wooden gun." Looking at the implements of street crime, the police told the press, "Mrs. Spinelli taught her young mobsters how properly to knife a man, how to handle an opponent in any kind of a fight and how to strike adversaries to 'lay them out.'"[13]

The jury selection process began with "Mrs. Spinelli, attired in a modish blue dress and apparently in gay spirits." When Spinelli realized that Babcock sought the death penalty, she "sobered." The defense argued, "All of the gang, except Simeone, have entered double pleas of not guilty and not guilty by reason of insanity." Four court-appointed attorneys, Ralph T. Lui, Peter Mannino, Robert Schwab, and Gordon Fleury, represented the defendants. "Gypsy" served as a material witness, and the district attorney felt that he had insufficient evidence to link her to the homicide. "The Duchess" remained the sole member of the group who refused to confess to any crime.[14] The jury-selection process took less than two days with none of the thirty-six prospective jurors objecting to the death penalty. Superior court judge Raymond T. Couglin seated a jury of five women and seven men with a male alternate to hear the case.[15]

The trial opened with a clash over legal questions. The defense attempted to block the admission of confessions into evidence. A ninety-minute argument with the jury excused resulted in Judge Coughlin's ruling admitting the confessions and other statement made by the defendants to the police. The defense blocked the introduction of a photograph of Ives and Hawkins "standing on the bridge pointing to the spot where they said they tossed Sherrad's body into the river." Attorneys Schwab and Fleury closely questioned the autopsy surgeon and the county chemist regarding the use of chloral hydrate "apparently for the purpose of laying the groundwork for an 'accidental death' defense." Defense questions focused on addiction to the drug and included a literary quiz regarding Dante Rosetti. Both scientists admitted they had never heard of the poet.[16] The confessions put Juanita Spinelli slipping the knockout drops into the glass that Simeone, her common-law husband, filled with whiskey to give to Sherrad, an escapee from a mental institution. Those confessions became part of the trial record.[17]

Juanita Spinelli took the stand to tell an alternative tale closely tied to her statements to police. She was "an unwilling member of the gang." Spinelli, "shouting hysterically at times, placed full responsibility for Sherrad's slaying upon Ives. She declared Ives not only plotted, but carried out Sherrad's death." She claimed "all her activities in the ring were the result of a threat by Ives to place her 18 year old daughter Lorrain, in a Chinese house of prostitution unless she complied with his orders." She admitted to placing the knockout drops in the glass, making blackjacks, and providing the gun used in holdups and a murder in San Francisco. She chose these actions because she "was afraid of Al." Her attorney, Ralph Lui, focused on Ives and had her testify that Ives said, "'Bobby has got to die and right now.'" Attorney Fleury tried to rehabilitate his client, Ives, with character witnesses, but the testimony resulted in "a mild outburst of laughter" to one answer on cross-examination.[18] The alternative narrative was about to be dealt a deathblow when Albert Ives and Gordon Hawkins took the stand.

Both Hawkins and Ives pointed the finger at Juanita Spinelli and told the jury that she gave the order to kill Sherrad. Ives said, "I got my orders. That's all I know about it. They were going to get me too. They talked about dropping me off a cliff or sticking hot needles in my ear drum."[19] The jury found all four of the accused guilty of first-degree murder. Regarding Juanita Spinelli, district attorney Otis D. Babcock closed with a finger pointed at her, saying, "Look at her, this scheming, cold, cruel woman. She and Simeone were the moving forces in this whole plot to get rid of Sherrad." Finally, regarding the penalty, "If any verdict other than the death penalty is returned against each and every one of these people, then I say to you that we should wipe capital punishment off the statute books and humbly apologize to all those others who have paid for their crimes with their lives."[20] The jury agreed, setting Juanita Spinelli up as the first woman to die in the gas chamber.[21]

The politics of death intervened for a while. In June 1941 Governor Culbert Olson granted Spinelli a thirty-day reprieve.[22] The executive action irked Judge Coughlin, and that was worthy of print.[23] Governor Olson also listened to Spinelli's son, Joseph, and his tales of marginal people living marginal lives.[24] Governor Olson then went the extra green mile and listened to Juanita Spinelli.[25] Then the governor ordered another look at her sanity.[26] With all avenues traveled, the execution time clock ticked down to the end.[27] On November 21, 1941, she was executed in the gas chamber.[28]

The *Los Angeles Times* ran an editorial titled "Good Riddance" the day after Spinelli's execution. The editorial opined, "Even squeamish Governor Olson could find no extenuation for the deliberate murder of which Mrs. Spinelli was duly convicted, and which, indeed, she scarcely denied; and the Supreme Court also declined to interfere on the basis of last-minute assertions made on technical grounds." Regarding the meaning of the chamber of gas, the writer thought, "The knowledge that women are not exempt from the penalties of the law in this State comes tardily, but not too late, perhaps, to prove a deterrent."[29] Perhaps the editorial writer reflected on the first forty years of state experience with women who kill men.

Beulah Louise Overell

On March 19, 1947, the yacht *Mary E.* exploded and sank in Newport Harbor in Orange County, taking with it Walter

E. and Beulah Overell, a prominent Flintridge couple. Their daughter, Beulah Louise Overell, seventeen years of age, was their sole heir. Beulah and her fiancé, George Rector Gollum, a Navy veteran and premedical student, were arrested that fateful Saturday night. Newport police chief R. R. Hodgkinson and Orange County sheriff Jim Musick refused to reveal the basis for the charge, but the chief said, "It should be obvious that we wouldn't have put them in jail if we didn't think we had some evidence against them."[30] Police discovered thirty sticks of dynamite and a detonator attached to an alarm clock. They announced that "the blast apparently had been caused by gasoline."[31] The *Los Angeles Times* also disclosed that the couple was ashore in a bowling alley at the time of the blast. Beulah, an "attractive blond girl," burst into "tears when placed under arrest" and denied any part in the tragedy.[32]

Within days the police determined that the perpetrators "bludgeoned [the deceased couple] to death prior to the dynamite explosion." With equal expedition Beulah Overell retained Marcus B. Wellington, former president of the California Bar Association, and Otto Jacobs, former city attorney of Santa Ana. Chief Hodgkinson told of more witnesses and evidence.[33] However, Orange County district attorney James L. Davis was "reportedly at political loggerheads with the sheriff who was too 'busy' to be at the arraignment and refused to issue a complaint." Deputy district attorney J. Parley Smith opposed an immediate hearing and declared "on behalf of the county prosecutor that 'we are not going to be rushed into trial by a hullabaloo by newspapers.'" Overell's attorney Marcus Wellington called for an immediate hearing, arguing, "It is unfair to take a 17-year old girl, without parents or guardians, into a star chamber such as the grand jury room." Overell flashed crowds "a 'V' for victory sign," and Gollum, "handcuffed, crossed his fingers as he left" the courtroom.[34]

On March 26, 1947, the grand jury handed down indictments "after criminologists convinced" them that the "web of circumstantial evidence" caught the lovers up in its snare.[35] The transcript of the grand-jury proceedings released the next day contained evidence that Gollum had bloodstains on his clothing. Gollum exhibited no emotion, but Overell was "weeping and distraught." A search of Gollum's car also turned up "wire similar to that attached to the explosives." Meanwhile, the authorities searched for Beulah Overell's personal diary.[36]

Otto Jacobs, the Orange County half of Overell's defense team, announced that she would plead not guilty and not guilty by reason of insanity. Gollum's attorney, Dee Holder, gave no indication of his plea. Sheriff Musick told the press that Gollum had never denied owning the bloodstained clothing and the police chemist confirmed the blood was human. Meanwhile, Overell "tidied her cell, read books, and knitted socks . . . ate well and seemed at ease."[37]

Attorneys in the case were far from at ease. The California attorney general, Fred N. Howser, entered the case and dispatched two state investigators. Both Overell's and Gollum's attorneys protested any interrogation without their presence after the investigators had been secreted into the jail. "This climaxed a day of rumors that Dist. Atty. James L. Davis was resigning from the case and that Howser was preparing to appoint someone else to prosecute it."[38]

The police located Ben Smith, a San Bernardino dynamite entrepreneur and county night jailer, who identified Overell and Gollum as the couple who had purchased twenty-seven sticks of 40 percent dynamite.[39] Further police sleuthing turned up the sales slip for fifty pounds of dynamite secreted in Gollum's camera. The Orange County sheriff's crime laboratory and Capt. Tom McGaff found it in the camera "wadded up in the film chamber."[40] Sacramento weighed in with Roger S. Greene, criminologist for the State Department of Justice, who rambled to the outback of Orange County, stating, "We are convinced both parties are guilty" prior to reviewing the evidence.[41] Divers descended to the depths of Newport Harbor for new clues, and gravediggers brought the Overells to the surface again for a new look by experts.[42] That new look resulted in the attorneys for the defendants declaring that the six-hour autopsy "definitely refute[d] the testimony" offered the grand jury.[43]

The lawyers now took the stage. Eugene D. Williams, the special prosecutor, won round one on a motion to amend the indictment to charge two separate counts of murder in the bludgeoning deaths and conduct a single trial of the couple.[44]

Suddenly, letter after letter, love note after love note, graced the pages of the *Los Angeles Times*. Overell signed off as "Your slave, Louise." Gollum mentioned the crime, writing, "They might say that I did it and you loved me so much you were shielding me." Overell, however, revealed nothing in writing.[45] The attorney general was in a state of "bewilderment" at the publication of the letters held by the prosecution. Special prosecutor Williams "said he personally feels that the publication of the letters 'damaged our case,' although [Attorney General] Howser said he does not believe that it hurt the case very much."[46] Since April 4 the attorney general had taken charge of the case, so this evidence problem occurred during his tenure.[47] Defense lawyers immediately pounced on the leak, and Overell spent her eighteenth birthday in jail with gifts of orchids, two cakes, and perfume. "Beulah Louise's dream last Christmas of being married on her 18th birthday had been doomed to tragedy," mourned the lugubrious press.[48] The next bombshell burst on May 1 with the announcement that the defense had located Beulah Overell's personal diary, and it contained "details of her idyllic romance" as well as entries regarding her parents welcoming Gollum into their home. The prosecution had long maintained that the parents opposed the marriage, but the diary refuted that theory.[49] Relatives visiting Overell in the sweltering Orange County jail reported her calm and spending her time reading and knitting.[50] While Overell knitted, the prosecution searched for a demolitions expert reportedly seen with Gollum, and the defense found a wiretap on the telephone of Gollum's stepfather.[51] State special agent Ralph Davis and Newport Beach assistant police chief Kenneth Gorton found two mystery witnesses in Balboa and whisked them off to jail as material witnesses.[52] Overell's legal defense team signed up William B. Beirne, a Los Angeles criminal lawyer, and Z. B. "Bert" West, former Orange County district attorney.[53]

Days before the trial, now special assistant attorney general Eugene D. Williams gave the press the state's theory of the case. Gollum had perpetrated the crime with a four-foot length of pipe, and Overell had planned the caper.[54] Overell was a "mastermind murderess" in the state's case; the defense labeled it a "hideous strategy."[55] In the eyes of the *Los Angeles Times*, "the trial [would] culminate one of the strangest, most complex murder cases in California history." William Beirne, Gollum's attorney, asserted, "These children are both being used as footballs to further the political ambitions of certain people." In all his experience, he had "never seen such legal trickery and skullduggery indulged in for the purpose of building up a case which [had] no foundation in fact."[56]

While lawyers wrangled over the jury, the defendants made their appearances. On opening day "Louise's 18-year old face gleamed with cosmetics. Her reddish brown hair lay tightly nestled against neck." In her entrance "she stepped smartly along in new brown and white pumps, her thin ankles flashing under the calf-length skirt of a new aqua blue dress." In terms of poise, "she seemed unconquered and distant." The fashion report on Gollum was quite different. He made "his trial debut" in the same blue double-breasted suit he had worn previously. Most importantly, "blood-red woolen socks knitted for him by Louise oozed color over brightly polished black shoes."[57]

With a jury almost in place, the state moved its evidence from the Los Angeles crime laboratory to Orange County in an armored car.[58] Overell entered the courtroom day after day looking "younger, more girlish than before."[59] Jury selection droned on, but defense attorneys inserted the allegation that the attorney general had released the love letters in questions to prospective jurors and that the defense knew of a "Mr. X" who had killed the Overells.[60] After fourteen days and 194 prospective jurors, a panel of six men and six women walked into the jury box.[61]

Special prosecutor and assistant attorney general Williams opened with the motive. "The defendants enjoyed an illicit, perverted, sadistic sexual passion amounting to a frenzy," Williams bellowed. The girl's parents objected to a marriage, and their wealth added another element. "The Overells presented an obstacle to the fulfillment of the defendants' desires, and they were removed. Lust, greed, frustration—ladies and gentlemen—these are the raw materials of which murders are made," he declared.[62] The "largest crowd of spectators in the history of the red sandstone Santa Ana Courthouse overflowed the corridors."[63] The prosecution's opening spurred the defense to release the diary of a "timid, nervous, distraught girl."[64]

With medical experts on the stand for the state, the courtroom remained packed, "filled mostly with women."[65] After hearing from the police witnesses, the jury observed the physical evidence paraded before them, with the appropriate experts testifying regarding explosives, wires, and timing devices.[66] State criminologist Roger S. Greene, "one of the country's leading criminologists," testified on the "intricacies of the alarm clock" allegedly used by Gollum to set off the explosives. The cascade of "scientific" evidence poured into court, including a moulage (or death mask) of Walter Overell, slides of bloodstains, a stanchion, enlarged microphotographs, screws, skin samples, signatures on explosives sales documents, and Beulah Overell's diary.[67]

Turning from the "scientific" evidence to "romance," the prosecution maintained that the motive involved a love affair opposed by the parents. The defense opened with procedural moves, experts, and surprise witnesses.[68] One of the procedural moves successfully omitted the ball-peen hammer as evidence. Thus "the State . . . rested its case against the couple without a 'murder weapon' in evidence."[69] The defense also subpoenaed Attorney General Howser and district attorney Davis to the great surprise of the prosecution.[70] Meanwhile, defense experts dismantled prosecution experts one by one.[71] Attorney General Howser testified that he had received the jailhouse love letters from J. H. Mulvey, special agent for the State Department of Justice, and that no plot existed to release them to the public. Mulvey testified how he had obtained the "inflammatory and often obscene jail correspondence." He did refuse to answer a question regarding his delivery of the letters to Howser. Capt. Tom McGaff, the Orange County Sheriff's Office criminologist, gave Mulvey the letters. Mulvey professed a memory loss during testimony and asked the court's leave to get his notes. "Mulvey returned to court later carrying a huge cardboard carton which provoked gales of laughter for the jury and the spectators."[72]

Defense experts continued to shred prosecution experts. One dismantled the alarm-clock theory.[73] The defense called a prosecution witness to undercut another state theory with a model of the yacht *Mary E.*[74] Carl M. Hernandez, a special-effects man in the film industry since 1914, also blasted the alarm-clock theory.[75] Because of the need to inventory the Overell estate, Beulah Overell left jail for Flintridge during a recess of the court. The *Times* produced a picture on page 2 of Beulah with the family's "red cocker spaniel Shar."[76] Back in trial a United States Navy ordnance officer blew prosecution expert testimony out of the water.[77]

The defense put Overell on the witness stand. Then "Bud" Gollum told his story. They had purchased the dynamite for Walter Overell and had nothing to do with the couple's demise.[78] Walter used single sticks of dynamite to cause fish to rise to the surface for dinner. Gollum and Beulah Overell remained steadfast under cross-examination. The defense closed, and the prosecution produced a pastiche of rebuttal witnesses. Both sides closed, and the judge instructed the jury on October 3.[79] On October 5 the jury came back with a verdict:

not guilty on all charges for both defendants. "A tremendous ovation greeted the announcement of the verdicts, rising from a crowd of hundreds which virtually surrounded the Orange County Courthouse."[80] Twelve special deputy sheriffs assigned to maintain order in the court failed to stop the shouting and cheering. The first vote was 7 to 5 for acquittal, and after seventeen hours and forty-two minutes, all jurors agreed due to the failure of the prosecution to clearly establish a chain of evidence.[81] The trial lasted a record 133 days and cost the county $17,400.[82] It cost the state and its attorney general more in terms of reputation.

The press coverage proved both conventional and sensational. Julia Hazelton's letter to the *Los Angeles Times* editor printed October 19, 1922, pinned down the journalistic convention.

Some of us are getting properly braced for the heroine stuff that will soon be hitting us from the papers about the latest lady murderess. We expect to be told again about the length of her skirt, whether she has adopted the "sorrow make-up," and whether she likes her eggs soft boiled or poached on toast. I can see it coming. It did occur to me, however, that it might be good for my system to cough up a protest. Why does it have to be? Why ask the brainy men and women of the press to spill a lot of perfectly good English in such a cause? Why insult the intelligence of the reading public by thrusting at them columns of such piffle?

But even assuming that newspaper men and women enjoy writing feature articles on criminals, and that the hoi poloi find the perusal of them delectable, what about the moral responsibility of the press? One does not have to be a keen student of psychology to trace the results that will follow from attractive featuring of the perverted.

Henceforth, for commanding attention, one will have a choice between the movies and killing someone, the difference being that in the case of the movies the actor pays his own press agent—presumably, whereas in the case of the murderess, the newspapers pay. The extent and style of the publicity is the same for star actor and star killer.

A college course in expert killing will undoubtedly be the next thing, with a scientific exposition of how hammers, vacuum cleaners, garden hose—and mayhap even on the other kind—may be utilized in the process. A chair as head of the department of scientific killing will be one of the openings for the future college graduate.

This and yet more may be expected as the result of exploiting prison heroes and heroines. Must it continue to be, or shall we have a rest? Here's hoping—

Julia, not much had changed a quarter century after you lodged your protest. The coverage of the Overell case followed the pattern, and the press and the movies would soon transform serial killers into "natural born celebrities."[83]

Betty Ferreri

In October 1948 "playboy" Jerome Ferreri was shot and then hacked to death with a meat cleaver.[84] Police arrested Vincent D'Angelo and Marion James Graham, residents in the Ferreri mansion in the Wilshire District of Los Angeles. So too did Patricia Elizabeth "Betty" Ferreri land in jail accused of murder.[85] Within days the press dubbed Betty Ferreri the "cleaver widow."[86]

Charles Fauci, alias Vincent D' Angelo, loaded the gun that Allan Adron used to fire two shots into Jerome Ferreri on October 26, 1948. Adron worked as a handyman for the estate, and according to Betty Ferreri's first version of the events, she gave him the gun with "instructions to him to shoot if Ferreri resumed beating her."[87] Adron also changed his story indicating that Charles Fauci, Jerome's cousin, slipped him the weapon. Graham altered his account of events partially indicating that Fauci had produced the weapon. Fauci said the gun was Jerome's piece and hidden in the garage. On the day of Jerome's demise, Fauci had taken the gun from its hiding place, loaded it, and put it in his pocket. This followed an incident involving Jerome throwing scissors at Betty, striking her in the leg, and generally being abusive and "ugly." Later in the day Betty screamed, and Fauci ran to Adron's bedroom window and declared, "He's murdering Betty, Allan. Go open the [front] door." Adron rushed to the front door, seized the gun, and ran to Betty's defense, but his aim was poor. He only wounded Jerome. Jack R. Hardy, Betty's attorney, filled in the conclusion via a statement by his client. She stated, "I's convinced now that the best bet for me is the truth. I should have told it long ago." That said, she recounted, "Jerry went down. He cried out, 'Allan . . . Allan . . . what are you doing?' Then Jerry began to get up. Toward me. I was crazy with fear. I knew I couldn't let him get hold of me again. I only wanted to knock him out. I thought at first I had grabbed a small hammer." However, her grasp had hold of "the cleaver." She claimed, "After the first time, I have no memory of hitting him again. I was numb." In addition to the homicide caper, police booked Fauci on a fugitive warrant from New York for automobile theft.[88]

With these new stories the district attorney voided the original complaint and issued a new complaint charging Ferreri, Adron, and Fauci with murder. The complaint averred that Betty hacked Jerry twenty-three times with the meat cleaver. Adron told reporters, "They're still not telling the whole truth." A police officer told the press, "The place was a house of horrors" and "had someone not 'taken care' of Ferreri, the playboy would have slain his wife the night of Oct. 26."[89] These police statements regarding physical abuse and self-defense put a clear image in the public mind. Subsequent police statements gave the defendants further ammunition for a trial. The police indicated that Jerry might have been the target of a mob hit. A telegram stating that "the flowers will bloom in December" indicated that Murder, Inc. had slated Jerry for a "squealer" execution.[90]

Charles Fauci's alias complicated the case. Ex-convict Fauci possessed Vincent D'Angelo's driver's license.[91] New York police found D'Angelo at his home and discovered that he had reported his automobile stolen.[92] Brooklyn officials arrived from New York to investigate Fauci and interviewed him in his cell. Meanwhile, Jack Hardy told the press that Betty Ferreri would plead not guilty and not guilty by reason of temporary insanity. Striking Jerome Ferreri repeatedly with a meat cleaver only indicated "the derangement induced by fear in view of Ferreri's record of brutality toward her."[93] With all of this in print, the accused moved to the preliminary hearing.

The prosecution paraded science before municipal judge Louis W. Kaufman in the form of the chief county autopsy surgeon, Dr. Frederick W. Newbarr. Newbarr gave the court a three-hour chalk talk on Jerry's wounds, and defense attorney Jack Hardy spent most of his time trying to pry testimony casting doubt on whether any of the meat-cleaver blows had caused death, whether cuts on the hands could have been caused by something other than the meat cleaver, and whether Jerry's basal skull fracture resulted from a fall rather than a blow from a meat cleaver. The doctor stuck to his interpretation that either the gunshot wounds or the cleaver wounds separately were enough to kill Jerry and that the victim was alive when struck by the meat cleaver. Jerry's blood alcohol was .13 percent.[94] Marion "Val" Graham, a singer and lodger at the estate, testified about the events leading up to the killing, including Jerry attacking Betty with a poker. Graham commented that the fur hat Betty Ferreri conveniently wore to the preliminary hearing "saved her from being knocked out by the poker."[95] The three-day preliminary hearing proved "one of the longest on record" there. At its conclusion Judge Kaufman denied defense motions, and the three defendants moved on to the arraignment.[96]

At the arraignment Ferreri donned her "lucky hat," and the *Los Angeles Times* printed an excellent picture of her, Jack Hardy, and the lucky hat with the story.[97] Legal maneuvering and the holiday season pushed further proceedings into 1949. Adron dismissed his attorney, L. R. Baker, and substituted Gladys Towles Root, one of Los Angeles's most flamboyant criminal defense lawyers. Adron maintained, "I have not been ably represented by these attorneys. They are trying to send me to an insane institution."[98]

The entry of Gladys Root changed the complexities of the proceedings. Adron entered a plea of guilty and a plea of not guilty by reason of insanity. Root asked that the two pleas be heard separately and waived a jury on the former plea. Superior court judge Charles W. Fricke accepted the plea and set

March 7 as the date for the separate hearing. The *Los Angeles Times* noted, "Mrs. Root's modish attire—she wore a trim blue suit and heavy jewelry—was in great contrast to the somber widow's weeds which the accused Mrs. Ferreri was wearing for the opening of the trial." Root also wore her signature "white feather hood and silver fox coat." Ferreri "went almost unnoticed" in her "simple black dress with high neck and long sleeves." She carried "a black hat and a black patent-leather purse."[99]

During the second day of trial, Ferreri broke down as Jack Hardy described the "brutal treatment" her son had suffered at the hands of Jerry. "When she began to cry, she attempted to shield her face from the spectators in the courtroom." She also tried to keep her distress from her lawyer and hid behind him "without attracting undue attention. She brushed away her tears with her handkerchief." Ferreri's attorney, Jack Hardy, in clashes with the prosecution and in questioning veniremen, established his client as a "champion of the home" and characterized the meat cleaver as "a repulsive weapon." Hardy also pushed the self-defense issue. He asked the jurors whether the fact that "regardless of the disposition and reputation of her husband, she still stood by him, stayed with him through trying circumstances and still tried to keep her home intact" would prejudice them against her.[100] On the third day of the trial, Ferreri cried audibly, and Jack Hardy shouted that Jerry Ferreri had acted "like a wild animal when in a rage." Every time Hardy referred to Jerry's request that Betty engage in a "life of shame," her tears started. Fauci became "the forgotten man."[101] The *Los Angeles Times* gave the trial page 2 coverage and frequently illustrated the day's events with one or two pictures.

The judge swore in a jury of seven men and five women on February 11, 1949.[102] The prosecution relied on Dr. Newbarr as lead witness, and he repeated his testimony from the preliminary hearing. Defense counsel won concessions that Jerry was able to stand and advance despite the gunshot wounds, that the wounds on Jerry's back could have been made by Betty's fingernails, and that Jerry was intoxicated "enough to make some people belligerent."[103] Val Graham altered her story when deputy district attorney J. Miller Leavy caught her in inconsistent testimony. This was a prosecution stratagem of "quasi-impeachment" of its own witness. Graham also testified about Betty's long history of physical and mental abuse by Jerry.[104] When Graham, under cross-examination, told of threats against Betty's life, Betty started "sobbing hysterically. Her body trembled as her weeping became audible. Then she pitched over in a faint." The court recessed, and then Graham resumed his testimony of beatings, Jerry's demand that Betty "enter into prostitution," and Jerry's parading his girlfriends before Betty. Finally, Graham told the jury that the lights were dim in the house that night.[105]

The prosecution next turned to investigating officer George W. Stockley. His testimony indicated that Betty Ferreri had admitted to taking a roundabout route to the meat cleaver. His notes also indicated that she said, "Mr. Ferreri had turned the lights off. He dragged me into the pantry and beat me about the face."[106] On February 21, 1949, Allan Adron took the stand and testified that the homicide "was planned in detail an hour before the actual slaying." Adron, born George Wilson Raleigh, told a tale of a deliberate meat-ax attack that stunned the courtroom. Perhaps more stunning was Gladys Root's hat, which "caused a minor sensation among the women in the courtroom. It was all silk and a yard wide."

Despite the fashion flare, Jack Hardy made Adron recount his past in mental hospitals and allowed Adron's bungled syntax to bring "forth hearty laughter from the spectators." Adron also recounted how his first wife tried to poison his chicken soup and how "his family wanted to get rid of him because he talked contrary to them." Yet despite his flights of fancy, Adron did remember that Betty Ferreri had "swish[ed] past" him, indicating that she took a direct route to the kitchen.[107] Adron also admitted that the story he told for the prosecution was not the same as a ten-page memorandum he had written for his attorney. In that document Adron wrote, "I never saw any pocket gun nor any weapon nor was there any plan for me to interfere when Jerry did return."[108] Adron did testify that he beat Jerry over the head with the gun barrel "at the same time [Betty] was beating him with the cleaver." Adron was uncertain how he came to possess the gun.[109] He and Hardy mixed it up to the amusement of the jury. The insane witness debated his former lawyer over the meaning of truth.[110] If the prosecution's case was full of public interest, the defense proved much more lurid.

The defense's version of the events featured an abused woman's self-defense case with ample evidence of Jerry Ferreri's violence and infidelity. In addition to presenting photographs of Jerry with other women, the defense had Betty take the stand; she shocked the jury with an allegation that Jerry had attacked her that night "to extract a promise . . . that she would enter into interracial prostitution."[111] His prior physical abuse had caused miscarriages.[112] These abuse stories found support in anti-character testimony from Jerry's acquaintances from New Jersey. In their eyes "Jerky Jerry" often "pitched knives" at Betty, beat dogs to death with a baseball bat, and "looked like a maniac" when angry.[113] Another former resident at the Ferreri estate, Peter Baum, testified that Jerry possessed a dual personality. A long parade ranging from doctors to bus drivers told similar tales.[114] Model Flo Smock, who was with Jerry on the day of his death, appeared, but "her appearance . . . was more noteworthy than her testimony."[115] Far more noteworthy was Charles Fauci's testimony that Jerry had planned to kill Betty and dispose of "her body in the desert." In addition to this plan, Fauci told of increased violence against Betty and recounted Adron grabbing the gun from him.[116] The usual cross-examination and rebuttal witnesses followed his testimony.

The defense and the prosecution summed up their cases to the jury, and deliberations started in earnest.[117] After more than one hour of discussion, the first ballot was 9 to 3 for acquittal. The fifth ballot yielded agreement on acquittal for both defendants. Jury foreman Charles J. Raggio explained the jury's verdict to the press. Betty's "obvious sincerity and her statement, corroborated by other witnesses, that she had been attacked three times" that day "was the most impressive point in the case in the minds of the jurors." Further, "the very character of the slain Jerome Ferreri was a factor, . . . all testimony had presented him as a man who might be dangerous," and he had "neither respect nor regard for his wife." The jury saw Betty Ferreri's cleaver attack in terms of "hysterical self-defense."[118] The victim clearly deserved killing, and the widow clearly perpetrated the crime in self-defense. The prosecution had failed to break the nexus with credible evidence.

The 1940s witnessed a revolution in the workplace with women at machines, in the military in a variety of specializations, and in America's image of women and their capabilities. This cultural shift impacted women accused of homicide in California. The professionalization of journalism and criminal lawyers changed the image of the feminine on trial. Elite women, love letters, and love triangles still caught the readers and sold papers, but change was evident in three areas: reporters got out of the detective business; police managed their "news" more carefully; and criminal defense attorneys used the press to put their story into newsprint early and often. The language of misogyny slipped from the trial stories. War was on the front page, while women were in the courtroom and on juries. Battered women had self-defense firmly grounded in the public mind and agency to defend themselves. The partner beatings, David Peterson Del Mar's "white noise," were now in print and in courtrooms. World War II had put women in positions of responsibility, and they had performed ably. Attorneys crafted their female clients in different feminine images that juries could sympathize with while deliberating in a jury room. The reality of interpersonal violence was a recognized fact of social life and an intolerable behavior.

CHAPTER SIX

Celebrity on Trial

Tinseltown Tarnished

American spectators love a good show, and the trial of a celebrity is the best spectacle. Thane Rosenbaum argues, "The courtroom as theater is as old as 'Oedipus Rex.' We have come to organize our lives around the law, and our cultural consumption is overwhelmingly fed by the calories of courtrooms."[1] In 1955 Broadway brought theatergoers the Scopes Monkey Trial via *Inherit the Wind. Twelve Angry Men* was on stage in 1954 and in movie theaters in 1957. Rosenbaum notes, "That 'Inherit the Wind' and 'Twelve Angry Men' have undergone so many creative incarnations demonstrates the litheness of law as spectacle and that the public seemingly never tires of trials."[2] Further, "we are drawn to the spectacle of trials, with lawyers as cunningly disarmed gladiators and elevated judges who can resolve all conflicts peaceably, with brains and a gavel rather than blood and gore." Rosenbaum also suggests, "The adversarial nature of the legal system also appeals to Americans' tendency to reduce everything to a competition. Trials also speak of our desire to believe in a single truth, that reasonable doubt can be overcome and that what actually happened is, indeed, knowable."[3] Susan

Jacoby, a journalist-author, writes that media have had a celebrity-making role because "the pressure to 'personalize' was directly proportional to the bigness of the story, and the story grew bigger the more it was personalized."[4] Further, "the insistence on celebrity personalization . . . intensified with the birth of the new feminist movement, because judging women on the basis of their appearance is as acceptable in the culture of journalism as it is throughout American culture."[5] Clearly this trend began in the 1920s; in the 1950s a killing involving a celebrity sharpens this focus and mesmerizes the audience. Such was a case in 1958.

Lana Turner

In April 1958 Beverly Hills police were summoned to film star Lana Turner's bedroom, where Johnny Stompanato, the former bodyguard of Mickey Cohen, had been killed. The convergence of film, celebrity, and homicide produced media frenzy as well as multiple books on the subject.[6] The fact that the criminally accused was Cheryl Crane, the minor child of Lana and Stephen Crane, proved secondary, yet it was the focus of the legal proceedings that followed.[7] This whirlwind homicide case was much like Turner's marriage to Stephen Crane. In 1942 she eloped with the "wealthy tobacco heir and stock broker" to Las Vegas.[8] Discovering that Crane's divorce was not final at the time of the wedding and that she was pregnant, Turner obtained an annulment.[9] Crane and Turner soon remarried.[10] Three months later Lana gave birth to Cheryl.[11] Lana and Stephen committed themselves to parenthood.[12] Parenthood lasted, but the marriage did not. Stephen and Lana divorced in 1944.[13] Then came the killing, and their lives converged again.

Distinguishing this case from prior cases was the presence of seasoned counsel immediately on the scene, providing the media with information favorable to his client. Lana Turner and Stephen Crane retained Jerry Giesler within one hour of the homicide. The day after the stabbing, Giesler told the press, "Lana's daughter acted out of extreme fear of Stompanato and said that she obviously struck at him in an attempt to defend her mother from an attack which had been repeatedly threatened by Stompanato." Giesler also informed the press that a police report contained information of Stompanato's beatings of "Miss Turner" with his fists and threats to cut her face.[14] In a 1963 interview California Supreme Court chief justice Phil Gibson remarked, "[Giesler] was one of the best trial lawyers I ever knew."[15] Giesler also understood the power of the media.

The April 6, 1958, edition of the *Los Angeles Times* provided readers with a visual tabloid of Turner and Jerry Giesler, Stompanato and mob figures, and a few photos of Cheryl Crane. The stories focused on Lana and Johnny. Lana saw her daughter whisked off to Juvenile Hall because of "a violent bedroom scene" leaving her "handsome friend Johnny Stompanato dead." The "slaying" took place in Lana's "pink bedroom" and "climaxed a gossip-strewn romance between the screen's onetime Sweater Girl and the dark-haired former underworld figure." The location of the homicide was "the master bedroom of Miss Turner's rented home at 730 N. Bedford Drive." The press made certain that the curious could easily find the scene of the crime. Beverly Hills police chief Clinton H. Anderson repeated Cheryl Crane's statement of the facts, saying, "The girl's sudden act climaxed a noisy quarrel between the actress and Stompanato" during which he "threatened to disfigure and kill her and her daughter." Cheryl then "had gone to her defense."[16] The law privileged a killing in defense of another as self-defense.

Chief Clinton H. Anderson told *Los Angeles Times* reporter Ray Herbert that Cheryl's story was consistent with the one she had told Capt. P. R. Smith at the scene of the homicide. Her recounting of the events included her spending the day with her father and Lana arriving home around 9:30 p.m. after shopping. Lana and Johnny got into a "violent argument." Lana told Johnny that they were through, and he threatened to kill her or disfigure her. Cheryl remembered Johnny declaring, "I'll get you. If I can't, some of my gang will. There aren't enough cops in the world to stop me." At this point Lana retreated to Cheryl's bedroom, and Cheryl pleaded with Lana to "make Stompanato leave." Lana replied, "I am going to. This is the showdown." Lana started down the hall only to have Johnny charge into Cheryl's bedroom. Lana convinced him to return to her pink parlor to have it out. There "the argument was renewed. It grew louder." In this context Cheryl armed herself with "a new butcher knife."

According to Chief Anderson, "Cheryl walked into her mother's room and approached Stompanato, who was shouting at the actress." Cheryl screamed, "You leave my mother alone." Then "as he turned toward her, Chief Anderson related, she plunged the knife into his abdomen." Johnny fell "with a surprised look on his face" on a "pink shag wall-to-wall carpet." Cheryl put the knife on "a small marble-topped table," ran to her room, threw herself on her bed, and called her father, who immediately retained Jerry Giesler. Lana started wiping up Johnny's blood and called her mother, who called a doctor. The doctor summoned an ambulance, and the police were thereby notified.[17]

Johnny, "the dapper Adonis of the underworld, and friend and one-time associate and bodyguard of Mickey Cohen," arrived in the morgue, with Mickey Cohen not far behind attempting to claim the body. The coroner's office refused the claim and told Cohen that the family must appear to recover his remains. Carmine Stompanato arrived from Woodstock, Illinois, and, accompanied by Mickey Cohen, drove to Chief Anderson's office in Beverly Hills. To mend Johnny's image, Carmine pleaded with the press, "Please don't call him a hoodlum." Johnny attended public school in Illinois followed by a hitch at the "Kemper Military School in Booneville, Mo." After graduating in 1943 Johnny joined the United States Marine Corps and served with the First Division until his discharge in 1946. That said, the *Times* cited police sources regarding his California career. "In 1949 he was arrested in Beverly Hills on a vagrancy charge and was found guilty." The prosecuting attorney in the case "described Stompanato as an associate of 'Mickey Cohen and his 40 thieves.'" Stompanato successfully appealed the conviction, won a new trial, and had charges dismissed. When police arrested Stompanato in 1952 on armed robbery charges, officers investigating the case "found two guns in his apartment, released him four days later." Johnny married and divorced three times. His romance with Lana took him to London while she performed on a movie set. "Scotland Yard detectives . . . had advised Stompanato to leave Britain for reportedly threatening the actress while they were in London." Back in California Chief Anderson "had 'always' been suspicious of Stompanato's associations with women." He told the press, "We questioned him about his activities. He was the gigolo type." Finally, Lana confided in Chief Anderson that "Stompanato had beaten her and that she was afraid of him."[18] Johnny's image was clearly tarnished.

Lana's past was not perfect either, including four failed marriages, and the press turned a "Love Photo" into more front-page news. The Beverly Hills police released "a picture on which she had written of her love for the slain former mobster." The photo resulted in more speculation. "Friends theorized that the break between the couple came when the actress, under pressure from friends," refused to take Johnny to the "fanciest party of the year—the Academy Awards." The police believed that this touched off "the series of bitter arguments." Police also quoted Lana as saying that five days after the Academy Awards, "John said he would cut my face with a razor. He told me that if a man makes a living with his hands, he would destroy his hands. You make a living with your face." The police also related Lana's statement that "Stompanato had choked her during an argument in their London hotel room last year." The last lines of the *Los Angeles Times* story told of Cheryl being "accorded special treatment in Juvenile Hall" and "audibly" praying "for her mother and herself."[19] Jerry Giesler's attempt to have her released to a relative failed, and she remained in Juvenile Hall.[20]

If the photograph was not enough to stir reader interest, Mickey Cohen grabbed front-page headlines with "Lana's Love Notes to Johnny." Cohen released the "love notes" to refute Lana's story that Johnny had chased her to London, Mexico, and California. Cohen called a press conference and "said Miss Turner's passionate missives to her boyfriend [that] came from Denmark, England, and other European points last year were sprinkled with 'My Dearest, Darling Love, Honey Pot, Darling Papito, Daddy Darling,' and the like." Carmine chimed in with his doubts about how a slip of a girl could fell a six-foot Marine and wanted Lana to take a lie-detector test. Carmine also refuted Lana's "chase" thesis. He asserted that the Beverly Hills police "were biased in Miss Turner's favor." The Beverly Hills police reacted with district attorney McKesson dispatching his chief investigator Julian Blodgett to determine how Mickey Cohen had obtained the letters from Johnny's locked apartment. The police told McKesson that they had allowed Mickey and Carmine into the apartment. McKesson speculated, "If someone could get in there and get letters, who knows what else might have been removed?" Mickey simply told reporters that he had the letters long before Johnny fell on the pink shag. He also mentioned paying for Johnny's funeral and his distaste for Lana.[21]

In addition to the *Los Angeles Times*'s printing of a few "love notes," the *Los Angeles Herald Examiner* printed the "text of twelve letters, a telegram, and several gift cards . . . across 450 column inches." The letters set out in Lana's words "our love, our hopes, our dreams, our sex and longings."[22] The letters were the product of a burglary. Mickey Cohen had released them to the press. The love letters in this case must be distinguished from those admitted into evidence in legal proceedings. Here they were privately acquired, albeit illegally, and released to impugn the reputation of a witness rather than the criminally accused. Yet they elicited the same public interest that Laura Fair's love letters had garnered when they hit newsprint in 1870.[23] Love letters gave readers a glimpse of private lives, personal emotions, and hidden events. Love letters sold newspapers.

Lana, in turn, was incommunicado, "near collapse," attended by a nurse, and listening to her attorneys. Louis C. Blau and Jerry Giesler announced, "It would be highly unethical, if not unlawful, for her [Turner] to issue statements or attend any press conference" because Cheryl Crane was a juvenile. Further, Lana had "been advised to testify freely and to the full extent of her knowledge only at a legal session such as a Coroner's inquest or a juvenile hearing." The witness list for the inquest included Lana's mother; Cheryl's father; Capt. Ray Borders, chief of Beverly Hills detectives; Chief Anderson; Dr. John McDonald, the family physician; and Dr. Harold Kade, the county surgeon who had performed the autopsy. Not called but afforded a good deal of print was Molly McMurry, Cheryl's eighty-year-old nursemaid interviewed in Edinburgh, Scotland. Since hearing of the tragedy, McMurry had declared, "I cannot believe my darling could have been responsible for this terrible thing. I feel so hopeless. I can do so little for Cheryl, and Lana now. All I can do is pray."[24]

Her prayers were answered at the coroner's inquest. The front page of the April 11, 1958, edition of the *Los Angeles Times* reported that Jack Jones told of Chief Anderson's "11th hour visit" to Lana Turner's home "as Lana prepared to deliver the most important lines of her career—a recital of the moments of horror a week ago when her 14-year old daughter Cheryl took the life of Johnny Stompanato." Capt. Ray Borders accompanied the chief, Lana Turner, and her attorney, Louis Blau. To handle "the expected mob of curiosity seekers," the sheriff assigned deputies to crowd control. Further, "special arrangements [had] been made to handle the pack of reporters and photographers who intend[ed] to be present for the inquest into the most spectacular Hollywood killing in many years." Meanwhile, more letters surfaced, including one riddled with smitten phrases such as, "You know baby, I'm so lonesome for the touch of you, I could die. I try to think of when you were here and those precious minutes I wasted when my lips were not on yours." Police detectives were still trying to determine how those letters had found their way to the press. It was "somewhat reminiscent of the old *Confidential* magazine format." Detectives discovered fingerprints, but the mystery continued.[25]

Page 2 news proved equally sensational as more evidence confirming Chief Anderson's characterization of Stompanato as a gigolo appeared. "Support for Anderson's description came from as far away as Europe yesterday," the *Times* informed its readers. The information involved Mickey Cohen's unpaid bills in Copenhagen, Brussels, Amsterdam, and Paris. Stompanato had instructed the creditors to post them to Lana Turner, and "the love-blinded actress paid—hundreds of dollars worth." Stompanato had also signed a promissory note for $2,800 that he never intended to pay. "Strangely enough, the note was turned over to Beverly Hills police by private detective Fred Otash, a figure not unfamiliar to those who have followed the *Confidential* magazine trial and other recent matters." A statement from "Ted Stauffer, former husband of Hedy Lamarr," also confirmed Lana's characterization of Johnny as chasing her. Further, Lana had told Ted and Hedy that she feared Johnny. The story carried a photograph of Lana with Sean Connery, "her leading man in 'Another Time, Another Place.'" The caption included the observation, "It was while making this movie that she wrote a series of passionate love letters to former Mobster Johnny Stompanato."[26]

Tucked away on the same page was Carmine Stompanato's continued insistence on a lie-detector test for Lana Turner. District attorney McKesson saw no reason for the test. "McKesson pointed out that Miss Turner will be under oath while testifying at today's inquest."[27] Law and procedure ruled that day.

On April 11, 1958, deputy coroner Charles C. Langhauser conducted the inquiry and asked the open-ended question, "Please tell the series of events that took place from your first meeting with Mr. Stompanato until the conclusion and his death." Lana Turner started the narrative at 2:00 p.m. on the fatal day with a shopping trip with Johnny. About 8:30 p.m. Johnny launched into an argument about a contemplated dinner with Lana's friends sans Johnny. He continued quarreling and grew more violent. Lana told the jury, "I was just finding out too many lies, and that this one more that I had found was just not the worst lie." The argument escalated into physical violence. "Mr. Stompanato grabbed me by the arms and started shaking me and cursing me very badly." Johnny declared that "he would never leave me, that if he said jump, I would jump; if he said hop, I would hop, and would have to do anything and everything he told me or he'd cut my face or cripple me." He also threatened to kill Lana, Cheryl, and Lana's mother. At this point on the night in question, Lana observed Cheryl in the room and told her to leave.[28]

Lana then told of Cheryl leaving the room, closing the door behind her, and Johnny coming at her "holding the jacket on the hanger in a way that he was going to strike [her] with it." Lana said, "Don't—don't ever touch me again. I am—I am absolutely finished. This is the end. And I want you to get out." Lana recalled, "[I] was walking toward the bedroom door, and he was right behind me, and I opened it, and my daughter came in." She said, "I swear it was so fast, I—I truthfully thought she had hit him in the stomach. The best I can remember, they came together and they parted (indicating). I still never saw a blade." Johnny fell to the floor, and the chaotic process of calling for help commenced.[29]

Lana remembered Cheryl exclaiming, "Mamma, I did not mean to do it. I didn't mean to do it." Langhauser silenced the courtroom. Lana resumed her testimony, recalling the amazingly quick arrival of Stephen Crane responding to a call from Cheryl. Then her mother entered the scene.[30]

The inquest continued with deputy district attorney William McGinley joining the interrogation. McGinley focused on the knife, its location in the bedroom, and how it arrived in the bathroom sink. He then asked who had called the police. Lana recalled, "I don't think I telephoned the police; I know that I telephoned for the ambulance, and the resuscitator and I telephoned Dr. Weber and Mr. Giesler, but I don't remember calling actual police."[31]

Perhaps the most significant evidence offered at the inquest was Beverly Hills police captain Ray Borders's testimony regarding Cheryl's statement at police headquarters on April 4, 1958. Present at the time of the interrogation were Jerry Giesler, Lana Turner, Chief Anderson, detective Polakov, and policewoman Stella Bertoglio. Cheryl said, "He kept threatening her and I thought he was going to hurt her, so I rushed into the room and struck him with the knife." Lana told police, "Everything she said is true." She added, "She just came inside the door, and the door was open. He was standing there with a jacket and shirt over his shoulders and he kept on and on and on with these threats, and Cheryl said, 'John, don't talk to mother like that.'" Lana thought Johnny retorted, "I will talk to her or anyone else." Then "he went on even more viciously verbally. The next thing I knew—this sounds strange—it happened so fast—it did, and I truthfully thought Cheryl had just poked him in the stomach. And then he pulled away from her." In the end Borders testified that every time Cheryl told her story it was identical with previous telling.[32]

The coroner's jury was out twenty-five minutes before returning a verdict of justifiable homicide.[33] The verdict, of course, earned front-page headlines with the *Times* offering a five-photograph sequence of Lana on the witness stand in her "Greatest Role." The caption continued, "Lana Turner is torn by emotion as, on the brink of collapse, she tells a Coroner's jury of the horror-filled moment when 'her baby,' 14-year old Cheryl, stabbed Johnny Stompanato." Jack Jones's story used the H-word in announcing the verdict: "The crackling emotion of a near-riotous inquest was climaxed in tears and spectator applause yesterday when a Coroner's jury ruled that the kitchen knife stabbing of Hoodlum Johnny Stompanato by Cheryl Crane, was 'justifiable homicide' in the belief her mother, Lana Turner, was in danger." More than one hundred reporters and photographers as well as newsreel cameramen mobbed the courtroom and the participants after the verdict. The story contained a fashion statement on Lana: "Her short blonde hair [was] combed back. She wore a gray coat and gray silk, tweed-type dress. She took one white glove off to expose silvered fingernails." Print also revealed, "She trembled, put her hands to her face from time to time and fought to control tears that threatened to overcome her."[34] Press coverage of the feminine had changed little since Laura Fair's trial in 1870. However, Lana Turner was already famous, while the press made Laura Fair into a celebrity.

The verdict of the coroner's jury atomized press coverage. Cheryl's fate in Juvenile Hall was undecided. Attorney Arthur J. Crowley represented her on Stephen Crane's behalf and promised to cooperate with juvenile authorities.[35] Despite visits from Lana and Stephen Crane, Cheryl suffered from homesickness.[36] Lana's visits with her mother drew the press corps and provided splendid photographs for readers.[37] Stephen Crane's visits drew column coverage in section B with a single-column photograph in the *Times*.[38] The interlude awaiting the juvenile court hearing afforded creative reporters opportunity.

Jack Jones followed the money. Beverly Hills police turned up Stompanato bank books, clothing, records, jewelry, and mementos in a storage warehouse. Albeit appearing on page 2, pictures of Lana Turner and Ray Borders with a jailhouse display were prominent in the story. A checking account in the names of John or Rosemary Stompanato bearing the address of Rosemary Trimble had been cleaned out, and another bankbook bore the same names. Rosemary "was unable to explain the happenstance." A memento in Johnny's stash was a wedding ring bearing the inscription "From Here to Eternity—Rosemary and John." Rosemary, the wife of Dr. David Trimble, was "dumbfounded." Also, a mysterious "oil painting of silk of Stompanato with a blond woman and a small girl" surfaced. "There was further mystery attached to this in that police didn't feel the portrayed woman resemble[d] any of his three former wives." Jones mused, "The possibility remained that it could be his first wife, Sarah, whom he married in China. But that marriage resulted in a son—not a daughter." Jones also uncovered a failed business deal that left another creditor with worthless promissory notes. Finally, back in Woodstock, Illinois, Carmine Stompanato contemplated a civil action.[39] Jones followed up on the worthless notes and "a pretty, red-haired Mar Vista widow" who had loaned Johnny $8,150. "She never got back a dime," Jones reported. Meanwhile, Beverly Hills police followed the Trimble lead. Jones noted, "Everywhere police turned, they seemed to be stumbling over evidence that Stompanato managed to turn friendships into profit." The number of promissory notes grew, and along with the worthless paper, the soiled reputation of Johnny and his acquaintances grabbed page 2 news.[40]

California's reputation suffered as well. The Reverend Dr. John Sutherland Bonnell preached against degeneration in an April 20 sermon in New York's Fifth Avenue Presbyterian Church. The Lana Turner case gave evidence of America's moral standards in decline. Bonnell declared, "We still are in the aftermath of World War II; we are under the influence of the late Dr. Alfred Kinsey," and "we are living in a period of insecurity induced by the atomic age." The "recent West Coast incident" dramatizes "the present moral degeneration and reveals the unhidden perils of the nation." Bonnell asserted, "This woman who must carry the guilt of her daughter, will continue to receive the patronage of an adoring, blind American Public."[41] Thus Lana Turner led the public down a slippery slope to moral depravity, according to the reverend. This attack was part of the fundamentalist assault on all things liberal as well as what Susan Jacoby has called "the culture of distraction."[42] Bonnell, like fundamentalists today, wanted to remake American society and the world in his biblical image.[43]

While the blind American public kept its adoring eyes on Lana, Cheryl appeared in Judge Allen T. Lynch's court for a closed juvenile court hearing. After ninety minutes of hearing witnesses, Judge Lynch granted temporary custody of Cheryl to her grandmother, Mildred Turner.[44] As Cheryl left court with her grandmother, she was slapped with a summons involving a civil damage suit filed against her, Lana, and others.[45] Cheryl drew a page 3 story.

Stephen Crane and Lana Turner reappeared on page 1 of the

Times when Crane announced that he would fight Turner for complete custody of Cheryl. Jack Jones reported, "Although Jerry Giesler, Lana's attorney, reported that the actress herself will battle for custody of the couple's daughter . . . there seemed to be no ill feeling between Crane and his glamorous ex-wife." Giesler took another fork in the road, calling "Crane's decision to contest the ruling 'ridiculous' and said he [was] certain his glamorous client [felt] the same way." After all, "any mother" would fight for custody of a daughter.[46]

While the parties contested custody in one court, William Jerome Pollack, attorney for Johnny's ten-year-old son, John Jr., and his mother, Mrs. Sarah Ibaraim, Stompanato's first wife, gathered evidence for the civil suit. Pollack averred that when he put Johnny's clothes on a dummy and stabbed it with "another butcher knife," the wound substantiated his theory that Johnny was "lying down when assaulted." That made the act wrongful death. While Pollack collected evidence, the Beverly Hills police investigated numerous death threats against Lana Turner and Jerry Giesler.[47]

Depositions in the civil suit started in June and gave the press more legal fodder.[48] An amended complaint alleged that the plaintiff was uncertain "as to whether it was Defendant Cheryl Crane or Defendant Lana Turner who did the actual stabbing, or whether the one assisted the other therein. Because of said doubt, plaintiff allege[d] that both of said defendants did inflict the said stab wound in the body of John Stompanato." Regarding the liability of Stephen Crane, the suit alleged that he arrived at the Turner residence when Johnny was still alive and did not summon medical assistance.[49] Now the civil side of the law came to the fore, and Lana and Cheryl had a new attorney, Lowell Dryden.

On June 23, 1958, Lana, Cheryl, Jerry, and Lowell provided photographic excitement as they headed into the law office of William Jerome Pollack.[50] At the end of the day Pollack reported, "Cheryl told [me] yesterday that she cannot recall actually stabbing Stompanato in the pink-carpeted bedroom of Lana's rented Beverly Hills mansion." Further, "Cheryl apparently cannot recollect giving to Beverly Hills Police Chief Clinton Anderson a statement read at the inquest which resulted in a justifiable-homicide verdict."[51] The case drifted into the court of Walter Allen.[52]

Judge Lynch determined that Cheryl was to remain a ward of the court in the custody of her grandmother.[53] Cheryl lived with her grandmother, and in 1959 appeared with her mother at the premiere of *Imitation of Life*.[54] Jerry Giesler retold the story in "The Lana Turner Tragedy" in a 1959 *Saturday Evening Post*.[55]

Lana Turner recounted her version of events in 1982 in *Lana*. She prefaced the "nightmare" with 195 pages of movie stories, four husbands, and her daughter, Cheryl. The chain of events leading to homicide started "innocently enough" with a telephone call from John Steele, a person unknown to Lana, but which turned out to be an assumed name of Johnny Stompanato. Offers of lunch and a steady dose of flowers followed until Lana agreed to meet the mysterious man for a drink. She averred, "The blackest period of my life began . . . with flowers and an innocent invitation for a drink, and it was to end in screaming headlines, in tragedy and death."[56] Johnny's obsession with Lana and his persistent telephone calls bothered her at first. Then she feared that he would invade her apartment, writing, "I had a strange premonition that he might somehow manage to get into my apartment at night."[57] One night Johnny did enter her apartment via the fire escape and attacked her in bed with a pillow and a kiss. She screamed and he left the bedroom, but his departure did not end their relationship.

Johnny proved persistent. Lana confessed, "I wasn't strong enough to resist. And there was another reason I didn't get help, though for a while I couldn't even admit it to myself: His consuming passion was strangely exciting." At a deeper level of analysis, Johnny constituted "forbidden fruit." Lana enjoyed a "dangerous captivation" that perhaps related to her father, who, she explained, "was an occasional gambler and ... he was murdered—the connection seems obvious enough, but I can't say for sure that it's valid." In addition to captivation, Lana experienced "fear." She "felt trapped" and recalled, "John took pains to remind me that he had the power to harm me and my family."[58] She embarked on a strategy of flight, but Johnny mysteriously appeared place after place in pursuit. Finally, Lana consented to see him in public.

Then came the Academy Award nomination for best actress for her role in *Peyton Place*. Lana observed, "John was so impressed by my Academy Award nomination that for a while he behaved." Yet Lana knew "the reality was that [she] remained John's captive."[59] Johnny underscored his power by brandishing a gun when they were in Acapulco prior to the Oscar ceremony.[60] The threats of violence became reality the night of the Academy Awards when Lana returned home. She had attended sans Johnny.

Johnny, "the irrational, violent monster lurking underneath the charming suitor," started an evening of violence with "one panther like spring" upon her.[61] The first swat "had caught one of my earrings and driven it painfully into my cheek."

The second time, "he cracked me." Lana hit the floor. Then fists blasted her from the walls to the floor and finally to the bed.[62] Pinned to the bed, Lana heard Johnny declare, "You will never leave me out of anything. If you go anywhere, I'll always go there, too. I let you get away with it this time, but never again as long as you live." Lana admitted defeat and retreated to the bathroom to "rinse [her] mouth out with cold water, spitting out the blood."[63] She did everything to prevent Cheryl from seeing her in her battered state.

Turner took two pages to explain why she did not seek interventions to stop the beatings, intimidation, and threats. Most of the excuses were about negative publicity ending her career or Cheryl's sensibilities.[64] Her narrative was self-serving and did not attempt a battered partner excuse of codependency.

The evening of the homicide, Johnny started an argument that grew in intensity. Lana attempted to shield Cheryl from the brouhaha, but the girl persisted in her demand to enter the bedroom and confront the couple. When Cheryl entered, Lana recounted, "what she saw was me sitting on the pink marble counter, and John coming toward me, his arm upraised, with something in his hand." What Cheryl could not perceive was "the fact that he was carrying clothing on hangers over his shoulder." Instead, Cheryl recognized an "upraised, threatening hand, and what appeared to be some kind of weapon." Lana saw "out of the corner of [her] eye" Cheryl "make a sudden movement. Her right arm had shot out and caught John in the stomach." Lana thought "she'd punched him." Then "there was a strange little moment, locked in time, as each stood looking at the other." Johnny gasped, "Oh, my God, Cheryl, what have you done?" Cheryl retreated and Johnny "took three little circling steps away from her, in slow motion." Johnny "fell backward, like a board, straight to the floor."[65]

Lana recalled, "A shock wave hit me." She saw Cheryl drop the knife. Lana sent her to her room and turned "numbly" to Johnny, who "was making dreadful, soft, choking sounds." Lana did not see the wound until she lifted his sweater, and "it was a small wound, only a little slice. Strangely there was very little blood." Lana could not remember going to the bathroom to secure a towel, noting, however, "Since there was a towel there I must have." Lana recollected, "[I] moved in a dream. None of this could be real. What made me do it, I don't know, but I picked up the knife and dropped it into the sink." Despite her numb state, she recalled her mind "commanded" that she "do something." Lana called her mother to declare, "Mother, John is dead." Lana called "Dr. McDonald" who "called [her] right back."[66] Lana then went to Cheryl's side, not knowing that the girl had called her father.

Help started arriving. First, Mildred Turner appeared. Then Dr. McDonald, who declared Johnny deceased and said, "Call Jerry Giesler." Stephen Crane arrived on the heels of McDonald, followed by the police, an ambulance, and attorney Giesler. Lana "didn't even notice them." She did remember her mother sending the doctor to see Cheryl and the attorney finding her. She told Giesler, "Cheryl, thinking to protect me, had stabbed John with the knife. I took him to the bathroom and showed the knife still lying there in the sink." Chief Anderson arrived at the door of the pink bedroom, and Lana pleaded, "Please, let me say I did it."[67] The chief replied, "Lana, don't, we already know it was Cheryl." Cheryl told her father, "I did it, Daddy, but I didn't mean to. He was going to hurt Mommy." Lana next remembered that the police swarmed the home: "I was stunned at the number of blue uniforms all over the place." She thought, "The police photographers must have given pictures to the press, for later the newspapers printed shots of John's body lying on the floor. How cooperative with the press, the Beverly Hills police!"[68]

Lana, Cheryl, and Jerry Giesler proceeded to police headquarters "in his [Giesler's] chauffeured car." At the station, Chief Anderson asked for Cheryl's story, and Lana hardly "remember[ed] her words." She recalled, "She had heard John say he was going to destroy my face, and she had brought the knife to protect me. A young girl, a child, against a big man." The little slice pierced "the aorta [and] was fatal by chance." Cheryl "had been trying to protect me. She was now in terrible trouble. Nothing seemed to matter except protecting her." Lana, Stephen Crane, and Jerry Giesler left the stationhouse at the insistence of the police because "the press had gathered like vultures outside, cameras at the ready. And they got their damned pictures."[69] The media feast was only beginning.

The coroner's inquest was "a humiliating ordeal" because Turner had "to explain on the witness stand what [she] barely understood [herself]." Further, Lana had "to confess before the cameras that strange helplessness that bound [her] to John for so long." She "nearly broke down on the witness stand from the mixture of agony and shame, of grief and relief that [she] felt about John's death." Regardless of the emotional strain, Cheryl's freedom came first. The jury took only twenty-five minutes to arrive at the verdict of justifiable homicide.[70]

The next legal hurdle was Judge Allen T. Lynch's juvenile court, which Lynch "mercifully closed . . . to the public and the press."[71] Lynch put Lana, Cheryl, and Stephen into therapy. Lana thought that she had "gotten little out of it" and declared, "I've never believed in psychoanalysis as a way to solve my problems."[72] Lana moved into a period of contemplation after six weeks of therapy.

She read the newspaper stories about her tragedy, editorials, letters from readers, including "the slanderous ones, the moralistic ones, the sympathetic ones, the pathetic ones." Lana did all of this to "understand and then to step outside of it." She also faced death threats, a civil suit, and financial difficulty.[73] Her agent, Paul Kohner, and producer Ross Hunter saved her career and her bottom line with *Imitation of Life*. The remainder of the book details Lana's movies and adds to her list of husbands. Cheryl ended up in trouble with her juvenile court supervisor and retreated to a special school in the East for rehabilitation.

Wayne Lawson's review of the book in the *New York Times* was unsympathetic. Lawson wrote, "The 60 pages she spends on her affair with Stompanato, which lasted a year, and the 15 on the Tyrone Power affair read like B-movie scripts." He found it "difficult to understand why she couldn't get rid of Stompanato before it was too late." Lawson concluded, "The bulk of the book is the very gossip and drivel Miss Turner says drove her to take up her pen in the first place, and the story of her life is fleshed out with trivia, unembarrassed by many exact dates."[74] Lawson pans the book and the genre. Yet despite the lack of footnotes, dates of events, and frank analysis of motivation and causation, Lana Turner kept most of her testimony consistent with the trivial content of film and confession books. The testimony, under oath, was subject to cross-examination. Books only have reviewers.

In 1988 Cheryl Crane published her version of the events in *Detour: A Hollywood Story*. Cheryl recounted "a few violent arguments" prior to the night of the homicide. On one occasion

Johnny "smashed a door, slapped her [Mother] around, and held a gun to her head, mainly because she refused to sleep with him. Instead, she preferred to get drunk and blot everything out." Lana tried to minimize Johnny's links with her, but on February 22, 1958, Louella Parsons "scolded [Lana] in her international column" for her relationship with Johnny.[75] The newspapers made matters worse with headlines such as, "LANA TURNER RETURNS WITH MOB FIGURE."[76]

On the night of the Oscars, Cheryl noticed something different: "I had never seen Mother actually tremble before, not until that day." That made Cheryl edgy.[77] Cheryl did not mention the beating Johnny administered when Lana returned from the Oscars. Perhaps she did not know of it, but she clearly remembered the night of the homicide.

Cheryl's recollection of the night Johnny died comports well with Lana's testimony at the hearing and as presented in her book. Cheryl's recounting of the interrogation in Chief Anderson's office exhibits a general loss of memory but sound research. Cheryl wrote, "Then the chief asked me to tell what I knew." Not remembering, she noted, "It was later reported accurately that I told Anderson that I did what I did to protect Mother." Unfortunately, "somewhere in the retelling, damaging words were put in my mouth that had me saying at the instant of thrusting the knife, 'You don't have to take that, Mama!'" That utterance, she observed, "wrongly suggest[ed] premeditation." She did recall that "when she [Lana] yanked the bedroom door open, Stompanato was advancing from behind her with his arm raised to strike." To Cheryl "his silhouette only looked as though he were attacking." Following her testimony, she wrote, "I believe that, in my fright, I jabbed at him with the knife out of a split-second impulse to scare him." She maintained that she had "no forethought. The fact is, having never been permitted in a kitchen, [she] knew little of knives."[78] The retelling was consistent with Cheryl's 1958 testimony.

Cheryl's version of Lana's testimony adds to the drama. She characterized Lana's appearance as "the most important performance of her life."[79] The language was that of the newspaper caption with photographs of Lana on the witness stand. Cheryl recalled Lana's testimony: "Mother underplayed. She spoke slowly, often using the arcane syntax that she had learned from testifying at divorce hearings, and she showed schoolgirl good manners with the three men who questioned her."[80] Her retelling of the hearing mirrored the transcript.

Cheryl reveled in the "ironic discovery" of Johnny's "papers and personal items that revealed the unsavory side of his business affairs. A number of unpaid promissory notes to women showed a paper trail into heavy debt."[81] The civil suit for $752,250 brought by Carmine Stompanato on behalf of Johnny's son proved bothersome, but "most everything was refuted in the public record," she remarked, adding, "But the case kept the story alive at the time when we wanted to get it behind us."[82] Not unexpectedly, the civil suit settled quietly for $20,000 two years later.[83]

Sheila Paulos in a *New York Times* review of *Detour* termed the book "an implausibly detailed reconstruction" of Cheryl Crane's life with Lana Turner, "portrayed here as self-absorbed and distant." Cheryl wrote the book to "clarify the record," and its contents prompted Paulos to muse, "The book should make the rest of us glad we weren't born rich and famous in Hollywood."[84] Perhaps an even more insightful review of the Stompanato homicide hit the bookstores in 1995. Jane Ellen

Wayne gave the event 10 pages out of a 198-page book titled *Lana: The Life and Loves of Lana Turner*.[85] The homicide in court involved Cheryl, but in the media of the day, the story was about celebrity riding sidesaddle on a horse that just did not run far enough. *Imitation of Life* and the reality of Cheryl's case juxtaposed years later were no contest. Image, not the reality of homicide, held public interest.

Image also was very much a part of how lawyers created narratives for the jury. Jerry Giesler's 1960 book, *The Jerry Giesler Story*, written for a popular audience, told readers of a basic change in representation in criminal cases.[86] Measured behavior replaced the rhetorical flourish dominating nineteenth-century practice. Giesler wrote, "I have never made a bombastic address to a jury." Regarding rhetorical flourish, he did not make "an orator's gestures." He "impressed the jury with [his] thoroughness, [his] sincerity and [his] determination to present all of the facts."[87] His mentor, Earl Rogers, emphasized the trial lawyer's need to know psychology and medicine.[88] Of equal importance in the Turner-Crane-Stompanato case was Giesler's handling of the press. He put his client's story in print within a day. He kept the press distracted with the story that journalists wanted, Lana's stories. When it came to the critical juvenile court hearing, he had a closed hearing. Lawyering was now more than psychology and medicine as evidence; it was press relations working the psychology of reporters.

With the deceased Stompanato falling to the floor, the new machinery of justice started with a telephone call to Stephen Crane, who called Jerry Giesler into the service of a woman who had killed a man. Beverly Hills chief of police Clinton H.

Anderson arrived with equal speed to survey the scene and interrogate witnesses. Both the police and the defense attorney were putting facts, as they saw them, in the hands of the press with great speed and regularity. The celebrity at the center of the press coverage remained the focus particularly when her love notes suddenly became public love letters. Whether in the 1870s or the 1950s, people were fascinated with love letters. Prosecutors had offered love letters as evidence in prior cases because love letters were private expressions of deeply held emotion intended only for the eyes of the author's beloved. They were windows of personal motivation. Prosecutors had culled love letters in other cases and included passages touching on motive or the violation of cultural norms. They did this to influence juries filled with individuals who believed in the veracity of love letters. Newspapers in the Cheryl Crane case printed Lana Turner's letters because their voyeuristic readers viewed love letters as sexual expressions and tender personal emotions expressed in prose.[89] They wanted to peer into the life of a celebrity and would buy papers to do so.

Beyond the personal life of a star, the case was a vehicle for fundamentalist commentary. New York City's Rev. Dr. Bonnell's public condemnation of Lana's life was part of a broader condemnation of liberal thought. Yet this was only the beginning of a continuing attack to be played out in the late twentieth century.

Finally, the case was a vehicle for the parties to tell their side of the story profitably. Both Lana and Cheryl wrote books. Both books had wide appeal to a public fixated on celebrity, violence, and women who kill men.

CONCLUSION

The newspaper stories, editorials, and statements of counsel reveal much about the image of women caught up in California's criminal justice administration system. The trials involving middle- and upper-class deceased men and their alleged slayers highlighted dominant cultural norms of the times. This culture reflected the signs and practices of journalists and lawyers represented in words and behaviors.[1] Victorian values defining the feminine as existing in a domestic sphere, providing for the care of children, and educating the next generation in morality came under attack by the turn of the century. "Feminist scholars demolished Victorian ideas about female intuition, hysteria, prostitution, vapors, menstruation, masturbation, passionlessness, orgasms, pregnancy, motherhood, marriage, and the double standard."[2] Nonetheless, it is important to note that during the nineteenth century, these concepts and values exhibited remarkable tenacity. Yet the Fair retrial and the Abarta and Cook cases demonstrated that juries in the last three decades of the century were willing to accept what the Harris jury in 1865 accepted: insanity of some sort as a defense. Equally, the concept of honor played a part in journalistic language and jury deliberations. Men valued the purity of womanhood and felt obligated to protect women. Lawyers and journalists played on the special nature of women, the elements of femininity.[3] Lawyers in defense of their female clients claimed the "unwritten law" and frequently tied it to an insanity defense such as in the Abarta case.[4] In addition to insanity, defense attorneys also argued self-defense. This was, according to Stanford law professor Lawrence Friedman, "ideology in action" or the "working norms of the legal system—the behavior of the actors in the system—together with what these norms and actions mean to people."[5] Newsprint and jury verdicts reflected the ideology. In the long nineteenth century, insanity and women went hand in hand. Isaac Ray, the expert on the subject and frequently cited in the Laura Fair case, believed that "the larger proportion of insanity in the American people was contributed by the female sex."[6] The early twentieth-century advances of psychology altered that perception.

Class played a role in the nineteenth-century cases. The prosecution put Laura Fair into the lower class, making her assault on an upper-class attorney even more egregious. Her life on the edge of respectable society made her a threat to upper-class Victorian morality. Significantly, Crittenden's affair with Fair drew little journalistic notice. He was the victim. His family members were victims of a brutal killing. Class as a factor in trials continued in the twentieth century.

The end of World War I brought the "new woman" to American culture, and the battered woman and self-defense became closely associated in the defense of women who killed. The 1920s saw women's sexuality transformed. "Hemlines rose and colored underwear replaced traditional white linen."[7] World

War I also "created new modes of sexual violence."[8] The "unwritten law" lost favor, and "homicidal jealousy" bound to an insanity defense gained in legal popularity. "By the 1920s that reappraisal was based on a growing appreciation of the universality of sibling jealousy, . . . the destructive effects of the emotion, and a crescendo of criticism of its value in a society that viewed women as the property of men."[9] Women in California moved, in law, quickly away from such a construct due to favorable court decisions and the provision of the California constitution of 1879 guaranteeing them access to "any legal occupation."[10] The "new woman" of the 1920s had her start in the nineteenth century thanks to pioneers such as Laura De Force Gordon. Women were no longer Euripides's Medea with only the power to destroy.[11] Women also had economic and political power.

The 1920s saw a shift in press emphasis as well as legal defense tactics. Lawyers no longer raised issues of menstruation and hysteria characteristic of nineteenth-century expert testimony. Rather counsel emphasized science and women's activities and victimization. Reporters continued to focus on dress and female mannerisms. Yet if the defendant could pass herself off as virtuous or sympathetic, male reporters continued to pander to stereotypical female images. Reporters portrayed women gone astray far less sympathetically.[12] Class continued to matter because lower-class women, living on the fringe of proper society, constituted a threat to the image of California as a Garden of Eden.

The "new woman" of the 1920s turned to a feminine ideal in the 1930s. Female fashion featured long, flowing skirts, clearly defined bustlines, tiny waistlines, and new foundation garments. Movie stars such as Jean Harlow, Greta Garbo, Marlene Dietrich, and Bette Davis became cultural models of steamy sensuality. Dating replaced the courting behavior of the long nineteenth century. Women freely chose their men, and companionate marriage raised expectations in wedlock. Women continued in wage work and focused on "making do" with Depression-era wages and New Deal support.[13] Importantly, the idea that women could commit crime or murder no longer shocked the reading public. In addition to the women in our narrative analysis, Bonnie Parker and Clyde Barrow's crime spree in 1932–34 generated many headlines throughout California.[14] Both Parker and Barrow were from poor families, yet the press sometimes portrayed them as Robin Hood figures. Law enforcement and bankers thought otherwise. As members of the lower class and as enemy deviants, they had to be stopped and exterminated.

World War II pulled the nation out of the Depression and put women to work in record numbers. California experienced an influx of immigrants second only to the gold rush. The population explosion increased tensions as declining infrastructure and increased competition for jobs and housing pitted new immigrants against older ethnic groups.[15] Hollywood continued to prosper, and women fought the back-to-the-home mentality. Middle- and upper-class white women lived the "problem that has no name."[16] Sometimes, however, for women of all social classes the problem bore a male face.

Women who killed men did so for a variety of reasons, and attorneys and newspapers ascribed legal or cultural causes to the homicidal behavior. Women like Laura Fair, Lastencia Abarta, and Marie Leonard Bailey killed because their men lied about marriage prospects and despoiled them in the process of their respective affairs. Women claimed insanity, as did

Katie Cook, Beatrice Mallette, Betty Flay Hardaker, and Betty Ferreri. The defense of insanity changed over time due to advances in psychiatry and the legal basis of the defense. Defense lawyers painted women as victims; prosecution lawyers thought homicidal women undermined civilization. Prosecutors called on the jury in the Fair case to reject the defendant's claims because they were "against the law and against morality." To decide otherwise was to "uproot civilization." Bertha Talkington was "a mad dog" who deserved to die. Defense attorneys, in kind, portrayed enemy deviant men as deserving exactly what they received. Tom Cook was "a very immoral man." Clara A. Wellman's husband was a wife beater and a drunken threat to the community. Angela Maria De Vita killed to protect her family. Lea Delmon killed the man who tried to sell her into prostitution. Gabrielle Dardley and Betty Ferreri also extinguished the lives of men in need of killing. Many of these killings were what Susan Jacoby has called "sexual revenge." It was revenge, depicted in Euripides's *Medea*, by a woman with only the power to destroy.[17]

Following the end of the nineteenth century, a skilled criminal defense bar emerged, with Earl Rogers and Jerry Giesler standing out as notable examples.[18] The lawyers of the period 1870–1900, whether defense or prosecution, often relied on rhetorical flourish as demonstrated in the Laura Fair case. The specialists of the twentieth century, however, used skilled interrogation of witnesses as well as a wealth of compelling evidence.

The prosecuting attorneys often identified greed as the root of homicidal evil. The cases of Aurelia Scheck, Gertrude Gibbons, Louise Peete, Madalynne Obenchain, Rosa Tarlazzi, Bertha Talkington, and Beulah Louise Overell contained elements of greed as a motive for murder. However, as the Overell case demonstrated, jurors required irrefutable evidence before the alleged motive of greed resulted in a conviction. In that case the prosecution failed to overcome the explanation that Overell's boyfriend purchased dynamite for her father because Overell's father regularly fished with one stick of dynamite to blast fish to the surface. Regardless of the efforts of the prosecutors and the press to paint Overell and her boyfriend as murdering conspirators, the jury lacked sufficient evidence to convict. Painting female defendants as consumers who could not adjust their consumption to their income or desired higher status worked at the movies, but the law and evidence constrained jurors.[19]

Prosecutors persisted in criminal proceedings despite substantial evidence favoring the criminally accused. The Gertrude Gibbons case is the best example of mistaken obstinacy. Attorneys exhibited similar zeal in the Obenchain case with the same results: failure for the prosecution. These prosecutors seem driven by misogyny rather than skillful case management based on probative evidence. They claimed adherence to the law in the press and persisted in claims of guilt based on evidence, but failed to win their cases. Some players simply did not know when to fold.

Defense attorneys argued self-defense as grounds for a justifiable homicide finding. There was an important difference between insanity pleas and self-defense pleas. As Susan Jacoby notes, "By obfuscating the motive and questioning the rationality of one who commits an act of revenge, they deny the avenger . . . her dignity in exchange for freedom."[20] As early as 1901 partner violence, wife beating, or battering constituted valid grounds for a finding of justifiable homicide. Clara

Wellman shot her battering husband. Nettie Platz, Claire Toler, Alice Haggerty, Gabrielle Dardley, Bertha Talkington, Erma Blanda, Berry Ferreri, and Nellie Madison also asserted this defense. Not all defense strategies proved successful, and in the case of Nellie Madison, counsel's outlandish claim that the dead body found in the bloody bed was not Nellie's husband only broadcast desperation to the jury. Defense in the protection of another usually resulted in a verdict of justifiable homicide. Angela Maria De Vita, Blanche Lescault, Erma Blanda, Marjorie Ferguson, Rose Miceli, and Cheryl Crane all claimed to be defending another person with deadly force. Often the facts convinced coroner's juries to end the criminal-justice process prior to trial. Clearly, we have demonstrated that jurors accepted the defense of wife battering long before appellate courts or the legislature arrived at the same conclusion. Importantly, defense attorneys constructed the defense in cultural terms that made the woman the victim of outrageous conduct. Neither Lastencia Abarta nor Katie Cook were victims of violent beatings, but both were victims of culturally outrageous behavior. The deceased men's conduct was paraded before the jury to give them another reason to find the women not guilty.[21] The shotgun defense tactics in trial and the cultural construct of the times in the jury room worked to set free women accused of killing.

For some of the criminally accused, defense attorneys scrambled to manufacture a defense that a jury could believe. Louise Peete and Juanita "The Duchess" Spinelli had long-term criminal pasts. A jury convicted Peete of one murder before a second jury sentenced her to the gas chamber on a later murder charge. "The Duchess," a gang leader and unsavory character, suffered a similar fate. Nellie Madison, unlike Spinelli or

Peete, left her attorney with only an incredible claim. An element of class existed in all three cases. None of these women maintained a middle-class lifestyle. Their relations with men, other than killing them, did not reflect middle-class values. Regardless of Victorian morals extending from the nineteenth century into the twentieth century, these women committed homicide with no credible excuse.

Nellie Madison was different regardless of class because of postconviction events. Agnes Underwood of the *Los Angeles Evening Herald and Express* took an interest in Madison and other women serving time at the women's institution at Tehachapi. She penned a story in the March 30, 1935, edition painting Madison with softer pastels, clearly not "the cold and detached murder defendant from the previous year."[22] Madison insisted, "[I regret] the disgrace I brought on myself and on my family." She was hopeful: "I feel that everything will eventually come out right, God knows I have done no wrong, and God will see that justice is done to me and for me."[23] Madison's attorney, Joseph Ryan, lost his appeal before the California Supreme Court, but not in the governor's office. Ryan petitioned Governor Frank Merriam for a reprieve or a commutation to a life sentence. He convinced the jurors to sign a statement admitting that they regretted sentencing Madison to death.[24] Madison's attorneys then convinced her to confess to the killing and ask the governor for mercy. In the process "the proud and extraordinarily reticent Nellie Madison had to reveal her status as a battered woman, duped and victimized by a man whose charming and ingratiating manner had the soul of a sexual predator and psychopath."[25] Her confession was front-page news on June 21, 1935, in the *Herald and Express* and included the graphic tales of violence and abuse.

The confession and publicity produced a reprieve, and with Madison off the front page, Governor Culbert Olson commuted the sentence to fifteen years.[26] In the end Madison had an excuse, was not a gang leader, and was far from a vile creature. She served her time and slipped back into society.

Upper-class women with outstanding counsel regardless of lifestyle fared far better in criminal court and in the press. Wealthy women paid lawyers like Earl Rogers and Jerry Giesler substantial fees because seasoned attorneys hung juries or won acquittals. In the newspapers upper-class women won extensive press coverage before, during, and on occasion after their trials. Yet until the 1940s reporters portrayed most women in a negative light, particularly "fat" women. The press warned men to beware of women in general but used some defendants for moral lessons. The gains made by women in the 1940s and 1950s tempered editorial venom.

Newspapers were in the business of selling daily editions. Sensationalism brought readers to the newsstands day after day. Clarence Darrow, one of America's most accomplished criminal-defense attorneys, speaking to the sixth annual meeting of the American Society of Newspaper Editors in Washington DC on April 20, 1928, told the editors what they already knew: "A newspaper today is purely a commercial enterprise."[27] Focusing on journalistic content, Darrow argued that when newspapers discover a "crime wave," the public "believes them and pays no attention to facts or figures, or statements, or logic, or reason."[28] Regarding justice, he thought, "Nobody knows the meaning of justice, but cheating justice means getting somebody acquitted, or not hanged."[29] Darrow abhorred the death penalty, but he noted that the people "are crazy about hangings. The crueler it is, the better, because the public must have a kick, especially since prohibition."[30] When it came to the details of crimes, the newspapers print "all" and "point out the way in which they were committed, thus stimulating many uneducated minds and untrained boys to do the same thing."[31] Finally, newspapers must sell advertising to make money, and "they have got to be good, and being good means to conform to existing things, because there have always been these people who live on the outer edges, decrying the injustices of the day."[32] Those people, like Darrow, sought justice according to their own values, and all too often justice went unheard until it was "too late to do them any good. Then we settle down to those theories, until something new comes along."[33] Although Darrow spoke of his crusades for justice and his outcast image in the press, he perhaps forgot all the marginal people living marginal lives sometimes swept into the criminal-justice system. The upper class, the sensational, and the current cultural norms sold newspapers.

The fixation on love letters by counsel to demonstrate motive enabled the press to ride on love epistles and increase sales. Laura Fair's love letters purported to show her to be a heartless, degraded, and infamous woman. Aurelia Scheck's letters evinced the "fiery lust that indicated the strength of passion that the woman raised in [her lover's] breast."[34] The prosecution held Beulah Louise Overell's love letters, but when they suddenly appeared in the newspapers, the defense took advantage. The defense had Overell's diary filled with the "details of her idyllic romance."[35] Lana Turner's love letters and notes boosted sales, but they served Mickey Cohen's desire to impugn Turner's honesty regarding her relationship with Johnny Stompanato. Regardless of class, here ranging from the lower-class moral outcast Laura Fair to the upper-class celebrity Lana Turner, love letters retained their attraction for newspaper readers and jurors. They were a window on emotion and motivation.

Beyond love letters Lana Turner had a public following due to *Peyton Place* (1957), in which she played Constance MacKenzie, a character dealing with issues of illegitimacy and single motherhood and touching closely on her relationship with her daughter, Cheryl.[36] Cheryl Crane recognized the "weird similarities between her own life and *Peyton Place*."[37] Audiences got a full dose of the rigid moral code of the 1950s and Constance MacKenzie's proclamation of the importance of motherhood. Turner proclaimed her love of motherhood in public but rarely acted out the myth in her life.[38] *Peyton Place* was context for the public obsession with the Stompanato murder investigation, but Turner's role in *Imitation of Life* (1959) "weirdly mimicked her rise to stardom and her troubled relationship with her daughter."[39] The movie's plot twist of the film daughter, Sandra Dee, "fall[ing] in love with her mother's boyfriend pandered directly to the rumors that Cheryl Crane had an affair with Stompanato and killed him out of jealousy."[40] The viewing public found print coverage of a killing replayed on the screen.

In addition to love letters and negative editorial comment on women, the press fixated on women in the courtroom audience. The press regularly commented on women's rights activists in attendance at the Laura Fair case. Generally, women in the audience were fodder for newspaper accounts of the Louis Peete and Madalynne Obenchain cases. The Emma Le Doux case drew "the morbid curiosity of many women." At the Aurelia Scheck trial, "women, almost frenzied with curiosity, fought like demons to get into court." During the trial, the women spectators "craned their necks so as not to lose a word of the slangy, lustful and murderous allusions couched in coarse and sometimes indecent language." Reporters failed to observe the behavior of men and commit it to newsprint.[41]

The linkage between performance and trials as well as culture and legal proceedings is well established. In fact, in his festschrift, titled *Law as Culture and Culture as Law* (2000), John Phillip Reid finds law-culture linkages in words and behaviors outside the courtroom.[42] Other scholars have interpreted trials as performances with a constitutive role in American culture.[43] Clearly, many of the trials were performances testing the feminine. As Ariela J. Gross observes, in an honor culture "it was not enough . . . to be honest. In order to have one's word believed, one had to demonstrate the attributes of credibility: detachment, independence, self-control."[44] The honor culture of the antebellum South, which Gross so expertly surveyed, resonated with California culture in the nineteenth century and found new definition in California. Juries looked at the women in the defendant's box with a critical eye for the feminine attributes. Lawyers and journalists played off the same sheet of music to sway their respective audiences. Women in Victorian California were not to be disorderly, yet they could not be too much of an enigma, too self-controlled.[45] The culture of the times and the performances of the players in trial marked California's visions of women killing men.

Whether in 1870 or 1958 the cases of women accused of killing men and their trials have demonstrated that gender mattered. Women and their lawyers constructed contemporary gender stereotypes for the courtroom and the press. Women's agency was important to the outcome of the trial. Women's agency in dressing and acting the part of the victim of a patriarchal system or of middle-class values was significant. Good lawyering was important in the courtroom and with the press. Lawyers were important in the evidence they gathered, the way they presented it, and the arguments they offered. Good interrogation was important in many trials. Law was the setting for all these trials. Courtroom justice was part of the attraction to the reading public and the audience. The rulings of the judges were significant for the presentation of defense and prosecution cases. The law guided the judges in making these rulings.

The press commented on the performances of witnesses and lawyers but seldom on law. Brief note of cases before the California Supreme Court rarely appeared, and retrials of cases that once drew hundreds of column inches won little notice. Laura Fair won the second trial, but since the transcripts were in print, the money made, and justice finally served, the press lost interest. The defense of partner abuse regardless of how counsel couched it worked with juries, and lawyers argued it without explicit press notice. It was the kind of justice Clarence Darrow spoke of in 1928: on the margins, on the edge of sanity, and on the cusp of femininity.

NOTES

Introduction

1. Most of the literature ranges far more broadly. See Smart, *Crime and Criminology*; Brodsky, *Female Offender*; Gora, *New Female Criminal*; Odem, *Delinquent Daughters*; Feinman, *Women in the Criminal Justice System*.

2. See Barker-Benfield, *Horrors of the Half-Known Life*. In the second edition of the book, the author admits that the twentieth-century printing emphasized "reactionaries and middle-class professionals with particular fish to fry" (xi). His twenty-first-century introduction reviews the reviewers of his first edition and the emerging literature on the subject.

3. Ireland, "Insanity and the Unwritten Law"; Ireland, "Libertine Must Die."

4. Ireland, "Frenzied and Fallen Females."

5. Ireland, "Frenzied and Fallen Females," 99.

6. Ireland, "Frenzied and Fallen Females," 99.

7. Ireland, "Frenzied and Fallen Females," 99.

8. Ireland, "Frenzied and Fallen Females," 101–5. See also Lander, *Images of Bleeding*. Lander surveys three centuries of male ideologies and attempts to dismantle those traditional male concepts and replace them with female-centered understandings. Her objective is to make menstruation a "nonissue" (187). On more general issues, see Huckabee, *Lawyers, Psychiatrists and Criminal Law*. See also Prior, "Murder and Madness."

9. Jones, *Mammoth Book*, which contains a short bibliography and short tales of women who commit murder.

10. Robertson, "Seduction, Sexual Violence, and Marriage." See also Monkkonen, *Murder in New York City*.

11. Adler, *First in Violence*, 109–19.

12. Adler, *First in Violence*, 112.

13. Waldrep, "Law and Society," 319.

14. Waldrep, "Law and Society," 320.

15. McKanna, *Homicide, Race, and Justice*.

16. McKanna, *Trial of "Indian Joe"*; McKanna, *Race and Homicide*; McKanna, *White Justice in Arizona*. See also Carranco and Beard, *Genocide and Vendetta*.

17. Mullen, *Dangerous Strangers*.

18. Escobar, *Race, Police*; Pagán, *Murder at the Sleepy Lagoon*.

19. Adler, *First in Violence*, 112.

20. Butler, *Gendered Justice in the American West*; Butler, "In Penitentiaries."

21. Peterson del Mar, *What Trouble I Have Seen*; Peterson del Mar, *Beaten Down*.

22. Friedman and Percival, *Roots of Justice*, 183.

23. Friedman and Percival, *Roots of Justice*, 265.

24. Bakken, *Practicing Law in Frontier California*, 99–137.

25. Trope, *Once upon a Time*, 114.

26. "Slays Him to Stop Wedding; Woman Shoots Man She Says Deceived Her; Prompted to Act Because He Would Wed Another; News Broke to Fiancée by Telephone Message," *Los Angeles Times*, January 2, 1915.

27. "She Doesn't Know," *Los Angeles Times*, January 4, 1915.

28. "Murder Is the Charge," *Los Angeles Times*, January 21, 1915.

29. "Sees Fate of Killer Sealed," *Los Angeles Times*, January 18, 1915.

30. "Dardley Girl on the Stand; Witnesses Describe Brutal Treatment of Her; First Loved, Then Feared, Finally Killed Him," *Los Angeles Times*, January 19, 1915.

31. Alexander, *Notorious Woman*, 6, 182.

32. See also Black, *Black's Law*; Wishman, *Confessions of a Criminal Lawyer*; Henson, *Confessions of a Criminal Lawyer*; Pasley, *Not Guilty*.

33. Cohen, *Murder of Helen Jewett*, 27.

34. Cohen, *Murder of Helen Jewett*, 27.

35. Cohen, *Murder of Helen Jewett*, 27.

36. Cohen, *Murder of Helen Jewett*, 353.

37. Rowbothan and Stevenson, *Criminal Conversations*, xxiii–xxiv.

38. Fox, *Trials of Intimacy*.

39. Fox, *Trials of Intimacy*, 56.

40. Fox, *Trials of Intimacy*, 92.

41. Fox, *Trials of Intimacy*, 215.

42. Fox, *Trials of Intimacy*, 311.

43. Ferguson, *Trial in America Life*, 1.

44. Ferguson, *Trial in America Life*, 3.

45. Ferguson, *Trial in America Life*, 159–64.

46. Loerzel, *Alchemy of Bones*.

47. Hamm, *Murder, Honor, and Law*, 11.

48. Hamm, *Murder, Honor, and Law*, 156. See also Ayers, *Vengeance and Justice*; Hoffer, "Disorder and Deference"; Waldrep, *Roots of Disorder*; Edwards, "Law, Domestic Violence."

49. Hatfield, *Never Seen the Moon*, 110–39.

50. Hatfield, *Never Seen the Moon*, 196.

51. Hatfield, *Never Seen the Moon*, 254.

52. Halaas, *Boom Town Newspapers*, 10–11.

53. Halaas, *Boom Town Newspapers*, 63.

54. Halaas, *Boom Town Newspapers*, 63, 77–78, 86, 92.

55. See Lystra, *Searching the Heart*.

56. Dodge, "*Whores and Thieves.*"

57. Dodge, "*Whores and Thieves,*" 24–25, 58, 62–63.

58. Dodge, "*Whores and Thieves,*" 61.

59. Dodge, "*Whores and Thieves,*" 61–62.

60. Dodge, "*Whores and Thieves,*" 70.

61. Dodge, "*Whores and Thieves,*" 79. See also Rugh, "Civilizing the Countryside"; Garnett, "Ordering."

62. Melnick, *Justice Betrayed.*

63. Butler, *Gendered Justice*, 140. See also Edgerton, *Montana Justice.* Edgerton's analysis is less gendered but clearly establishes the nature of harsh punishment.

64. K. N. Gross, *Colored Amazons*, 156.

65. Halttunen, *Murder Most Foul*, 172–207.

66. Cairns, "'Enigma Women' Nellie Madison," 16. Popular crime history still maintains a large audience even for local violence. See Morrison, *Murder in the Garden*; Mitchell, *Dead and Buried.*

67. Holmlund, "Decade of Deadly Dolls," 151.

68. Bilder, "Bodies of Evidence."

69. Bilder, "Bodies of Evidence," 244.

70. Bilder, "Bodies of Evidence," 246.

71. Bilder, "Bodies of Evidence," 249.

72. Bilder, "Bodies of Evidence," 250.

73. Bilder, "Bodies of Evidence," 253.

74. Schofield, "Lizzie Borden Took an Axe." See also Webster, "'Lizzie Borden Took an Axe'"; Shaw, "New England Gothic."

75. Self-defense was well established in California law. In *People v. Iams*, 57 Cal. 119 (1880), the court articulated the defense in all its classic elements:

> To justify the killing of another in self-defense, it must appear that the danger was so urgent and pressing, that, in order to save his own life, or to prevent his receiving great bodily harm, the killing of the other was absolutely necessary, and it must appear that the person killed was the assailant, or that the slayer had really and in good faith endeavored to decline further struggle before the mortal blow was given.
>
> A bare fear of the commission of the offense, to prevent which a homicide may lawfully be committed, is not sufficient to justify it; but the circumstances must be sufficient to excite the fears of a reasonable man, and the party killing must have acted under the influence

of such fears alone. It is not necessary, however, to justify such killing, that the danger be actual. It is enough that it be an apparent danger: such an appearance as would induce a reasonable person in defendant's position to believe that he was in immediate danger of great bodily injury. Upon such appearances, a party may act with safety; nor will he be held accountable, though it should afterwards appear that the indications upon which he acted were wholly fallacious, and that he was in no actual peril.

The rule in such cases is this, What would a reasonable person—a person of ordinary caution, judgment, and observation—in the position of the defendant, seeing what he saw, and knowing what he knew, have supposed from this situation and these surroundings? If such reasonable person so placed would have been justified in believing himself in imminent danger, then the defendant would be justified in believing himself in such peril, and acting upon such appearances. The defendant is not necessarily justified, because he actually believed that he was in imminent danger. When the danger is only apparent, and not actual and real, the question is, Would a reasonable man, under all the circumstances, be justified in such belief? If so, the defendant will be so justified. If this was defendant's position, it was his right to repel the aggression, and fully protect himself from such apparent danger. If he could have withdrawn from the danger, it was his duty to retreat. Between his duty to flee and his right to kill, he must fly; or, as the books have it, must retreat to the wall. But by this is not meant that a party must always fly, or even attempt flight. The circumstances of the attack may be such, the weapon with which he is menaced [**9] of such a character, that retreat might well increase his peril. By "retreating to the wall" is only meant, that the party must avail himself of any apparent and reasonable avenues of escape by which his danger might be averted, and the necessity of slaying his assailant avoided.

76. "Bad Reputation of Tom Cook Aired in Court," *Los Angeles Times*, December 22, 1899.

77. On objectivity in journalism generally, see Schiller, *Objectivity*

and the News; Dicken-Garcia, *Journalism Standards*; Baldasty, *Commercialization of News*. Baldasty in particular considers the penny press a revolutionary development. For an alternative view, see Nerone, "Mythology of the Penny Press."

78. "Mrs. Le Doux Condemned," *San Jose Mercury News*, June 24, 1906.

79. "She Learned Her Lesson," *Los Angeles Times*, August 15, 1906.

80. "Case Count," *Los Angeles Times*, November 4, 1921.

Chapter One. Mirror, Mirror on the Wall

1. Deverell, *Whitewashed Adobe*.

2. Starr, *Inventing the Dream*, 76. See also Schiesl and Dodge, *City of Promise*.

3. Ethington, *Public City*, 237.

4. Ethington, *Public City*, 237.

5. See generally Schudson, *Origins of the Ideal*.

6. Welter, "Cult of True Womanhood." See also Chafe, *American Woman*, 199–23.

7. On sexual politics and acceptable women's roles, see Freedman, "Sexuality in Nineteenth-Century America."

8. Ethington, *Public City*, 210.

9. Ethington, *Public City*, 212; Bakken, *Practicing Law in Frontier California*, 15–16.

10. Ethington, *Public City*, 212–13.

11. Ethington, *Public City*, 216.

12. Gullett, *Becoming Citizens*, 153.

13. Gullett, *Becoming Citizens*, 157.

14. Grossberg, *Judgment for Solomon*, 100.

15. Ginzberg, "Pernicious Heresies," 142.

16. Hartog, *Man and Wife in America*, 312.

17. Hartog, *Man and Wife in America*, 219.

18. Hartog, *Man and Wife in America*, 231.

19. Lamott, *Who Killed Mr. Crittenden?*; Jackson, *San Francisco*

Murders. Both books recount the case and both for popular audiences.

20. "The Case of Mrs. Fair," *San Francisco Chronicle*, January 3, 1871; "The Crittenden-Fair Case: The Question of Jurisdiction Discussed in the County Court," *San Francisco Chronicle*, January 6, 1871; "The Fair-Crittenden Case: The Question of Jurisdiction Still a Disputed Point—Alameda County Still Claims Jurisdiction," *San Francisco Chronicle*, January 11, 1871.

21. "Trial of Laura D. Fair for the Killing of A. P. Crittenden," *San Francisco Chronicle*, March 28, 1871.

22. "Trial of Laura D. Fair."

23. "The Assassination," *San Francisco Chronicle*, March 29, 1871.

24. "The Assassination," *San Francisco Chronicle*, March 30, 1871.

25. "Assassination," March 30, 1871.

26. "Assassination," March 30, 1871.

27. Ethington, *Public City*, 236–37.

28. Lamont, *Who Killed Mr. Crittenden?* 49–122.

29. "The Assassination: Opening Speech by Elisha Cook," *San Francisco Chronicle*, March 31, 1871.

30. "The Assassination: A Hard Fight over the Admission of Crittenden's Letters in Evidence," *San Francisco Chronicle*, April 1, 1871.

31. "Assassination," April 1, 1871.

32. "The Assassination: The Court Adjourns on Account of the Illness of Defendant," *San Francisco Chronicle*, April 2, 1871.

33. "The Assassination: Long and Important Examination of Dr. Lyford, One of Mrs. Fair's Physicians," *San Francisco Chronicle*, April 3, 1871.

34. Lamott, *Who Killed Mr. Crittenden?* 178.

35. "The Assassination: Dr. Trask Swears She Was Insane When the Deed Was Done," *San Francisco Chronicle*, April 4, 1871.

36. "The Assassination: Mrs. Fair Pathetically Appeals to the Jury,

an Exciting Episode in Court, Two Strong Minded Females Fined for Applauding," *San Francisco Chronicle*, April 5, 1871; Lamott, *Who Killed Mr. Crittenden?* 190.

37. "The Assassination: The Cross-Examination of the Alleged Murderess," *San Francisco Chronicle*, April 5, 1871; "The Assassination: The Cross-Examination of Mrs. Fair Concluded," *San Francisco Chronicle*, April 6, 1871.

38. "The Assassination: The Day Consumed in Examining Letters," *San Francisco Chronicle*, April 7, 1871.

39. "The Letters: Love Letters of Crittenden Admitted in Evidence," *San Francisco Chronicle*, April 9, 1871.

40. Lamott, *Who Killed Mr. Crittenden?* 227.

41. "The Fatal Amour," *San Francisco Chronicle*, April 10, 1871. The edition ran a six-page story on the trial, mostly consisting of the love letters.

42. "Fatal Amour," April 10, 1871.

43. Lamott, *Who Killed Mr. Crittenden?* 226.

44. "The Fatal Amour: Witnesses Testify as to Mrs. Fair's Reputation for Chastity," *San Francisco Chronicle*, April 12, 1871.

45. "Amour: More Evidence as to Mrs. Fair's Unchastity," *San Francisco Chronicle*, April 13, 1871. On Tevis, see Igler, *Industrial Cowboys*, 42, 101.

46. "The Fatal Amour: Elisha Cook Testifies and Demolishes Snyder; Mrs. Fair Gives Evidence in Rebuttal, and Denies Everything," *San Francisco Chronicle*, April 14, 1871.

47. "The Fatal Amour" and "Women in Court: An Epistle from One of the Strong-Minded," both in *San Francisco Chronicle*, April 15, 1871.

48. "The Argument: Closing Scenes of the Fair-Crittenden Trial," *San Francisco Chronicle*, April 16, 1871.

49. Babcock, "Women Defenders in the West," 7–8; Cole, "Women & the Death Penalty."

50. "The Argument: A Vivid Picture of the Effects of Free-Love Doctrines; Campbell Closes His Argument with a Brilliant Peroration," *San Francisco Chronicle*, April 16, 1871.

51. "Argument," April 16, 1871.

52. "Argument," April 16, 1871.

53. "Argument," April 16, 1871.

54. "The Argument: Judge Quint Talking against Time All Day," *San Francisco Chronicle*, April 18, 1871.

55. "The Fatal Amour: The Argument for the Defense," *San Francisco Chronicle*, April 20, 1871.

56. "The Fatal Amour: Mr. Cook's Argument; The Question of Motive Ably Reviewed; The Relations between Mrs. Fair and Crittenden Explained; The Cunning of Crittenden and Infatuation of Mrs. Fair," *San Francisco Chronicle*, April 21, 1871.

57. "Women in Court," *San Francisco Chronicle*, April 21, 1871.

58. "The Fatal Amour: Mr. Cook Continues His Argument for the Defense," *San Francisco Chronicle*, April 22, 1871.

59. "Is It Murder!" *San Francisco Chronicle*, April 23, 1871.

60. "Cook Closes," *San Francisco Chronicle*, April 24, 1871.

61. Cole, "Women & the Death Penalty," 17; Lamott, *Who Killed Mr. Crittenden?* 268–77.

62. "The Fair Trial: Comments of the Press upon the Trial of Laura Fair," *San Francisco Chronicle*, April 28, 1871.

63. "Fair Trial," April 28, 1871.

64. *People v. Fair*, *California Reports*, vol. 43 (1872), 137, 140–44.

65. *People v. Fair*, 137, 158. See also "The Case of Laura Fair: New Trial Granted by the Supreme Court," *San Francisco Bulletin*, February 6, 1872.

66. Cole, "Women & the Death Penalty," 19; George Rathmell, "Scandal & Murder at Bush & Montgomery," *Nob Hill Gazette*, April 2006; Lamott, *Who Killed Mr. Crittenden?* 290–93.

67. Friedman, *American Law*, 243.

68. Reid, *Chief Justice*, 118.

69. "Fischer's Trial: Irresistible Impulse to Kill a Railroad Commissioner; Trial for Shooting C. J. Beerstecher; The Plea of Insanity—All

of the Usual Signs of Homicidal Mania and Some Unusual Ones," *San Francisco Chronicle*, May 20, 1881.

70. The deadly shooting of Charles de Young preceded the attack in this particular case. See McKee, "The Shooting of Charles de Young."

71. "Trial of Spreckels: Elaborate Opening of the Defense; The Law and the Jurors; Insanity, Self-defense and Justification Relied On for a Verdict of Acquittal," *San Francisco Chronicle*, June 3, 1885.

72. Mike Wallace, "The Press Needs a National Monitor," *Wall Street Journal*, December 18, 1996. In the nineteenth century newspaper editors faced contempt citations for criticism of sitting judges with their only remedy in the courts. "Assail A. P. Catlin, Czar," *Sacramento Bee*, June 5, 1896.

73. "The Murderous Assailant of Mr. De Young Goes Unpunished," *New York Times*, July 2, 1885.

74. See also *Los Angeles Herald*, March 16, 1881; Gray, *Forster v. Pico*, 228–29. Chico's mother was the sister of Pio Pico, one of the great Californios of the century. The *Los Angeles Express* reported her name as Lastania; others had it as Lastenia Abartachipi. Gray's research yielded Lastencia as the correct spelling of her name.

75. *Los Angeles Evening Express*, March 16, 1881; April 28, 1881. See also Bakken, "Limits of Patriarchy: Women's Rights," 709–13.

76. *Los Angeles Evening Express*, April 28, 1881.

77. *Los Angeles Evening Express*, April 29, 1881.

78. The following account is taken from the *Los Angeles Evening Express*, April 28–30, 1881.

79. *Los Angeles Evening Express*, April 29, 1881.

80. *Los Angeles Evening Express*, April 29, 1881.

81. *Los Angeles Evening Express*, April 29, 1881.

82. *Los Angeles Evening Express*, April 29, 1881.

83. *Los Angeles Evening Express*, April 29, 1881.

84. See *Los Angeles Times*, April 28–30, 1881.

85. Spiegel, "Temporary Insanity and Premenstrual Syndrome," 485.

86. Spiegel, "Temporary Insanity and Premenstrual Syndrome," 490–91. The question of moral insanity had been raised as early as 1863; Dr. Isaac Ray popularized the concept.

87. *Los Angeles Times*, April 30, 1881.

88. *Los Angeles Evening Express*, April 30, 1881.

89. *Los Angeles Evening Express*, April 30, 1881.

90. *Los Angeles Evening Express*, April 30, 1881.

91. *Los Angeles Evening Express*, April 30, 1881.

92. *Los Angeles Evening Express*, April 30, 1881.

93. *Los Angeles Evening Express*, April 30, 1881.

94. *Los Angeles Evening Express*, April 30, 1881.

95. *Los Angeles Evening Express*, April 30, 1881.

96. *Los Angeles Evening Express*, April 30, 1881.

97. *Los Angeles Evening Express*, April 30, 1881. See also Bakken, "Limits of Patriarchy: Women's Rights," 713–15.

98. Unless otherwise noted, the narrative is taken in whole or in part from *Los Angeles Times*, December 19–24, 1899. The microfilm of case no. 207, *People v. Cook*, is in microfilm box 1248, Orange County Clerk of Court Office, Santa Ana CA.

99. *Los Angeles Times*, December 19, 1899. The necessity of an acknowledgment on the transfer of property owned by a married woman was well established in California law. In *Rico v. Brandenstein*, 98 Cal. 465 (1893), the court at 481 held that "the evident policy of our law-makers, to loosen the chains which bound married women at the common law, so far as their separate property is concerned, to confer upon them like power of alienation with that possessed by their husbands." Also see *Mathews v. Davis*, 102 Cal. 202 (1894); *Lamb v. Harbough*, 105 Cal. 680 (1895); *Loupe v. Smith*, 123 Cal. 491 (1899).

100. *Los Angeles Times*, December 20, 1899.

101. *Los Angeles Times*, December 21, 1899.

102. *Los Angeles Times*, December 21, 1899.

103. *Los Angeles Times*, December 21, 1899.

104. *Los Angeles Times*, December 22, 1899.

105. *Los Angeles Times*, December 24, 1899.

106. *Los Angeles Times*, December 24, 1899. The *Orange News*, December 28, 1899, noted, "The defense was insanity; and Mrs. Cook's testimony of the marital infidelity and the cruelty and threats of her husband, coupled with his bestiality, did much to bring about the speedy verdict." Further, "Cook communicated a loathsome disease to his wife, and his treatment of her was most shocking and bestial."

107. For a view of the era focused on women, see Green, *Light of the Home*; Smith-Rosenberg, *Intimate Conduct*.

108. Hartog, "Lawyering, Husbands' Rights," 70.

109. Hartog, "Lawyering, Husbands' Rights," 70. See also Hoff, *Law, Gender and Injustice*.

110. Hartog, "Lawyering, Husbands' Rights," 83.

111. Hartog, "Lawyering, Husbands' Rights," 84.

112. Hartog, "Lawyering, Husbands' Rights," 87.

113. Hartog, "Lawyering, Husbands' Rights," 87.

114. Hartog, "Lawyering, Husbands' Rights," 95.

115. See Friedman and Percival, *Roots of Justice*, 239–44. The authors analyze the trial of Clara Fallmer, a pregnant fifteen-year-old who shot her lover to death when he refused to marry her. She was guilty on the facts, used the insanity defense, and made the trial about her plight and the dastardly deeds of her lover. The jury bought it. The authors also note an important book on this type of trial that puts it into the context of a morality play, Mary Hartman's *Victorian Murderesses* (239n).

116. A case very close to the facts that Hartog recites is that of Eloise Rudiger of Omaha, who in 1893 killed Henry Reiser after he "seduced" her and then turned his back on her. She, like Lastencia, purchased a handgun on the day of the killing and shot him on a public street. Her aim was not restrained, and she shot him three times. When her husband arrived on the scene, she told him that it was his duty to do the killing. Her jury acquitted her. McKanna, *Homicide, Race, and Justice*, 59–60.

117. Schuele, "Community Property Law."

118. Lothrop, "Rancheras and the Land," 79.

119. Matsuda, "The West and the Legal State," 55.

120. Fischer, "Women in California." Mental cruelty had been added to the list of grounds for divorce in California by 1890. See *Waldron v. Waldron*, 85 Cal. 251 (1890). On these developments, see Griswold, "Evolution of the Doctrine of Mental Cruelty," 131–33. Deadly force had been applied and spousal abuse used as justification for homicide in the case of William Rubottom. On September 7, 1858, Rubottom shot and killed his son-in-law because of his abuse of Rubottom's daughter. He was not charged with the homicide because the killing was ruled justifiable. *Los Angeles Star*, September 11, 1858. The suffrage campaign, begun in the 1870s, was in full swing in the 1890s. Chandler, "In the Van"; Cooper, "California Suffrage Campaign of 1896." See also Pascoe, *Relations of Rescue*.

121. For other attempts at this task, see Merry, *Getting Justice and Getting Even*; Rosen, *Courts and Commerce*.

122. For alternative theories of causation, particularly on twentieth-century sentencing behavior and the images of female felons, see Bloom, "Triple Jeopardy." Of particular interest for nineteenth-century studies is her analysis of the "chivalry hypothesis" at pages 57–58.

Chapter Two. Good Riddance

1. "Bad Husband Made Good," *Los Angeles Times*, August 6, 1901.

2. "Bad Husband Made Good."

3. Bakken, "Limits of Patriarchy: The 'Unwritten Law,'" 100–101.

4. "Bad Husband Made Good."

5. "Bad Husband Made Good."

6. "I Shot Him; He Is Dead," *Los Angeles Times*, November 22, 1910.

7. "She's Still Calm," *Los Angeles Times*, November 24, 1910.

8. "Unwritten Law Woman's Plea," *Los Angeles Times*, February 21, 1911.

9. "Son's Evidence Frees Mother: Jury Renders Verdict Three Minutes after Retiring; Unwritten Law Invoked on Behalf of Mrs. De Vita, Accused of Murder, Who according to Testimony of Her Boy, Was Threatened by Bove More than Once," *Los Angeles Times*, February 22, 1911.

10. "Such Homicide Justifiable; Members of Panel Shake Hands with Woebegone Figure Who Cherished Recovered Honor above Great Love for Man Who Would Have Driven Her to Slavery," *Los Angeles Times*, July 30, 1913.

11. "Free Woman Who Killed Her Kinsman; Jurors Return Verdict of Justifiable Homicide in Attack Case," *Los Angeles Times*, July 16, 1921.

12. "Corpse Found in Trunk," *Los Angeles Times*, March 26, 1906.

13. "Woman Had No Accomplice in Her Crime," *San Jose Mercury News*, March 27, 1906.

14. "Woman Expected to Soon Confess," *San Jose Mercury News*, March 28, 1906.

15. "Given Knock-out Drops and Morphine," *San Jose Mercury News*, March 30, 1906.

16. "Threw Officers on the Wrong Trail," *San Jose Mercury News*, March 31, 1906.

17. "Threw Officers."

18. "Not Guilty the Plea of Emma Le Doux; Stockton Courtroom Crowded When Woman Was Arraigned Today," *San Jose Mercury News*, April 16, 1906.

19. "Le Doux Jury Selected; Woman's Defense Technical," *Los Angeles Times*, June 9, 1906.

20. "Le Doux Case Nearing End, Prosecution Rest in Murder Trial: Motive for Deed Is Shown in Reading of Letters to Le Doux Which Speak in Endearing Terms and Which Were Read to Him by Nineteen-Year-Old Brother," *Los Angeles Times*, June 19, 1906.

21. "Laughs at Death," *Los Angeles Times*, June 24, 1906

22. "Mrs. Le Doux Condemned," *San Jose Mercury News*, June 24, 1906.

23. "Mrs. Le Doux Condemned."

24. "Le Doux Woman Doomed to Hang," *Los Angeles Times*, August 8, 1906.

25. "Mrs. Le Doux Condemned"; "Laughs at Death," artwork depicts her in a suit and hat.

26. "Laughs at Death."

27. "Woman and Capital Punishment," *San Jose Mercury News*, June 24, 1906.

28. "Show That Juror Was Prejudice[d]," *San Jose Mercury News*, July 10, 1906.

29. "Wanted Her Neck Broken," *Los Angeles Times*, July 10, 1906.

30. "Wanted Her Neck Broken."

31. "Le Doux Woman Doomed to Hang."

32. "To Save Emma Le Doux," *Los Angeles Times*, September 26, 1906.

33. "Confident of Acquittal," *Los Angeles Times*, February 2, 1909.

34. *People v. Emma Le Doux*, 155 Cal. 535 (1909). Justice Henshaw's opinion reviewed all the evidence established in the trial prior to his analysis of the defense claims of trial-court error.

35. "New Trial for Mrs. Le Doux; State Supreme Court Decides Error Made in Jury Venire to Try Woman for Murder," *Los Angeles Times*, May 20, 1909.

36. "Fighting New Trial," *Los Angeles Times*, May 23, 1909.

37. "Alleged Murderess Very Ill; Attorney for Mrs. Emma Le Doux Says Client Will Not Be Able to Stand Trial," *Los Angeles Times*, January 7, 1910.

38. "Pleads to See Mother; Mrs. Le Doux, 'Trunk' Murderess, Is Granted Boon before Entering Prison for Life," *Los Angeles Times*, January 28, 1910; "Trunk Murderess Is in San Quentin Cell," *San Jose Mercury News*, February 3, 1910.

39. "Woman in Old Trunk Murder Is Paroled," *Los Angeles Times*, July 30, 1920.

40. "Woman Slayer Denied Parole," *Los Angeles Times*, November 12, 1934.

41. "Mrs. Glab Asks for Parole; Thirty-nine Inmates of Tehachapi Prison File Applications," *Los Angeles Times*, January 4, 1937.

42. "Pair under Arrest in Scheck Murder," *Los Angeles Times*, June 15, 1906.

43. "Say They Have a Confession," *Los Angeles Times*, June 16, 1906.

44. "Bond of Love Was Murder," *Los Angeles Times*, June 17, 1906.

45. "Murderess at Victim's Grave," *Los Angeles Times*, June 18, 1906.

46. "Scheck-Stackpole Evidence Grows," *Los Angeles Times*, June 19, 1906.

47. "Murderess Is So Bashful," *Los Angeles Times*, June 21, 1906.

48. "Stackpole Long a Low Criminal," *Los Angeles Times*, June 27, 1906. See also "Dark Record of Stackpole," *Los Angeles Times*, June 26, 1906.

49. "Morbid Crowd Was Fooled," *Los Angeles Times*, June 23, 1906.

50. "Snarls in Despair When Held For Trial," *Los Angeles Times*, June 29, 1906.

51. "Snarls in Despair."

52. "Jury Gotten to Try Stackpole: Four Witnesses Testify to Circumstances of Case," *Los Angeles Times*, August 11, 1906.

53. "Scheck Murder Plots Recited," *Los Angeles Times*, August 14, 1906.

54. "She Learned Her Lesson," *Los Angeles Times*, August 15, 1906.

55. "Weaving the Woof of Evidence," *Los Angeles Times*, August 16, 1906.

56. "Weaving the Woof of Evidence."

57. "Noose Opens for Stackpole," *Los Angeles Times*, August 17, 1906.

58. "Stackpole Jury Verdict Today," *Los Angeles Times*, August 18, 1906.

59. "Stackpole Jury Deliberating," *Los Angeles Times*, August 19, 1906.

60. "A Creditable Solution," *Los Angeles Times*, September 18, 1906.

61. "Mrs. Scheck's Way of Escape," *Los Angeles Times*, October 6, 1906.

62. "Scheck Hearing Postponed," *Los Angeles Times*, September 20, 1906.

63. "No Bail for Mrs. Scheck," *Los Angeles Times*, September 26, 1906.

64. "Murder Charge on Mrs. Scheck," *Los Angeles Times*, September 29, 1906.

65. "Mrs. Scheck Is Released: Perjury Indictment Declared Not Maintained; Judge Trask Holds That Requirements of Law Are Not Fulfilled in That Grand Jury Received No Testimony, Except the Woman's, to Disprove Her Original Story," *Los Angeles Times*, November 24, 1906.

66. "Seek New Trial: Stackpole Will Make Fight," *Los Angeles Times*, August 26, 1906.

67. "Sentenced for Life: Stackpole to San Quentin," *Los Angeles Times*, August 31, 1906.

68. "Rushed In for Life: Stackpole Bound for Penitentiary," *Los Angeles Times*, April 5, 1907.

69. "On Suspicion of Murder; Woman Arrested Charged with Giving Her Husband Poison as Medicine," *Los Angeles Times*, December 18, 1918. The story observed, "No woman has ever been convicted of murder in the first degree in the Los Angeles county criminal courts."

70. "Alleged Borgia Plot Spreads," *Los Angeles Times*, December 19, 1918.

71. "Alleged Crime Made Useless," *Los Angeles Times*, December 20, 1918.

72. "Mrs. Gibbons Still Held: New and Startling Evidence Bared When Experts Declare Death Natural," *Los Angeles Times*, December 21, 1918.

73. "Dual Marriage Proven; Herrick Says He Never Divorced Mrs. Gibbons; Poison Case Complex," *Los Angeles Times*, December 22, 1918.

74. "Statement Is Startling; Mrs. Kurtz Bares Evidence upon Which Mrs. Gibbons Was Arrested," *Los Angeles Times*, December 24, 1918.

75. "Extraordinary Situation Looms: Expected Conflict of Analysts in Gibbons Poison Case Leaves Authorities at Odds on Prosecution of the Woman; One Side Reports No Cyanide," *Los Angeles Times*, December 27, 1918.

76. "Experts Find Cyanide; Stookey and Swain of Stanford Report Poison in Gibbons' Body," *Los Angeles Times*, December 28, 1918.

77. "May Free Alleged Poisoner: 'Reasonable Doubt' in Gibbons Case Very Likely to Prevent Conviction for Murder and No Other Charge Will Lie; All Up to the Grand Jury," *Los Angeles Times*, January 5, 1919.

78. "Mrs. Gibbons to Grand Jury," *Los Angeles Times*, January 16, 1919.

79. "Mrs. Gibbons Free Today," *Los Angeles Times*, January 17, 1919.

80. "Grand Jury May Decide," *Los Angeles Times*, January 1, 1919.

81. "Mrs. Gibbons Freed, Will Change Name," *Los Angeles Times*, January 18, 1919.

Chapter Three. Toward the New Woman

1. See in general Cott, *No Small Courage*.

2. See Peiss, "Making Faces."

3. Ahmad, *Opium Debate*, 5.

4. See Starr, *Material Dreams*; Sitton and Deverell, *Metropolis in the Making*; Bottles, *Los Angeles and the Automobile*; Lotchin, *Fortress California*.

5. Staiger, *Bad Women*, 147.

6. "Bride Is Charged with Foothill Road Murder: Taunts at Her Plans to Die Made Her Fire on Man She Had Intended to Wed, Says Young Mrs. Bailey," *Los Angeles Times*, December 23, 1920.

7. "Arraign Mrs. Bailey: Bride Accused of Murder Dazedly Faces Formal Charge," *Los Angeles Times*, December 24, 1920.

8. "Mutely Faces Murder Charge: Girl Hears Blood Accusation in Impassive Silence; Slayer of Sweetheart Is Held to the Superior Court; 'Told Me He Taunted Her,' Says Arresting Officer," *Los Angeles Times*, December 31, 1920.

9. "Woman Slayer Plans Defense," *Los Angeles Times*, May 18, 1921.

10. "Cool before Death Case Testimony: Mrs. Bailey, Facing Trial as Slayer, Hears Witness Say She Admitted Act," *Los Angeles Times*, May 26, 1921.

11. "Touch Aroused Death Thought: Weapon Felt 'Cold, Sinister,' Marie Bailey Testifies; Declares Lover's Proposal Made Life Barren; Points Revolver at Self but Unhappily Kills Man," *Los Angeles Times*, May 27, 1921.

12. "Find She Slew Man She Loved," *Los Angeles Times*, May 28, 1921.

13. "Mrs. Bailey Is Sentenced to Term in Prison," *Los Angeles Times*, June 1, 1921.

14. Streib, *Fairer Death*, 6.

15. Wolfe and Mader, "Louise Peete."

16. Wolfe and Mader, "Louise Peete," 343.

17. Wolfe and Mader, "Louise Peete," 344.

18. Wolfe and Mader, "Louise Peete," 344.

19. "Mrs. Peete Says Denton Must Have Had Double: Remarkable Explanation of Discrepancy about Arm; She Declines to Discuss Crowhurst Statement," *Los Angeles Times*, September 25, 1920.

20. "Expect Mrs. Peete in Salt Lake Today: Clue to Denton Murder Is Found When Walls of Home Are Ripped by Detectives," *Los Angeles Times*, October 1, 1920.

21. "Sharply Quizzed, Mrs. Peete Sticks to Story," *Los Angeles Times*, October 5, 1920.

22. "Habeas Corpus Writ Is Sought for Mrs. Peete: Attorney Declares He Will Also Ask Indictments of District Attorney's Men for 'Kidnapping' Her," *Los Angeles Times*, October 6, 1920.

23. "Mrs. Peete Weeps Where Denton Was Murdered," *Los Angeles Times*, October 7, 1920.

24. "Mrs. Peete Will Refuse Grand Jury Testimony," *Los Angeles Times*, October 27, 1920; "'Spanish Woman' Story Mrs. Peete's Defense," *Los Angeles Times*, October 28, 1920; "Contradictions Found: Grand Jury Transcript in Denton Case Is Released; New Defense Planned," *Los Angeles Times*, November 4, 1920; "Mrs. Peete Owned Gun like Denton-Case Find," *Los Angeles Times*, November 26, 1920.

25. "Plan to Fill Jury Box in Peete Case Today," *Los Angeles Times*, January 20, 1921.

26. "Mrs. Peete and Jury Go to Murder House Today," *Los Angeles Times*, January 21, 1921.

27. "Woman's Testimony Hits Hardest at Mrs. Peete," *Los Angeles Times*, January 25, 1921.

28. "Lent Mrs. Peete Shovel Says Surprise Witness: State Flashes Trump Cards in Denton Murder Trial; Lawyers Clash over Damaging New Evidence," *Los Angeles Times*, January 27, 1921.

29. "Mrs. Peete Daily 'Free Show': Extraordinary Phase of Sensational Murder Trial Supplied by the Thousands Who Mass on the Street to Catch Brief Glimpse of Her on Way to Courtroom," *Los Angeles Times*, January 30, 1921.

30. "Crisis in Peete Case to Be Reached Today," *Los Angeles Times*, February 3, 1921.

31. Wolfe and Mader, "Louise Peete," 350; "Record Shows Mrs. Peete Posed as Logan's Sister," *Los Angeles Times*, December 24, 1944.

32. "Judson, Husband of Mrs. Peete, Leaps to Death," *Los Angeles Times*, January 13, 1945.

33. "Defense Hints Mrs. Peete May Not Testify at Trial," *Los Angeles Times*, April 24, 1945.

34. "Denial Voiced by Mrs. Peete at Death Trial," *Los Angeles Times*, May 2, 1945.

35. "Parallels Drawn in Peete Case," *Los Angeles Times*, May 3, 1945; "Witness Reveals Peete Hat Dance," *Los Angeles Times*, May 8, 1945.

36. "Louise Peete, Found Guilty, Faces Death," *Los Angeles Times*, May 29, 1945.

37. "Mrs. Peete Cold and Calm as She Pays with Her Life," *Los Angeles Times*, December 22, 1947.

38. "Son of Minister Arrested as Man Who Killed Kennedy," *Los Angeles Times*, August 7, 1921.

39. "Says Kennedy Given Beating: Mrs. Obenchain Reveals Other Love Affair of Broke; Thinks Death Can Be Traced through Unnamed Rival; Declares Burch Only College Chum; 'Never a Suitor,'" *Los Angeles Times*, August 8, 1921.

40. "Hunt Kennedy Death Gun; Mystery Auto Is Found," *Los Angeles Times*, August 9, 1921.

41. "Hunt Kennedy Death Gun."

42. "Grand Jury to Dig into Kennedy Murder Case," *Los Angeles Times*, August 10, 1921.

43. "Mrs. Obenchain Is Championed: Mother Assails Father of Victim in Murder; Says His Bitterness Will Play Part in Case; Tells of Younger Kennedy's Romance with Woman," *Los Angeles Times*, August 10, 1921.

44. "Love Tragedy Letters Read: Missive from Mrs. Obenchain to Kennedy Wrathful; Broke Upbraided as Trifler with Woman's Heart; Better Opposition of Slain Man's Family Shown," *Los Angeles Times*, August 10, 1921.

45. "'She's One Woman for Me': Obenchain Says He Will Aid Ex-wife in Murder Case, but Must Remain in Chicago," *Los Angeles Times*, August 10, 1921.

46. "Mrs. Obenchain and Burch Are Indicted in Kennedy Murder Case," *Los Angeles Times*, August 12, 1921.

47. "Sentiment Versus Sense," *Los Angeles Times*, August 18, 1921.

48. Barker-Benfield, *Horrors of the Half-Known Life*, 49.

49. Ahmad, *Opium Debate*, 78.

50. "Husband's Aid Sermon Topic: Is Obenchain Justified, Asks Ministerial Union Head; Not Unless Wife Repents of Past Life, He Decides; Kennedy Case Discussed in Last Night's Sermon," *Los Angeles Times*, August 22, 1921.

51. "'Mystic Love' Death Motive? Occult Influence Figures in Kennedy Case," *Los Angeles Times*, August 23, 1921.

52. "'Mystic Love.'"

53. "Mrs. Burch Gets Divorce: Wins Suit against Husband Accused in Kennedy Murder Case," *Los Angeles Times*, September 1, 1921.

54. "Kennedy Death Defense Split," *Los Angeles Times*, September 9, 1921.

55. "To Appeal No Bail Decision: Mrs. Obenchain's Lawyer Will File Writ in High Court; Lack of Transcript Called Prejudicial to Woman; Judge Reeve Hold Cannot Go Beyond Indictment," *Los Angeles Times*, September 17, 1921.

56. "See New Turn to Burch Case," *Los Angeles Times*, September 19, 1921.

57. "Seeks Women Jurors," *Los Angeles Times*, October 17, 1921.

58. "Woolwine Hurls Charges: Here Is District Attorney's Statement Made in Court Assailing Chicago Attorney," *Los Angeles Times*, October 25, 1921.

59. "History's Famous Charmers Outdone by Madalynne," *Los Angeles Times*, October 30, 1921.

60. Harry Carr, "Burch Suddenly Old Man: Wilts Under Shock of Insanity Plea, but Regains His Composure; Madalynne Study in Contrasts," *Los Angeles Times*, November 2, 1921.

61. Carr, "Burch Suddenly Old Man."

62. Barker-Benfield, *Horrors of the Half-Known Life*, 198.

63. "Woolwine Ouster Asked; Bar Rules for Erbstein," *Los Angeles Times*, November 2, 1921.

64. "Decides Burch Is Sane: Los Angeles Judge Rejects Plea for Slayer of J. Belton Kennedy," *New York Times*, November 8, 1921. The trial was covered in New York and Chicago.

65. "Obenchains Licensed to Wed; Plan Held Up: Burch, Down on His Knees, Pleads with Madalynne as Former Husband Looks On," *Los Angeles Times*, November 15, 1921.

66. "'Death Vigil' of Burch and Madalynne Told: State Witnesses Related Asserted Watch over Kennedy from Hotel before Murder," *Los Angeles Times*, December 2, 1921.

67. "Madalynne's Hot Love Notes Jar Obenchain: Ex-husband Groans as Letters of Woman to Kennedy Reveal Heart Won by Broker," *Los Angeles Times*, December 7, 1921.

68. "Elder Burch Threatens Newspaper Reporter," *Los Angeles Times*, December 16, 1921.

69. "Insanity Battle Opens in Kennedy Death Case: Burch's Past Revealed as Women Deny He Carried Gun; New Defense Surprise Today," *Los Angeles Times*, December 22, 1921.

70. "Father Fights for Burch," *Los Angeles Times*, December 28, 1921.

71. "The Lancer," *Los Angeles Times*, January 1, 1922.

72. "Madalynne Wrecker of Three Men, Keyes Says," *Los Angeles Times*, January 10, 1922.

73. "Woman Is Assailed in Burch Mistrial; Prosecutor Says Mrs. De Mott, a Juror, Deliberately Blocked the Ends of Justice," *New York Times*, January 17, 1922.

74. "Exhibitors to Consider Film Ban: Theatre Owners Will Discuss Picture Which Features Obenchain," *Los Angeles Times*, February 17, 1922.

75. "Theater Owners to Bar 'Notorieties,'" *Los Angeles Times*, February 18, 1922.

76. "The Lancer," *Los Angeles Times*, March 12, 1922.

77. "Nine Jurors Believe Madalynne Is Guilty," *Los Angeles Times*, March 18, 1922.

78. "Madalynne Is Court Victor," *Los Angeles Times*, June 20, 1922.

79. "Jail Visitors Allowed If All Goes Smoothly," *Los Angeles Times*, July 13, 1922.

80. "Clara Pal of Madalynne: Women Accused of Murder Form Intimate Friendship in Jail, Says Girl Prisoner," *Los Angeles Times*, July 19, 1922.

81. "Fists Fly for Madalynne: Dark-Hued Inmates Battle When 'White Gals' Slur Jail Beauty for Smuggling in Sweets," *Los Angeles Times*, August 9, 1922.

82. "Madalynne Is Given Freedom; Burch in Custody Pending Mind Examination," *Los Angeles Times*, December 5, 1922.

83. "Burch Gains Freedom after His Four Trials; All Juries Disagree on Charge That He and Mrs. Obenchain Slew Kennedy," *New York Times*, December 10, 1922.

84. Alma Whitaker, "The Last Word: Blood," *Los Angeles Times*, May 1, 1923.

85. "Back to Prison on March Bent," *Los Angeles Times*, June 13, 1924.

86. "Elder Kennedy Attacks Burch," *Los Angeles Times*, February 2, 1927.

87. "Burch's Will Gives Estate to Mrs. Obenchain," *Los Angeles Times*, August 1, 1944.

88. "Fiction Outdone Again," *Los Angeles Times*, April 10, 1930.

89. Parish, *For the People*, 54.

90. Parish, *For the People*, 41–42.

91. Parish, *For the People*, 54; Giesler as told to Martin, *Jerry Giesler Story*, 58–63.

92. Wolf and Mader, *Fallen Angels*, 51–57.

93. "Mourns Murdered Man: Intimate of Slain Clothing Man-

ufacturer Puts Blame for His Friend's Death upon Burglars," *Los Angeles Times*, August 24, 1922.

94. "Police Obtain Murder Clue," *Los Angeles Times*, August 24, 1922.

95. "Trap Set for Man's Killers," *Los Angeles Times*, August 25, 1922.

96. "No Enemy Slew Oesterreich: Spite Theory Abandoned in Murder Cause," *Los Angeles Times*, August 30, 1922.

97. "Hold Widow in Murder," *Los Angeles Times*, July 13, 1923.

98. "Widow of Oesterreich Is Arraigned as Slayer," *Los Angeles Times*, July 14, 1923; "Find New Murder Evidence," *Los Angeles Times*, July 15, 1923; "Oesterreich Net Tightens," *Los Angeles Times*, July 17, 1923; "Decorator Is Quizzed in Slaying," *Los Angeles Times*, July 16, 1923; "Take Widow to Murder Scene," *Los Angeles Times*, July 18, 1923.

99. "Assail Widow's Defense; State Attempts to Show Oesterreich Was Alone with Wife at Time of Slaying," *Los Angeles Times*, July 27, 1923.

100. "Jail Threat for Witness: Two Testify Widow Had Them Dispose of Pistols," *Los Angeles Times*, July 28, 1923.

101. "Depicts Mrs. Oesterreich: Rich and Dangerous Age but She Fails to Attract Attention as Murder Suspect," *Los Angeles Times*, August 1, 1923.

102. "Depicts Mrs. Oesterreich."

103. "Depicts Mrs. Oesterreich."

104. "Mrs. Oesterreich Freed," *Los Angeles Times*, January 16, 1925.

105. Giesler as told to Martin, *Jerry Giesler Story*, 51–52.

106. "Secret Room May Solve Famous Murder Puzzle," *Los Angeles Times*, April 8, 1930.

107. "Klein [Walter Klein was an alias of Otto Sanhuber] Confesses Murder of Oesterreich in 1922," *Los Angeles Times*, April 9, 1930; "'Attic Slayer' Tells Motive," *Los Angeles Times*, April 10, 1930.

108. "Jury Will Sift 'Attic' Slaying," *Los Angeles Times*, April 11, 1930.

109. "Woman Denies Attic Murder," *Los Angeles Times*, April 22, 1930.

110. "Oesterreich's Widow Bonded," *Los Angeles Times*, June 2, 1930; "Trip of Widow East Resumes," *Los Angeles Times*, June 4, 1930; "Murder Trial Slated Today," *Los Angeles Times*, June 10, 1930.

111. "Attic-Murder Shots Related," *Los Angeles Times*, June 14, 1930.

112. "'Ghost' Guides Jury to Attics," *Los Angeles Times*, June 17, 1930; "Trial Marked by Sensations," *Los Angeles Times*, June 17, 1930; "Story of Attic Ghost Halted," *Los Angeles Times*, June 19, 1930; "Former Words Face Sanhuber," *Los Angeles Times*, June 21, 1930.

113. "Sanhuber Denies Slaying," *Los Angeles Times*, June 26, 1930; "'Ghost of Garrets' Unshaken in Denial of Oesterreich Murder," *Los Angeles Times*, June 27, 1930; "Attic Man Clings to His Revised Story of Oesterreich Slaying in Cross-Examination," *Los Angeles Times*, June 28, 1930.

114. "'Bat Man' Case to Jury Today," *Los Angeles Times*, July 1, 1930; "Manslaughter Verdict Voted," *Los Angeles Times*, July 2, 1930; "Sanhuber Fate Decided Today," *Los Angeles Times*, July 3, 1930.

115. "'Garret Ghost' Out of Shadow: Sanhuber Liberated under Statute of Limitations; Defense Motion for Arrest of Judgment Granted," *Los Angeles Times*, July 12, 1930.

116. "Oesterreich Case in Snag," *Los Angeles Times*, August 1, 1930; "'Threat' Witness Sought: State Renews Efforts to Obtain Testimony of Milwaukee Woman in Oesterreich Murder Case," *Los Angeles Times*, August 3, 1930.

117. "Jury Battle Develops as Oesterreich Murder Trial Opens," *Los Angeles Times*, August 5, 1930; "Murder Jury Uncompleted: Questioning Continues in Oesterreich Case; Several Women Excused

for Death Opposition," *Los Angeles Times*, August 6, 1930; "Sexes Equal in Jury Chosen for Oesterreich Murder Trial," *Los Angeles Times*, August 7, 1930.

118. *Los Angeles Times*, August 8, 9, 11, 12, 13, 14, 15, 1930.

119. *Los Angeles Times*, August 19, 20, 21, 1930.

120. "Attic Murder Jury Divided," *Los Angeles Times*, August 24, 1930; "Attic Murder Jury Still Out," *Los Angeles Times*, August 25, 1930; "Attic Murder Jury Dismissed," *Los Angeles Times*, August 26, 1930.

121. "'Attic Murder' Case Dropped," *Los Angeles Times*, December 9, 1930.

122. Holmlund, "Decade of Deadly Dolls."

123. This was the combination of the provocation doctrine and self-defense tied to the reasonable-man concept. See Lee, *Murder and the Reasonable Man*.

124. *Melvin v. Reid*, 297 P. 91 (Cal. Dist. Ct. App. 1931); "Sues Mrs. Wallace Reid," *New York Times*, June 9, 1928; "Film Suit Asks Damages," *Los Angeles Times*, June 9, 1928; "Woman's Past Her Own: Appellate Court Gives Gabrielle Melvin Judgment against Mrs. Wallace Reid, et al. for Film," *Los Angeles Times*, March 3, 1931. Also see Friedman, "The One-Way Mirror," 319, 332–33; Friedman, *Private Lives*, 149–50.

125. Staiger, *Bad Women*, 165.

Chapter Four. The Haves and the Have Nots

1. Starr, *Endangered Dreams*.

2. Read, *New Avengers*, 76.

3. Read, *New Avengers*, 76.

4. Read, *New Avengers*, 83.

5. Staiger, *Bad Women*, 150–51.

6. Hughes-Warrington, *History Goes to the Movies*, 38–71.

7. Staiger, *Perverse Spectators*, 81.

8. See Barker-Benfield, *Horrors of the Half-Known Life*, 84–85, on nineteenth-century male concerns.

9. "Ghost Haunts Hanging Scene," *Los Angeles Times*, February 22, 1930.

10. "Woman Hunted in Murder," *Los Angeles Times*, January 12, 1930.

11. "Murder Case Arrest Nears," *Los Angeles Times*, January 14, 1930.

12. "Woman to Face Jury as Poisoner," *Los Angeles Times*, February 7, 1930.

13. "Harman Charge Dropped," *Los Angeles Times*, June 30, 1930.

14. "Woman to Face Murder Charge," *Los Angeles Times*, February 14, 1931.

15. "Murder of Son Laid to Mother," *Los Angeles Times*, November 21, 1930.

16. "Murder of Son."

17. "Death Suspect to Face Court," *Los Angeles Times*, December 22, 1930.

18. "Mother Faces Murder Trial," *Los Angeles Times*, March 2, 1931.

19. "Jury Acquits Mrs. Tarlazzi," *Los Angeles Times*, March 7, 1931.

20. "Brutal Murder Third Slaying in County in Space of Three Days," *Merced Sun-Star*, October 16, 1934; "Barber Is Slain En Route to Modesto," *Modesto Bee*, October 16, 1934.

21. "Story of Bandit Slaying Doubted in Merced Probe: Mrs. Talkington Grilled by [District Attorney Stephen P.] Galvin; No Blame Placed at Inquest," *Merced Sun-Star*, October 17, 1934.

22. "Widow Repeats Story of Mate's Gangster Death," *Sacramento Bee*, October 17, 1934.

23. "Former Sutteran Is Quizzed about Husband's Death: Merced County Officers Doubt Woman's Story of Road Killing," *Sacramento Bee*, October 17, 1934.

24. "Mrs. Talkington Resists Grilling Despite Gun Ruse," *Merced Sun-Star*, October 18, 1934; "Murder Charge Is Discussed in Talkington Case," *Modesto Bee*, October 18, 1934.

25. "Mrs. Talkington Confesses She Is Husband Slayer," *Sacramento Bee*, October 20, 1934; "Talkington Widow Admits She Killed Mate with Pistol," *Modesto Bee*, October 19, 1934; "Barber's Widow Cracks, Tells of Slaying Husband," *Merced Sun-Star*, October 19, 1934; "Body of Slain Man Is to Be Exhumed," *Modesto Bee*, October 20, 1934.

26. "Slayer's First Mate's Death under Probe," *San Francisco Chronicle*, October 21, 1934; "Death Tale Confession Announced," *Los Angeles Times*, October 20, 1934; this is an Associated Press wire story.

27. "Circumstantial Case Built against Widow in Talkington Death," *Merced Sun-Star*, October 22, 1934; "Officers Think Man Purchased Talkington Gun," *Modesto Bee*, October 22, 1934.

28. "Death of Girl in 1925 Checked in Talkington Case," *Merced Sun-Star*, October 23, 1934.

29. "Mrs. Talkington to Face Murder Hearing Tuesday," *Merced Sun-Star*, October 24, 1934.

30. "Tests Made of Death Evidence," *Merced Sun-Star*, October 25, 1934; "Sale of Murder Gun Traced, New Version Claimed," *Merced Sun-Star*, October 27, 1934.

31. "DeMoss Enters Insanity Plea," *Merced Sun-Star*, October 30, 1934.

32. "Widow Indicted by Grand Jury in Highway Murder," *Merced Sun-Star*, November 3, 1934.

33. "Widow to Face Trial Dec. 18," *Merced Sun-Star*, November 5, 1934.

34. "Galvin to Ask Woman's Death," *Merced Sun-Star*, December 15, 1934.

35. "Mrs. Talkington Goes to Trial in Battle for Life," *Merced Sun-Star*, December 17, 1934; "Seven Men and Five Women Seated on Jury," *Merced Sun-Star*, December 19, 1934.

36. "Jury of 7 Men And 5 Women Selected to Decide Widow's Fate: Courtroom Dispute Breaks Out Immediately over Admission of Testimony on Her Two Children Who Are Dead," *Merced Sun-Star*, December 19, 1934.

37. "Self Defense Version of Talkington Death Attacked by Chemist," *Merced Sun-Star*, December 20, 1934; "Bullet Angle Is Feature in Merced Trial," *Sacramento Bee*, December 21, 1934.

38. "State Rests Case as Surprise Witness Is Called at Trial Here," *Merced Sun-Star*, December 21, 1934; "Witnesses in Merced Trial Favor Defense," *Sacramento Bee*, December 23, 1934.

39. "Talkington Shot in Auto Quarrel; Threat Related," *Merced Sun-Star*, December 24, 1934; "Defendant Is Witness in the Merced Trial," *Sacramento Bee*, December 26, 1934.

40. "Two Defense Letters Prove Boomerang at Talkington Hearing," *Merced Sun-Star*, December 27, 1934.

41. "Death Demanded: Talkington Case to Go to Jury by Nightfall Today," *Merced Sun-Star*, December 28, 1934.

42. "Merced Trial Nears End as Counsel Argue," *Sacramento Bee*, December 31, 1934.

43. "Defense Flays Court After Guilty Verdict Is Returned By Jury," *Merced Sun-Star*, January 2, 1935.

44. "Widow Ready to Go to Prison for Slaying Husband," *Merced Sun-Star*, January 3, 1935; "Sentencing of Widow Delayed," *Merced Sun-Star*, January 4, 1935; "Widow's Counsel Asks New Trial in Murder Case," *Merced Sun-Star*, January 5, 1935; "Widow to Hear Fate Saturday," *Merced Sun-Star*, January 10, 1935; "Convicted Widow Refused Retrial of Death Charge," *Merced Sun-Star*, January 12, 1935; "Mrs. Talkington Taken to Prison on Life Sentence," *Merced Sun-Star*, January 14, 1935.

45. "What Judges May Not Say," *Los Angeles Times*, August 5, 1935; "Death Case Appeal Won," *Los Angeles Times*, June 27, 1935.

46. "Widow of Slain Man Marries," *Los Angeles Times*, August 6, 1936.

47. "Woman's Career Traced by County Authorities," *Los Angeles Times*, March 27, 1934.

48. "Death Case Widow Mum: Slain Film Man's Mate Found; Mrs. Nellie Madison, Booked on Suspicion of Murder, Balks Police

Queries; Officers Discover Her at Ranch House near Lebec; Victim Shot-Riddled," *Los Angeles Times*, March 27, 1934.

49. Cairns, "'Enigma Woman' Nellie Madison." For a complete and insightful analysis of the case, see Cairns, *Enigma Woman*.

50. "Widow Veils Death Tale: Defense Perfect, Says Counsel," *Los Angeles Times*, March 28, 1934.

51. "Murder Charge against Mrs. Madison Due Today: Former Mate of Widow Pledges Support to Her; Autopsy Shows Shot Fired near Victim's Head," *Los Angeles Times*, March 29, 1934.

52. "Widow to Keep Defense Hidden: No Contention Planned at Mrs. Madison's Hearing; Death Case Counsel Tells Program for Secrecy; Accused Woman's Brother to Return for Trial," *Los Angeles Times*, April 8, 1934.

53. "Widow Will Face Trial; Mrs. Madison Bound Over," *Los Angeles Times*, April 13, 1934.

54. "State to Exhibit Shot-torn Bed Today in Trial of Madison Widow, Accused of Murder: Jury Query Stirs Move; Counsel Hint at Self-Defense," *Los Angeles Times*, June 7, 1934.

55. "Strange Events on Night of Madison Killing Told," *Los Angeles Times*, June 9, 1934.

56. "Judge Called as Witness in Madison Murder Trial: Jurist Overrules Objection to Own Testimony and Estimates Time between Shots as Told by Another," *Los Angeles Times*, June 13, 1934.

57. "Doubt Cast on Identity; Testimony Hints Madison Alive," *Los Angeles Times*, June 14, 1934.

58. "Mrs. Madison on Stand Denies Killing Husband," *Los Angeles Times*, June 15, 1934.

59. "New Move in Death Trial: Widow Faces Gun Charge; Mrs. Madison Testifies She Did Not Chase and Fire at Ex-husband," *Los Angeles Times*, June 19, 1934.

60. "Death Plea Hits Widow: Mrs. Madison's Hanging Asked; Closing Arguments Begun in Murder Case with End Possibly Tomorrow," *Los Angeles Times*, June 20, 1934.

61. "Madison Trial May End Today: Murder Case Likely to Go

to Jury This Afternoon; Prosecutor Likens Stoical Widow to Lady Macbeth; Defense Stresses Lack of Powder Odor Evidence," *Los Angeles Times*, June 21, 1934.

62. The sentencing produced widespread page 1 coverage in the local press. See *Los Angeles Times*, July 6, 1934; *Los Angeles Evening Herald and Express*, July 5, 1934; *Los Angeles Evening Post-Record*, July 5, 1934; *Los Angeles Examiner*, July 6, 1934.

63. *People v. Nellie May Madison*, 3 Cal. 2d 668 (1935).

64. "Mrs. Madison Admits Killing Her Husband: Iron Woman Confesses; Slaying Told by Mrs. Madison; Prisoner Facing Gallows Asserts She Shot Mate in Self-Defense," *Los Angeles Times*, June 21, 1935.

65. Cairns, "'Enigma Woman' Nellie Madison," 24.

66. "Mrs. Madison to File Plea for Retrial: Move Due Today on Confession; Doomed Woman's Story of Knife-Throwing Scouted; Insanity Claim Seen," *Los Angeles Times*, June 22, 1935. In this story Joseph Ryan denied Nellie's version regarding the trial strategy and washed his hands of her as a client. William J. Brown "still retain[ed] high respect for her," insisting, "As a lawyer I am doing everything in my power to assist her." Nellie drew a two-column picture from the newspaper's file.

67. "'Mercy Lie' in Madison Case Told," *Los Angeles Times*, September 5, 1935.

68. "O'Brien's Kindly Lie," *Los Angeles Times*, September 6, 1935.

69. "Saved from the Noose, She Wants to Repay; Mrs. Madison Seeking to Be Nurse in Prison," *Los Angeles Times*, September 18, 1935.

70. "Getting Away with Murder," *Los Angeles Times*, September 18, 1935.

71. Cairns, "'Enigma Woman' Nellie Madison," 25.

72. "Invalid Held in Mate's Death," *Los Angeles Times*, May 29, 1939.

73. "Trial Urged for Widow," *Los Angeles Times*, June 3, 1939.

74. "Widow Facing Shooting Trial," *Los Angeles Times*, June 13, 1939.

75. "Sanity Test Ordered for Slayer Suspect," *Los Angeles Times*, June 29, 1939. The story was on page 11, column 2, next to ads for gloves and silverware.

76. "Insanity Pleaded by Slayer Suspect," *Los Angeles Times*, July 6, 1939.

77. "Husband Slayer Ruled Insane," *Los Angeles Times*, August 8, 1939.

78. "Widow to Face Trial in Slaying," *Los Angeles Times*, November 29, 1939.

79. "Mrs. Mallette Back for Trial," *Los Angeles Times*, December 2, 1939.

80. "Trial Ordered for Mrs. Mallette," *Los Angeles Times*, December 7, 1939.

81. "Woman Relates Mate Slaying," *Los Angeles Times*, January 10, 1940.

82. "Insanity Plea Again Invoked as Woman Convicted in Killing," *Los Angeles Times*, January 12, 1940.

83. "Wife Found Sane After Jury Convicts Her of Slaying," *Los Angeles Times*, January 13, 1940.

84. "Wife Gets Life in Mate Slaying," *Los Angeles Times*, January 17, 1940.

85. *People v. Beatrice Mallette*, 39 Cal. App. 2nd 294 (1940).

86. "Mrs. Mallette Wins Acquittal," *Los Angeles Times*, August 30, 1940.

87. "Sanity Affirmed in Slaying Case," *Los Angeles Times*, December 7, 1940.

Chapter Five. War Women of the 1940s

1. See May, *Homeward Bound*.

2. Vev, *Transforming the Screen*, 218–49.

3. "Daughter Trailed in Canyon after Slaying of Mother," *Los Angeles Times*, January 29, 1940.

4. "Woman Who Confessed Killing Own Daughter Pictured at Inquest," *Los Angeles Times*, February 24, 1940.

5. "Chloe Davis Released in Mass Murder; Father Regains Child, but She Will Remain Ward of Juvenile Court," *Los Angeles Times*, April 25, 1940.

6. "Suspected Robber Gang and Woman Chief Are Arrested," *Sacramento Bee*, April 15, 1940.

7. "Group Discussed Way of Killing 'Pa'; At Picnic Youth Marked for Death 'Talked About Murder Too Much,'" *Sacramento Bee*, April 16, 1940.

8. "River Yields Murder Gang Victim's Body; Gunmen Eliminate Young Member for Talking Too Much," *Sacramento Bee*, April 16, 1940.

9. "River Yields Murder Gang Victim's Body."

10. "Indictments Are Sought: Four of Five Members of Group Face Action in Slaying of Youth; Grand Jury to Meet; Special Session of Investigating Body Is Planned for Next Tuesday," *Sacramento Bee*, April 17, 1940.

11. "Gunmen Joke as They Lead Police to Death Scene; Youthful Pair Describe How They Did Away with Member of Gang," *Sacramento Bee*, April 17, 1940; "Robbery-Gang Killing Explained," *Los Angeles Times*, April 17, 1940.

12. "Two Cities Will Seek to Indict Murder Group," *Sacramento Bee*, April 18, 1940.

13. "Autopsy Reveals Murder Gang's Victim Drowned," *Sacramento Bee*, April 19, 1940.

14. "Jury Selection Begins in Trial of Murder Gang," *Sacramento Bee*, May 20, 1940.

15. "Jury Is Selected to Try Members of Murder Ring," *Sacramento Bee*, May 21, 1940.

16. "Murder Defense and State Clash on Confessions; Duchess Case Attorneys Fight to Block Introduction of Statement," *Sacramento Bee*, May 22, 1940.

17. "Confessions Are Read in Spinelli Murder Hearing; The

Duchess' Face Pales as Statements Are Introduced," *Sacramento Bee*, May 23, 1940.

18. "Woman Swears Death Gang Was Led by Youth," *Sacramento Bee*, May 24, 1940.

19. "'Killer' Gives Testimony against Duchess; Albert Ives Swears Mrs. Spinelli and Simeone Ordered Sherrad's Death," *Sacramento Bee*, May 27, 1940.

20. "Jury Agrees on Death Mob Guilt, Splits on Penalty," *Sacramento Bee*, May 29, 1940.

21. "Death Decreed for Woman Chief of Robber Gang," *Los Angeles Times*, May 29, 1940. Spinelli's appeal lost in the California Supreme Court. *People v. Ives, et al.*, 17 Cal. 2d. 459 (1941).

22. "Mrs. Spinelli Gets Reprieve," *Los Angeles Times*, June 20, 1941.

23. "Olson Aide and Judge Irked over Reprieve of 'Duchess,'" *Los Angeles Times*, June 21, 1941.

24. "Olson Hears Spinelli Son; Boy Recounts Sordid Story of Life in Plea to Save 'The Duchess,'" *Los Angeles Times*, July 10, 1941.

25. "Spinelli Execution Stayed by Governor Second Time," *Los Angeles Times*, July 17, 1941.

26. "Olson Orders Re-examination of Duchess Spinelli's Sanity," *Los Angeles Times*, October 14, 1941; "Death Awaits Mrs. Spinelli," *Los Angeles Times*, November 20, 1941.

27. "'Duchess' Pronounces Curse on Eve of Her Execution," *Los Angeles Times*, November 21, 1941; "'Duchess' Goes to Doom Today," *Los Angeles Times*, November 21, 1941.

28. "'Duchess' Dies in Gas Chamber," *Los Angeles Times*, November 22, 1941; "Woman Executed in Gas Chamber," *New York Times*, November 22, 1941.

29. "Good Riddance," *Los Angeles Times*, November 22, 1941.

30. "Victims' Daughter, Fiancé Jailed in Boat Blast Inquiry," *Los Angeles Times*, March 20, 1947.

31. "Victims' Daughter."

32. "Victims' Daughter."

33. "Murder Complaints to Be Sought in Yacht Deaths," *Los Angeles Times*, March 22, 1947.

34. "Girl and Fiancé Embrace, Hear Charges of Murder," *Los Angeles Times*, March 23, 1947.

35. "Couple Indicted in Overell Deaths," *Los Angeles Times*, March 27, 1947.

36. Maury Godchaux, "Bloodstains on Clothing Linker to Gollum in Inquiry of Overell Yacht Explosion Deaths," *Los Angeles Times*, March 28, 1947.

37. Maury Godchaux, "Overell Girl's Attorney Discloses Plan for Double Plea to Charges," *Los Angeles Times*, March 29, 1947.

38. Maury Godchaux, "Row Halts Efforts to Quiz Two Overell Defendants," *Los Angeles Times*, April 1, 1947.

39. Maury Godchaux, "New Clues on Dynamite Found in Overell Deaths," *Los Angeles Times*, April 3, 1947.

40. Maury Godchaux, "Sales Slip for Dynamite Found in Gollum Camera," *Los Angeles Times*, April 4, 1947.

41. Maury Godchaux, "Family of Overell Girl Trying to Arrange Bail," *Los Angeles Times*, April 6, 1947.

42. Maury Godchaux, "Divers Send Up Sacks in Overell Death Clue Hunt," *Los Angeles Times*, April 11, 1947; "Overell Bodies Disinterred for Post Mortems," *Los Angeles Times*, April 24, 1947.

43. Maury Godchaux, "Overell Defense Declares New Autopsy 'Wins Case,'" *Los Angeles Times*, April 25, 1947.

44. Maury Godchaux, "One Trial Decreed in Overell Deaths," *Los Angeles Times*, April 29, 1947.

45. "Notes Tell Love of Accused Pair," *Los Angeles Times*, April 30, 1947.

46. Maury Godchaux, "Howser Suspects Theft of Overell Love Letters," *Los Angeles Times*, April 30, 1947.

47. Maury Godchaux, "Howser Takes Charge of Overell Prosecution," *Los Angeles Times*, April 5, 1947.

48. Maury Godchaux, "Lawyers Demand Inquiry into Overell-Gollum Letters," *Los Angeles Times*, May 1, 1947.

49. Maury Godchaux, "Story of Her Blossoming Young Love Confided to Diary by Beulah Overell," *Los Angeles Times*, May 3, 1947.

50. "Relatives Visit Defendants in Overell Case," *Los Angeles Times*, May 4, 1947; Maury Godchaux, "Calmness of Overell Girl Baffles Closest Relatives," *Los Angeles Times*, May 5, 1947.

51. "Radio Earphone Found at Home of Gollum Kin," *Los Angeles Times*, May 7, 1947.

52. "Gollum Reported in Cafe Prior to Night of Blast," *Los Angeles Times*, May 14, 1947.

53. Maury Godchaux, "Beirne Added to Overell Case Defense Force," *Los Angeles Times*, May 20, 1947.

54. Maury Godchaux, "State May Concentrate Its Fire on Beulah Overell," *Los Angeles Times*, May 24, 1947.

55. Maury Godchaux, "'Innocent,' Beulah Overell Protests on Eve of Trial," *Los Angeles Times*, May 25, 1947.

56. Maury Godchaux, "Overell Girl Jovial on Eve of Trial," *Los Angeles Times*, May 26, 1947.

57. Gene Sherman, "Curious Line Overell Girl's Path to Court; Murder Trial Setting Assumes Morbid Color," *Los Angeles Times*, May 27, 1947.

58. Maury Godchaux, "Overell Evidence to Be Moved in Armored Car," *Los Angeles Times*, June 1, 1947.

59. Gene Sherman, "Notoriety Fans Add Drab Drama to Overell Trial," *Los Angeles Times*, June 2, 1947.

60. Gene Sherman, "Defense Infers Howser Released Overell Letters," *Los Angeles Times*, June 18, 1947.

61. Gene Sherman, "Overell Murder Trial Jury Sworn In; Six Men and Six Women Accepted," *Los Angeles Times*, June 20, 1947.

62. Gene Sherman, "Overell Murder Proof Promised," *Los Angeles Times*, June 25, 1947.

63. Gene Sherman, "July Told Overells Died before Blast," *Los Angeles Times*, June 27, 1947.

64. Maury Godchaux, "Overell Girl's Diary Made Public as Defense Move," *Los Angeles Times*, June 27, 1947.

65. Gene Sherman, "Credibility of Medical Testimony Attacked by Overell Case Defense," *Los Angeles Times*, July 1, 1947. See also "Redlands Pathologist Testifies in Overell Case," *Los Angeles Times*, July 2, 1947; "Overell Wounds Stressed at Trial," *Los Angeles Times*, July 3, 1947; "Mrs. Overell Head Blow after Death Held Possible," *Los Angeles Times*, July 4, 1947.

66. Gene Sherman, "Blast Data Given at Overell Trial," *Los Angeles Times*, July 10, 1947; "Expert Says Timing Device Set Off Two Blasts aboard Overell Yacht," *Los Angeles Times*, July 11, 1947; "Overell Jury May Look at 150 Exhibits," *Los Angeles Times*, July 13, 1947; "Pipe to Be Introduced in Overell Death Trial," *Los Angeles Times*, July 14, 1947; "State Offers Alleged Overell Death Weapon," *Los Angeles Times*, July 15, 1947; "Conflicts Alleged in Overell Defense: Prosecution in Yacht Slaying Case Loses Point as 'Murder Weapon' Evidence Ruled Out," *Los Angeles Times*, July 16, 1947.

67. "Cast of Overell's Head to Be Offered as Murder Evidence," *Los Angeles Times*, July 21, 1947; "Jurors Shown Slides of Bloodstains Expert Links with Gollum's Clothes," *Los Angeles Times*, July 23, 1947; "Prosecution Loses Battle to Have Pipe Accepted as Overell Evidence," *Los Angeles Times*, July 24, 1947; "State Planning Dramatic Move in Overell Case," *Los Angeles Times*, July 26, 1947; "Overell Case to Feature Scientific Testimony," *Los Angeles Times*, July 27, 1947; "Clock, Screw and Skin Figure in Overell Case," *Los Angeles Times*, July 29, 1947; "Explosives Sales Told Overell Jury," *Los Angeles Times*, July 30, 1947; "Expert Testifies Gollum Signed Dynamite Receipt," *Los Angeles Times*, July 31, 1947; "Beulah's Attempt to Split Case from Gollum Fails: Girl Not Linked with Evidence Yet, Attorney States," *Los Angeles Times*, August 1, 1947.

68. "Defense to Call Its Own Experts at Overell Trial," *Los Angeles Times*, August 18, 1947; "Beulah's Lawyers Lose Plea to Strike Testimony," *Los Angeles Times*, August 20, 1947; "Prosecution May Reopen Its Case against Overell Girl and Gollum,"

Los Angeles Times, August 21, 1947; "Overell Trial Prosecution Reopening Still Uncertain," *Los Angeles Times*, August 22, 1947; "Overell Defense Maps Surprises," *Los Angeles Times*, August 23, 1947; "Fighting Defense Due for Beulah and Gollum," *Los Angeles Times*, August 24, 1947.

69. "State May Not Reopen Overell Prosecution," *Los Angeles Times*, August 25, 1947.

70. Gene Sherman, "Overell Defense Spring Surprise; Subpoenas State Atty. Gen. Howser," *Los Angeles Times*, August 26, 1947; "Overell Defense Subpoenas Dist. Atty. Davis as Witness," *Los Angeles Times*, August 30, 1947.

71. Gene Sherman, "Witness Says Overells Were Alive at Time of Explosion Aboard Yacht," *Los Angeles Times*, August 27, 1947; "Doctors Hit State Overell Testimony," *Los Angeles Times*, August 29, 1947

72. Gene Sherman, "Overell Defense Queries Howser," *Los Angeles Times*, September 3, 1947.

73. Gene Sherman, "Overell Yacht Blast Premature, Defense Explosives Expert Says: Witness Riddles Alarm Clock Theory; Bears Out View Yachtsman Was Alive," *Los Angeles Times*, September 4, 1947.

74. Gene Sherman, "Mechanic Who Visited Yacht Says Overell Was Irrational before Blast," *Los Angeles Times*, September 5, 1947.

75. Gene Sherman, "Overell Witness Calls Yacht Blast Premature: Explosives Expert Also Asserts Alarm Clock Could Not Have Set Off Dynamite Charge," *Los Angeles Times*, September 6, 1947.

76. Gene Sherman, "Beulah Overell Leaves Jail for Day to Assist in Inventory of Her Home: Heiress Taken to Flintridge Estate, but Bud Gollum Remains in His Cell," *Los Angeles Times*, September 10, 1947.

77. Gene Sherman, "Navy Man Backs Overell Defense," *Los Angeles Times*, September 11, 1947.

78. Gene Sherman, "Overell Girl Relates Her Own Story of Events Up to Parent's Death: Defense Attorney Questions Posed to Confident

Heiress but Saves Climax for Today," *Los Angeles Times*, September 16, 1947; "Beulah and Bud Testify They Bought Dynamite for Overell," *Los Angeles Times*, September 17, 1947; "Gollum Remains Cool and Unshaken in Denial of Slaying Overell Couple: Slashing Cross-Examination Ends; Defense May Close Its Case Today," *Los Angeles Times*, September 18, 1947.

79. "Judge Instructs Jurors on 14 Possible Verdicts," *Los Angeles Times*, October 4, 1947; Gene Sherman, "Jury Debates Fate of Bud and Beulah," *Los Angeles Times*, October 4, 1947; "Prosecutor Runs Emotional Gamut in Overell Case," *Los Angeles Times*, October 4, 1947.

80. Gene Sherman, "Beulah, Bud Acquitted; Crowd at Court Cheers," *Los Angeles Times*, October 6, 1947.

81. "Weary Jurors Give Way to Emotion; Tell of Five Ballots during Ordeal," *Los Angeles Times*, October 6, 1947.

82. "Record 133-Day Trial Cost County $17,400," *Los Angeles Times*, October 6, 1947.

83. Schmid, *Natural Born Celebrities*.

84. "Widow and Janitor to Face Inquest in 'Playboy' Killing," *Los Angeles Times*, October 28, 1948; "Two Beautiful Women Tell Stories in Playboy Killing," *Los Angeles Times*, October 31, 1948; "Ferreri's Threats to Wife Described: Attack with Poker before Slaying Told by Witness on Eve of Inquest," *Los Angeles Times*, November 1, 1948; "Two Star Witnesses Held in Playboy Ferreri Slaying," *Los Angeles Times*, November 2, 1948.

85. "Lodgers Told Truth, Says Mrs. Ferreri," *Los Angeles Times*, November 3, 1948.

86. "Cleaver Widow Asks to Visit Home," *Los Angeles Times*, November 6, 1948.

87. "Cousin Said to Admit Loading Gun Used in Killing of Ferreri: His Alleged Confession Changes Tangled Case," *Los Angeles Times*, November 16, 1948.

88. "Cousin Said to Admit."

89. "Joint Charge Hits Trio in Ferreri Case," *Los Angeles Times*, November 17, 1948.

90. "Ferreri Case Linked with Gang Hinted," *Los Angeles Times*, November 20, 1948.

91. "Vincent D'Angelo Mystery Deepens," *Los Angeles Times*, November 21, 1948.

92. "Missing Man in Ferreri Case Found," *Los Angeles Times*, November 22, 1948.

93. "Crime Link Sought in Fauci Inquiry," *Los Angeles Times*, November 23, 1948.

94. "Ferreri's Wounds Center of Inquiry," *Los Angeles Times*, November 24, 1948.

95. "Ferreri Cleaver Witness Heard," *Los Angeles Times*, November 25, 1948.

96. "Trial Set for Trio in Ferreri Killing: Judge Bars Pleas for Dismissal, Reduction to Manslaughter, Bail," *Los Angeles Times*, November 27, 1948.

97. "Trio Arraigned on Charles in Ferreri Slaying," *Los Angeles Times*, December 14, 1948.

98. "Counsel Shift Approved in Ferreri Case," *Los Angeles Times*, February 2, 1948.

99. "Adron Pleads Guilt in Ferreri Slaying," *Los Angeles Times*, February 9, 1949.

100. "Mrs. Ferreri Weeps during Jury Picking: Mother Breaks Down as Counsel Tells of Brutal Treatment Son Received," *Los Angeles Times*, February 10, 1948.

101. "Ferreri Widow Weeps in Court," *Los Angeles Times*, February 12, 1948.

102. "Jury Sworn In for Trial of Ferreri Murder Case," *Los Angeles Times*, February 12, 1949; the case was now on page 5. "Ferreri Testimony Begins Tomorrow," *Los Angeles Times*, February 13, 1949; the story moved back to page 18. "Betty Ferreri Finds Only Solace at Court with Father and Brother," *Los Angeles Times*, February 14, 1949.

103. "Ferreri Case Hints Self-Defense Plea," *Los Angeles Times*, February 15, 1949. The case was now back on page 2.

104. "Singer Admits Lie in Ferreri Trial," *Los Angeles Times*, February 16, 1949; story on page 2 with two photographs.

105. "Ferreri Widow Faints on Hearing Testimony," *Los Angeles Times*, February 17, 1949.

106. "Ferreri Defense Hit by Officer's Story," *Los Angeles Times*, February 18, 1949.

107. "Adron Testifies Ferreri Death Plotted Hour before Slaying," *Los Angeles Times*, February 22, 1949; story on page 2 with two pictures.

108. "Lawyer's Hand over Mouth Halts Ax Widow's Outcry," *Los Angeles Times*, February 25, 1949. This story was on page 4; the story cited in the next note was on page 2.

109. "Judge in Ferreri Trial to Be Called as Witness," *Los Angeles Times*, February 25, 1949.

110. "Ferreri Trial Sees Flaring of Tempers: Leavy, Hardy and Adron Engage in Lively Repartee at Session," *Los Angeles Times*, February 26, 1949.

111. "Mrs. Ferreri Gives Lurid Testimony," *Los Angeles Times*, March 1, 1949.

112. "Ax Widow Calls Husband Beast with 'Puppy Eyes,'" *Los Angeles Times*, March 2, 1949; story on page 2 with three pictures, including one with Jerry and two girl friends.

113. "Ferreri Declared Bully in Boyhood," *Los Angeles Times*, March 4, 1949.

114. "Ferreri's Complex Revealed at Trial," *Los Angeles Times*, March 5, 1949.

115. "Model Tells of Seeing Ferreri before Murder: Red-Haired Floy Smock Creates Sensation among Spectators of Trial of Widow," *Los Angeles Times*, March 8, 1949.

116. "Fauci Says Ferreri Ready to Kill Wife," *Los Angeles Times*, March 9, 1949.

117. "State Asks Life Sentences for Mrs. Ferreri and Fauci: Prosecutor Contends Ax Murder Was Deliberately Planned Affair," *Los Angeles Times*, March 17, 1949; "Ferreri Case May Be Given Jury

Today: Defense Completes Arguments for Widow and Cousin of Slain Man," *Los Angeles Times*, March 18, 1949; "Ferreri Fate Goes to Hands of Jury: Four Possible Verdicts Faced by Ax Widow and Fauci in Slaying," *Los Angeles Times*, March 19, 1949.

118. "Jury Agreement Bars Ballot Check," *Los Angeles Times*, March 20, 1949.

Chapter Six. Celebrity on Trial

1. Rhone Rosenbaum, "We the Jury Find We Can't Get Enough," *Los Angeles Times*, April 12, 2007.

2. Rosenbaum, "We the Jury."

3. Rosenbaum, "We the Jury."

4. Jacoby, *Age of American Unreason*, 179–80.

5. Jacoby, *Age of American Unreason*, 180.

6. Turner, *Lana*; Morella and Epstein, *Lana*; Crane with Jahr, *Detour*; Wayne, *Lana*.

7. "Suitor of Lana Turner Is Killed by Her Daughter, 14, with Knife," *New York Times*, April 6, 1958.

8. "Lana Turner Becomes Bride to Tobacco Heir in Elopement," *Los Angeles Times*, July 18, 1942.

9. "Lana Turner, Mother-to-Be, Wins Annulment of Marriage," *Los Angeles Times*, February 5, 1943.

10. Hedda Hopper, "Lana Turner Discloses Remarriage to Crane," *Los Angeles Times*, April 6, 1943.

11. "Actress Lana Turner Becomes Mother of Girl," *Los Angeles Times*, July 26, 1943.

12. Edwin Schallert, "Idol of Youth Puts Baby before Films: Lana Turner Regards Picture-Making as Job Second to Her Motherhood," *Los Angeles Times*, November 7, 1943.

13. "Lana Turner's Divorce Suit to Be Uncontested," *Los Angeles Times*, August 16, 1944.

14. "Child Acted Out of Fear, Says Giesler," *Los Angeles Times*, April 5, 1958.

15. Lascher, "An Interview with Phil Gibson," 8.

16. Ray Hebert, "Lana's Daughter Held for Slaying; Girl in Juvenile Hall to Await Hearing in Stompanato Stabbing," *Los Angeles Times*, April 6, 1958.

17. Hebert, "Lana's Daughter Held for Slaying."

18. "Stompanato Brother Here to Claim Body of 'Adonis,'" *Los Angeles Times*, April 6, 1958.

19. "Lana Turner's 'Love' for Slain Stompanato Revealed by Photo," *Los Angeles Times*, April 7, 1958.

20. "Cheryl Crane Detained; Daughter of Lana Turner to Get a Hearing April 24," *New York Times*, April 8, 1958.

21. "Cohen Discloses Lana Love Notes to Johnny," *Los Angeles Times*, April 9, 1958.

22. Crane with Jahr, *Detour*, 217.

23. See Lystra, *Searching the Heart*.

24. Lystra, *Searching the Heart*.

25. Jack Jones, "Lana Will Tell Today How Stompanato Died," *Los Angeles Times*, April 11, 1958.

26. "New Sides of Stompanato's Bizarre Life Come to Light," *Los Angeles Times*, April 11, 1958.

27. "Stompanato's Brother Presses for Lie Tests," *Los Angeles Times*, April 11, 1958.

28. "Complete Testimony of Inquest," *Los Angeles Times*, April 12, 1958.

29. "Complete Testimony of Inquest."

30. "Complete Testimony of Inquest."

31. "Complete Testimony of Inquest."

32. "Complete Testimony of Inquest."

33. "Lana Turner's Child Is Cleared at Inquest," *New York Times*, April 12, 1958.

34. Jack Jones, "Jury Clears Cheryl after Lana's Story," *Los Angeles Times*, April 12, 1958.

35. "Cheryl's Release Still Undecided; Belief Is That Girl Will Stay in Juvenile Hall Pending Hearing," *Los Angeles Times*, April 12, 1958.

36. "Crane Visits Cheryl; She's Homesick," *Los Angeles Times*, April 14, 1958.

37. "Lana and Mother Have Happy Visit with Cheryl," *Los Angeles Times*, April 20, 1958.

38. "Won't Try to Get Cheryl, Crane Says; Pledges to Support Lana in Seeking Release of Child," *Los Angeles Times*, April 21, 1958.

39. Jack Jones, "Stompanato's Bank Books, Jewelry Located by Police; Doctor's Wife Mystified by Check Account," *Los Angeles Times*, April 15, 1958.

40. "Widow Lent Stompanato $8150 to Buy Gift Shop," *Los Angeles Times*, April 16, 1958.

41. "Morals on Decline, Dr. Bonnell Asserts," *New York Times*, April 21, 1958.

42. Jacoby, *Age of American Unreason*, 243.

43. Jacoby, *Age of American Unreason*, 193.

44. Jack Jones, "Cheryl May Get Word of Fate Today," *Los Angeles Times*, April 24, 1958; "Judge Gives Daughter of Lana Turner to Grandmother Pending Final Ruling," *New York Times*, April 25, 1958.

45. "Cheryl, Free Again, Handed Summons for Damage Suit," *Los Angeles Times*, April 25, 1958; "Stompanato's Son to Seek $750,000 in Suit," *Los Angeles Times*, April 22, 1958; story on page 22.

46. Jack Jones, "Crane to Fight Lana to Get Full Custody over Cheryl," *Los Angeles Times*, April 30, 1958.

47. "Stompanato's Son to Seek $750,000."

487. "Lana, Cheryl to Testify in Slaying Suit," *Los Angeles Times*, May 17, 1958.

49. "Suit Voices Doubt on Who Killed Stompanato; Amended $750,000 Suit by Dead Man's Son Hints Lana Turner Did Stabbing," *Los Angeles Times*, May 29, 1958.

50. "Miss Crane Questioned," *New York Times*, June 24, 1958; Jack Jones, "Can't Remember Stabbing Stompanato, Cheryl Says; Girl Gives Her Deposition at Hearing on Suit," *Los Angeles Times*, June 24, 1958.

51. Jones, "Can't Remember Stabbing Stompanato."

52. "Walter Allen Named Judge in Glendale," *Los Angeles Times*, June 11, 1959.

53. "Cheryl Crane Ruling; Lana Turner's Daughter Will Remain with Grandmother," *New York Times*, September 26, 1958; "Grandmother to Keep Cheryl Crane's Custody," *Los Angeles Times*, December 12, 1958.

54. "Lana and Cheryl Take in Premiere," *Los Angeles Times*, February 20, 1959.

55. Jerry Giesler, "The Lana Turner Tragedy," *Saturday Evening Post*, December 5, 1959.

56. Turner, *Lana*, 198.

57. Turner, *Lana*, 204.

58. Turner, *Lana*, 205.

59. Turner, *Lana*, 221.

60. Turner, *Lana*, 222.

61. Turner, *Lana*, 227.

62. Turner, *Lana*, 228.

63. Turner, *Lana*, 229.

64. Turner, *Lana*, 232–33.

65. Turner, *Lana*, 240–41.

66. Turner, *Lana*, 241.

67. Turner, *Lana*, 243.

68. Turner, *Lana*, 244.

69. Turner, *Lana*, 244–45.

70. Turner, *Lana*, 249.

71. Turner, *Lana*, 249.

72. Turner, *Lana*, 251.

73. Turner, *Lana*, 254.

74. Wayne Lawson, "Screen Beauty Tells All," *New York Times*, September 5, 1982.

75. Crane with Jahr, *Detour*, 197.

76. Crane with Jahr, *Detour*, 199.

77. Crane with Jahr, *Detour*, 200.

78. Crane with Jahr, *Detour*, 206.

79. Crane with Jahr, *Detour*, 220.

80. Crane with Jahr, *Detour*, 221.

81. Crane with Jahr, *Detour*, 226.

82. Crane with Jahr, *Detour*, 239–40. See also "Crane Joins Lana to Fight Stompanato Suit," *Los Angeles Times*, May 23, 1958; "Stephen Crane Upheld in Stompanato Suit," *Los Angeles Times*, July 19, 1958; "Objections Overruled in Stompanato Death Suit," *Los Angeles Times*, August 2, 1958; "Stompanato 'Assets' Ordered Given to Son," *Los Angeles Times*, November 29, 1958.

83. Wayne, *Lana*, 130.

84. Sheila Paulos, "Review 9," *New York Times*, March 13, 1988.

85. Wayne, *Lana*, 120–29.

86. For an example of the same genre, see Olender, *For the Prosecution*. Giesler wrote the foreword, observing, "In Los Angeles County where I have practiced law for the past 40 years, the Bar has been slow in accepting women lawyers on an equal basis. It is but a little over 20 years since slim, twinkle-eyed Terrys T. Olender broke through the stone-wall barriers to become the first woman Deputy District Attorney to prosecute major felonies in our courtrooms" (vii–viii). On women in the criminal defense bar, see Rice, *Counsel for the Damned*.

87. Giesler as told to Martin, *Jerry Giesler Story*, 307.

88. Giesler as told to Martin, *Jerry Giesler Story*, 310.

89. See Lystra, *Searching the Heart*.

Conclusion

1. On law and culture, see McEvoy, "A New Realism for Legal Studies," 435.

2. Kern, *Cultural History of Causality*, 186.

3. See also Hamm, *Murder, Honor, and Law*, 204.

4. Hamm, *Murder, Honor, and Law*, 205. Hamm notes that the

unwritten law for men standing alone was insufficient for an acquittal if not tied to an insanity defense.

5. Friedman, "A Dead Language," 1535.

6. Barker-Benfield, *Horrors of the Half-Known Life*, 33.

7. Kern, *Cultural History of Causality*, 181.

8. Kern, *Cultural History of Causality*, 182.

9. Kern, *Cultural History of Causality*, 192.

10. Bakken, "Constitutional Convention Debates in the West"; Bakken, "California's Constitutional Conventions Create Our Courts"; Bakken, "Looking Back"; Bakken, "Limits of Patriarchy: Women's Rights," 703–16.

11. Jacoby, *Wild Justice*, 206.

12. For the context of film, see Staiger, *Bad Women*, 165.

13. See Ogden, *Great American Housewife*; Kessler-Harris, *Out to Work*; Scharf, *To Work and to Wed*; Wandersee, *Women's Work and Family Values*; Ware, *Holding Their Own*; Bergman, *We're in the Money*.

14. See Phillips, *Running with Bonnie and Clyde*; Milner, *Lives and Times*; Block, *Gangsters, Swindlers, Killers and Thieves*.

15. Lotchin, *Way We Really Were*.

16. Matthews, *"Just a Housewife"*; Hoff, *Unequal before the Law*; May, *Homeward Bound*.

17. Jacoby, *Wild Justice*, 206.

18. This development was part of a national trend. See Leibowitz, *Defender*. In 1928 he successfully defended three women accused of murder in New York (50–51). Joel Moldovsky was a criminal defense attorney in Philadelphia and devoted a chapter of his book to women clients; see Moldovsky and DeWolf, *Best Defense*, 178–87.

19. Staiger, *Bad Women*, 165–74. Staiger observes that the bad woman could morph into a "new woman" who followed her own intuitions, became intelligent, independent, mildly aggressive, and a moderate consumer. Sam Stoloff argues that a deeper social paranoid style was afoot in American popular culture that demonized lower-class people who found instant wealth in sports and cinema. Stoloff, "Fatty Arbuckle and the Black Sox."

20. Jacoby, *Wild Justice*, 214–15.

21. This tactic continued well into the late twentieth century and beyond. Susan Jacoby uses the 1977 case of Francine Hughes, a Michigan mother of four; though she was divorced from her husband, he continued to live with her and abuse her regularly. Hughes poured gasoline around her ex-husband's bed and burned him to death in his alcoholic stupor. A Lansing, Michigan, jury acquitted her on the basis of temporary insanity. After a short period of psychiatric testing, she was declared sane and released from custody. Jacoby, *Wild Justice*, 211–13.

22. Cairns, *Enigma Woman*, 171.

23. Cairns, *Enigma Woman*, 172.

24. Cairns, *Enigma Woman*, 174–75.

25. Cairns, *Enigma Woman*, 182.

26. Cairns, *Enigma Woman*, 222–38.

27. Weinberg and Weinberg, *Clarence Darrow*, 401.

28. Weinberg and Weinberg, *Clarence Darrow*, 403.

29. Weinberg and Weinberg, *Clarence Darrow*, 406.

30. Weinberg and Weinberg, *Clarence Darrow*, 406.

31. Weinberg and Weinberg, *Clarence Darrow*, 407.

32. Weinberg and Weinberg, *Clarence Darrow*, 408.

33. Weinberg and Weinberg, *Clarence Darrow*, 408.

34. "Noose Opens for Stackpole," *Los Angeles Times*, August 17, 1906.

35. Maury Godchaux, "Story of Her Blossoming Young Love Confided to Dairy by Beulah Overell," *Los Angeles Times*, May 3, 1947.

36. Kashner and MacNair, *Bad & the Beautiful*, 257.

37. Kashner and MacNair, *Bad & the Beautiful*, 258.

38. Kashner and MacNair, *Bad & the Beautiful*, 259.

39. Kashner and MacNair, *Bad & the Beautiful*, 264,

40. Kashner and MacNair, *Bad & the Beautiful*, 266.

41. See Dary, *Red Blood & Black Ink*, 243–54, on women editors. Genre rather than gender in the nineteenth-century practice

prevailed. By the mid-twentieth century women reporters had far more critical pens.

42. Hartog and Nelson, *Law as Culture*.

43. Richard Wightman Fox, cited earlier for his book on the Beecher-Tilton affair, also wrote "Intimacy on Trial." See also Clifford, *Predicament of Culture*; Binder and Weisberg, "Cultural Criticism of Law"; Lazarus-Black and Hirsch, *Contested States*.

44. A. J. Gross, *Double Character*, 49.

45. See Smith-Rosenberg, *Disorderly Conduct*; Cairns, *Enigma Woman*.

BIBLIOGRAPHY

Adler, Jeffrey S. *First in Violence, Deepest in Dirt: Homicide in Chicago, 1875–1920.* Cambridge MA: Harvard University Press, 2006.

Ahmad, Diana L. *The Opium Debate and Chinese Exclusion Laws in the Nineteenth-Century American West.* Reno: University of Nevada Press, 2007.

Alexander, Elizabeth Urban. *Notorious Woman: The Celebrated Case of Myra Clark Gaines.* Baton Rouge: Louisiana State University Press, 2001.

Ayers, Edward L. *Vengeance and Justice: Crime and Punishment in the 19th-Century American South.* New York: Oxford University Press, 1984.

Babcock, Barbara Allen. "Women Defenders in the West." *Nevada Law Journal* 1, no. 1 (Spring 2001): 1–18.

Bakken, Gordon Morris. "California's Constitutional Conventions Create Our Courts." *1994 California Supreme Court Historical Society Yearbook* 1 (1994): 33–54.

———. "Constitutional Convention Debates in the West: Racism, Religion, and Gender." *Western Legal History* 3 (Summer/Fall 1990): 213–44.

———. "The Limits of Patriarchy: The 'Unwritten Law' in California Legal History." In *California History: A Topical Approach*, edited by Gordon Morris Bakken, 84–107. Wheeling IL: Harlan Davidson, 2003.

———. "The Limits of Patriarchy: Women's Rights and the 'Unwritten Law' in the West." *Historian* 60, no. 4 (Summer 1998): 703–16.

———. "Looking Back: The Court and California Law in 1897." *1996–97 California Supreme Court Historical Society Yearbook* (1998): 121–45.

———. *Practicing Law in Frontier California*. Lincoln: University of Nebraska Press, 1991.

Baldasty, Gerald J. *The Commercialization of News in the Nineteenth Century*. Madison: University of Wisconsin Press, 1992.

Barker-Benfield, G. J. *The Horrors of the Half-Known Life: Male Attitudes toward Women and Sexuality in Nineteenth-Century America*. New York: Routledge, 2000.

Bergman, Andrew. *We're in the Money: Depression America and Its Films*. Chicago: Ivan R. Dee, 1993.

Bilder, Tiffany Johnson. "Bodies of Evidence: Inquest Photography in the Trial of Lizzie Borden." In *Murder on Trial, 1620–2002*, edited by Robert Asher, Lawrence B. Goodheart, and Alan Rogers, 235–69. Albany: State University of New York Press, 2005.

Binder, Guyora, and Robert Weisberg. "Cultural Criticism of Law." *Stanford Law Review* 49 (1997): 1149–1220.

Birch, Helen, ed. *Moving Targets: Women, Murder and Representation*. Berkeley: University of California Press, 1994.

Black, Roy. *Black's Law*. New York: Touchstone Book, 1999.

Block, Lawrence. *Gangsters, Swindlers, Killers and Thieves*. New York: Oxford University Press, 2004.

Bloom, Barbara Ellen. "Triple Jeopardy: Race, Class and Gender as Factors in Women's Imprisonment." PhD diss., University of California, Riverside, 1996.

Bottles, Scott L. *Los Angeles and the Automobile: The Making of the Modern City*. Berkeley: University of California Press, 1987.

Brodsky, Annette M., ed. *The Female Offender*. Beverly Hills CA: Sage, 1975.

Butler, Anne M. *Gendered Justice in the American West: Women Prisoners in Men's Penitentiaries*. Urbana: University of Illinois Press, 1997.

———. "In Penitentiaries." In *Encyclopedia of Women of the American*

West, edited by Gordon Morris Bakken and Brenda Farrington, 145–52. Thousand Oaks CA: Sage, 2003.

Cairns, Kathleen A. *The Enigma Woman: The Death Sentence of Nellie May Madison*. Lincoln: University of Nebraska Press, 2007.

———. "'Enigma Woman' Nellie Madison: Femme Fatales & Noir Fiction." *Montana: The Magazine of Western History* 54, no. 1 (Spring 2004): 14–25.

Carranco, Lynwood, and Estle Beard. *Genocide and Vendetta: The Round Valley Wars of Northern California*. Norman: University of Oklahoma Press, 1981.

Chafe, William H. *The American Woman: Her Changing Social, Economic, and Political Role, 1920–1970*. New York: Oxford University Press, 1972.

Chandler, Robert J. "In the Van: Spiritualists as Catalysts for the California Women's Suffrage Movement." *California History* 73 (Fall 1994): 188–201, 252–54.

Clifford, James. *The Predicament of Culture: Twentieth-Century Ethnography, Literature and Art*. Cambridge MA: Harvard University Press, 1988.

Cohen, Patricia Cline. *The Murder of Helen Jewett: The Life and Death of a Prostitute in Nineteenth-Century New York*. New York: Alfred A. Knopf, 1998.

Cole, Holly. "Women & the Death Penalty in Victorian San Francisco." *Newsletter of the California Supreme Court Historical Society* (Spring/Summer 2006): 5–7, 17–20.

Cooper, Donald G. "California Suffrage Campaign of 1896: Its Origin, Strategies, Defeat." *Southern California Quarterly* 71 (Winter 1989): 311–25.

Cott, Nancy F. *No Small Courage: A History of Women in the United States*. New York: Oxford University Press, 2000.

Crane, Cheryl, with Cliff Jahr. *Detour: A Hollywood Story*. New York: Arbor House, 1988.

Dary, David. *Red Blood & Black Ink: Journalism in the Old West*. New York: Alfred A. Knopf, 1998.

Deverell, William. *Whitewashed Adobe: The Rise of Los Angeles and the Remaking of Its Mexican Past*. Berkeley: University of California Press, 2004.

Dicken-Garcia, Hazel. *Journalism Standards in Nineteenth-Century America*. Madison: University of Wisconsin Press, 1989.

Dodge, L. Mara. *"Whores and Thieves of the Worst Kind": A Study of Women, Crime, and Prisons, 1835–2000*. DeKalb: Northern Illinois University Press, 2002.

Edgerton, Keith. *Montana Justice: Power, Punishment and the Penitentiary*. Seattle: University of Washington Press, 2004.

Edwards, Laura. "Law, Domestic Violence, and the Limits of Patriarchal Authority in the Antebellum South." *Journal of Southern History* 65 (November 1999): 733–70.

Escobar, Edward J. *Race, Police, and the Making of a Political Identity: Mexican Americans and the Los Angeles Police Department, 1900–1945*. Berkeley: University of California Press, 1999.

Ethington, Philip J. *The Public City: The Political Construction of Urban Life in San Francisco, 1850–1900*. New York: Cambridge University Press, 1994.

Feinman, Clarice. *Women in the Criminal Justice System*. New York: Praeger, 1986.

Ferguson, Robert A. *The Trial in America Life*. Chicago: University of Chicago Press, 2007.

Fischer, Christine. "Women in California in the Early 1850s." *Southern California Quarterly* 64 (1978): 231–53.

Fox, Richard Wightman. "Intimacy on Trial: Cultural Meanings of the Beecher-Tilton Affair." In *The Power of Culture: Critical Essays in American History*, edited by Richard Wightman Fox and T. J. Jackson Lears, 103–34. Chicago: University of Chicago Press, 1993.

———. *Trials of Intimacy: Love and Loss in the Beecher-Tilton Scandal*. Chicago: University of Chicago Press, 1999.

Freedman, Estelle B. "Sexuality in Nineteenth-Century America: Behavior, Ideology, and Politics." *Reviews in American History* 10, no. 4 (December 1982): 196–215.

Friedman, Lawrence M. *American Law in the 20th Century.* New Haven CT: Yale University Press, 2002.

———. "A Dead Language: Divorce Law and Practice Before No-Fault." *Virginia Law Review* 86 (2000): 1497–1537.

———. "The One-Way Mirror: Law, Privacy, and the Media." *Washington University Law Quarterly* 82, no. 2 (2004): 319–43.

———. *Private Lives: Families, Individuals, and the Law.* Cambridge MA: Harvard University Press, 2004.

Friedman, Lawrence M., and Robert V. Percival. *The Roots of Justice: Crime and Punishment in Alameda County, California, 1870–1910.* Chapel Hill: University of North Carolina Press, 1981.

Garnett, Nicole Stelle. "Ordering (and Order in) the City." *Stanford Law Review* 57 (October 2004): 1–58.

Giesler, Jerry, as told to Pete Martin. *The Jerry Giesler Story.* New York: Simon and Schuster, 1960.

Ginzberg, Lori D. "Pernicious Heresies: Female Citizenship and Sexual Respectability in the Nineteenth Century." In *Women in the Unstable State in Nineteenth-Century America*, edited by Alison M. Parket and Stephanie Cole, 139–62. College Station: Texas A&M University Press, 2000.

Gora, JoAnn Gennaro. *The New Female Criminal: Empirical Reality or Social Myth?* New York: Praeger, 1982.

Gray, Paul Bryan. *Forster v. Pico: The Struggle for the Rancho Santa Margarita.* Spokane: Arthur H. Clark, 1997.

Green, Harvey. *The Light of the Home: An Intimate View of the Lives of Women in Victorian America.* New York: Pantheon Books, 1983.

Griswold, Robert. "The Evolution of the Doctrine of Mental Cruelty in Victorian American Divorce, 1790–1900." *Journal of Social History* 20 (Fall 1986): 127–48.

Gross, Ariela J. *Double Character: Slavery and Mastery in the*

Antebellum Southern Courtroom. Princeton NJ: Princeton University Press, 2000.

Gross, Kali N. *Colored Amazons: Crime, Violence, and Black Women in the City of Brotherly Love, 1880–1910.* Durham NC: Duke University Press, 2006.

Grossberg, Michael. *A Judgment for Solomon: The D'Hauteville Case and Legal Experience in Antebellum America.* New York: Cambridge University Press, 1996.

Gullett, Gayle. *Becoming Citizens: The Emergence and Development of the California Women's Movement, 1880–1911.* Urbana: University of Illinois Press, 2000.

Halaas, David Fridtjof. *Boom Town Newspapers: Journalism on the Rocky Mountain Mining Frontier, 1859–1881.* Albuquerque: University of New Mexico Press, 1981.

Halttunen, Karen. *Murder Most Foul: The Killer and the American Gothic Imagination.* Cambridge MA: Harvard University Press, 1998.

Hamm, Richard H. *Murder, Honor, and Law: 4 Virginia Homicides from Reconstruction to the Great Depression.* Charlottesville: University of Virginia Press, 2003.

Hartman, Mary. *Victorian Murderesses.* New York: Schocken Books, 1977.

Hartog, Hendrik. "Lawyering, Husbands' Rights." *Journal of American History* 84 (June 1997): 67–96.

———. *Man and Wife in America: A History.* Cambridge MA: Harvard University Press, 2000.

Hartog, Hendrik, and William E. Nelson, eds. *Law as Culture and Culture as Law.* Madison WI: Madison House, 2000.

Hatfield, Sharon. *Never Seen the Moon: The Trials of Edith Maxwell.* Urbana: University of Illinois Press, 2005.

Henson, Allen Lumpkin. *Confessions of a Criminal Lawyer.* New York: Vantage Press, 1959.

Hoff, Joan. *Law, Gender and Injustice: A Legal History of U.S. Women.* New York: New York University Press, 1991.

———. *Unequal before the Law: A Legal History of U.S. Women.* New York: New York University Press, 1991.

Hoffer, Peter C. "Disorder and Deference: The Paradoxes of Criminal Justice in the Colonial Tidewater." In *Ambivalent Legacy: A Legal History of the South,* edited by David J. Bodenhamer and James W. Ely Jr., 187–201. Jackson: University Press of Mississippi, 1984.

Holmlund, Christine. "A Decade of Deadly Dolls: Hollywood and the Woman Killer." In *Moving Targets: Women, Murder and Representation,* edited by Helen Birch, 127–34. Berkeley: University of California Press, 1994.

Huckabee, Harlow M. *Lawyers, Psychiatrists and Criminal Law.* Springfield IL: Charles C. Thomas, 1980.

Hughes-Warrington, Marnie. *History Goes to the Movies: Studying History On Film.* New York: Routledge, 2007.

Igler, David. *Industrial Cowboys: Miller & Lux and the Transformation of the Far West, 1850–1920.* Berkeley: University of California Press, 2001.

Ireland, Robert. "Frenzied and Fallen Females: Women and Sexual Dishonor in the Nineteenth-Century United States." *Journal of Women's History* 3 (Winter 1992): 95–117.

———. "Insanity and the Unwritten Law." *American Journal of Legal History* 32 (April 1988): 157–72.

———. "The Libertine Must Die: Sexual Dishonor and the Unwritten Law in the Nineteenth-Century United States." *Journal of Social History* 23 (Fall 1989): 27–44.

Jackson, Joseph Henry, ed. *San Francisco Murders.* New York: Duell, Sloan and Pearce, 1947.

Jacoby, Susan. *The Age of American Unreason.* New York: Pantheon Books, 2008.

———. *Wild Justice: The Evolution of Revenge.* New York: Harper and Row, 1983.

Jones, Richard Glyn, ed. *The Mammoth Book of Women Who Kill.* New York: Carroll and Graff, 2002.

Kashner, Sam, and Jennifer MacNair. *The Bad & the Beautiful: Hollywood in the Fifties*. New York: W. W. Norton, 2002.

Kern, Stephen. *A Cultural History of Causality: Science, Murder Novels, and Systems of Thought*. Princeton NJ: Princeton University Press, 2004.

Kessler-Harris, Alice. *Out to Work: A History of Wage-Earning Women in the United States*. New York: Oxford University Press, 1982.

Lamott, Kenneth. *Who Killed Mr. Crittenden?* New York: David McKay, 1963.

Lander, Louise. *Images of Bleeding: Menstruation as Ideology*. New York: Orlando Press, 1988.

Lascher, Edward L. "An Interview with Phil Gibson." *Newsletter of the California Supreme Court Historical Society* (Autumn/Winter 2006): 2–21.

Lazarus-Black, Mindie, and Susan F. Hirsch, eds. *Contested States: Law, Hegemony and Resistance*. New York: Routledge, 1994.

Lee, Cynthia K. *Murder and the Reasonable Man: Passion and Fear in the Criminal Courtroom*. New York: New York University Press, 2007.

Leibowitz, Robert. *The Defender: The Life and Career of Samuel S. Leibowitz, 1893–1933*. Englewood Cliffs NJ: Prentice-Hall, 1981.

Loerzel, Robert. *Alchemy of Bones: Chicago's Luetgert Murder Case of 1897*. Urbana: University of Illinois Press, 2003.

Lotchin, Roger W. *Fortress California, 1910–1961: From Warfare to Welfare*. New York: Oxford University Press, 1992.

———, ed. *The Way We Really Were: The Golden State in the Second Great War*. Urbana: University of Illinois Press, 2000.

Lothrop, Gloria Ricci. "Rancheras and the Land: Women and Property Rights in Hispanic California." *Southern California Quarterly* 76 (Spring 1994): 59–84.

Lystra, Karen. *Searching the Heart: Women, Men, and Romantic*

Love in Nineteenth-Century America. New York: Oxford University Press, 1989.

Matsuda, Mari J. "The West and the Legal Status of Women: Explanations of Frontier Feminism." *Journal of the West* 24 (January 1985): 47–56.

Matthews, Glenna. *"Just a Housewife": The Rise and Fall of Domesticity in America*. New York: Oxford University Press, 1987.

May, Elaine Tyler. *Homeward Bound: American Families in the Cold War Era*. New York: Basic Books, 1988.

McEvoy, Arthur F. "A New Realism for Legal Studies." *Wisconsin Law Review*, no. 2 (2005): 433–54.

McKanna, Clare V., Jr. *Homicide, Race, and Justice in the American West, 1880–1920*. Tucson: University of Arizona Press, 2001.

———. *Race and Homicide in Nineteenth-Century California*. Reno: University of Nevada Press, 2002.

———. *The Trial of "Indian Joe": Race and Justice in the Nineteenth-Century West*. Lincoln: University of Nebraska Press, 2003.

———. *White Justice in Arizona: Apache Murder Trials in the Nineteenth Century*. Lubbock: Texas Tech University Press, 2005.

McKee, Irving. "The Shooting of Charles de Young." *Pacific Historical Review* 16, no. 3 (August 1947): 271–84.

Melnick, Ralph. *Justice Betrayed: A Double Killing in Old Santa Fe*. Albuquerque: University of New Mexico Press, 2002.

Merry, Sally Engle. *Getting Justice and Getting Even: Legal Consciousness among Working-Class Americans*. Chicago: University of Chicago Press, 1990.

Milner, E. R. *The Lives and Times of Bonnie and Clyde*. Carbondale: Southern Illinois University Press, 1996.

Mitchell, Corey. *Dead and Buried: A Shocking Account of Rape, Torture, and Murder on the California Coast*. New York: Kingston, 2003.

Moldovsky, Joel, and Rose DeWolf. *The Best Defense*. New York: Macmillan, 1975.

Monkkonen, Eric H. *Murder in New York City*. Berkeley: University of California Press, 2001.

Morella, Joe, and Edward Z. Epstein. *Lana: The Public and Private Lives of Miss Turner*. New York: Dell, 1971.

Morrison, Scott. *Murder in the Garden: Famous Crimes of Early Fresno County*. Fresno: Craven Street Books, 2006.

Mullen, Kevin J. *Dangerous Strangers: Minority Newcomers and Criminal Violence in the Urban West, 1850–2000*. New York: Palgrave Macmillan, 2005.

Nerone, John. "The Mythology of the Penny Press." *Critical Studies in Mass Communications* 4, no. 4 (December 1987): 376–404.

Odem, Mary. *Delinquent Daughters: Protecting and Policing Adolescent Female Sexuality in the United States, 1885–1920*. Chapel Hill: University of North Carolina Press, 1995.

Ogden, Annegret S. *The Great American Housewife: From Helpmate to Wage Earner, 1776–1986*. Westport CT: Greenwood Press, 1986.

Olender, Terrys T. *For the Prosecution: Miss Deputy D.A.* Philadelphia: Chilton, 1961.

Pagán, Eduardo Obregón. *Murder at the Sleepy Lagoon: Zoot Suits, Race, and Riot in Wartime L.A.* Chapel Hill: University of North Carolina Press, 2003.

Parish, Michael. *For the People: Inside the Los Angeles County District Attorney's Office, 1850–2000*. Santa Monica CA: Angel City Press, 2001.

Pascoe, Peggy. *Relations of Rescue: The Search for Female Moral Authority in the American West, 1874–1939*. New York: Oxford University Press, 1990.

Pasley, Fred D. *Not Guilty! The Story of Samuel S. Leibowitz*. New York: Putnam's, 1933.

Peiss, Kathy. "Making Faces: The Cosmetics Industry and the Cultural Consumption of Gender, 1890–1930." *Genders*, no. 7 (March 1990): 143–69.

Peterson del Mar, David. *Beaten Down: A History of Interpersonal*

Violence in the West. Seattle: University of Washington Press, 2002.

———. *What Trouble I Have Seen: A History of Violence against Wives.* Cambridge MA: Harvard University Press, 1996.

Phillips, John Neal. *Running with Bonnie and Clyde: The Ten Fast Years of Ralph Fults.* Norman: University of Oklahoma Press, 1996.

Prior, Pauline M. "Murder and Madness: Gender and the Insanity Defense in Nineteenth-Century Ireland." *New Hibernia Review* 9 (Winter 2005): 19–36.

Read, Jacinda. *The New Avengers: Feminism, Femininity and the Rape-Revenge Cycle.* Manchester: Manchester Press, 2000.

Reid, John Phillip. *Chief Justice: The Judicial World of Charles Doe.* Cambridge MA: Harvard University Press, 1967.

Rice, Cy. *Counsel for the Damned: Gladys Towles Root.* New York: Citadel Press, 1964.

Robertson, Stephen. "Seduction, Sexual Violence, and Marriage in New York City, 1886–1955." *Law and History Review* 24, no. 2 (Summer 2006): 331–73.

Rosen, Deborah A. *Courts and Commerce: Gender, Law, and the Market Economy in Colonial New York.* Columbus: Ohio State University Press, 1997.

Rowbothan, Judith, and Kim Stevenson, eds. *Criminal Conversations: Victorian Crimes, Social Panic, and Moral Outrage.* Columbus: Ohio State University Press, 2005.

Rugh, Susan Sessions. "Civilizing the Countryside: Class, Gender, and Crime in Nineteenth-Century Rural Illinois." *Agricultural History* 76 (Winter 2002): 58–81.

Scharf, Lois. *To Work and to Wed: Female Employment, Feminism, and the Great Depression.* Westport CT: Greenwood Press, 1980.

Schiesl, Martin, and Mark M. Dodge. *City of Promise: Race and Historical Change in Los Angeles.* Claremont CA: Regina Books, 2006.

Schiller, Daniel. *Objectivity and the News: The Public and the Rise of Commercial Journalism*. Philadelphia: University of Pennsylvania Press, 1981.

Schmid, David. *Natural Born Celebrities: Serial Killers in American Culture*. Chicago: University of Chicago Press, 2005.

Schofield, Ann. "Lizzie Borden Took an Axe: History, Feminism and American Culture." *American Studies* 34, no. 1 (1993): 91–103.

Schudson, Michael. *Origins of the Ideal of Objectivity in the Professions: Studies in the History of American Journalism and American Law, 1830–1940*. New York: Garland, 1990.

Schuele, Donna C. "Community Property Law and the Politics of Married Women's Rights in Nineteenth Century California." *Western Legal History* 7 (Summer/Fall 1994): 245–81.

Shaw, S. Bradley. "New England Gothic by the Light of Common Day: Lizzie Borden and Mary E. Wilkins Freeman's 'The Long Arm.'" *New England Quarterly* 70, no. 2 (1997): 211–36.

Sitton, Tom, and William Deverell, eds. *Metropolis in the Making: Los Angles in the 1920s*. Berkeley: University of California Press, 2001.

Smart, Carol. *Crime and Criminology: A Feminist Critique*. Boston: Routledge, 1976.

Smith-Rosenberg, Carol. *Disorderly Conduct: Visions of Gender in Victorian America*. New York: Alfred A. Knopf, 1985.

———. *Intimate Conduct: Visions of Gender in Victorian America*. New York: Alfred A. Knopf, 1985.

Spiegel, Allen D. "Temporary Insanity and Premenstrual Syndrome: Medical Testimony in an 1865 Murder Trial." *New York State Journal of Medicine* 88 (September 1988): 482–92.

Staiger, Janet. *Bad Women: Regulating Sexuality in Early American Cinema*. Minneapolis: University of Minnesota Press, 1995.

———. *Perverse Spectators: The Practices of Film Reception*. New York: New York University Press, 2000.

Starr, Kevin. *Endangered Dreams: The Great Depression in California*. New York: Oxford University Press, 1996.

———. *Inventing the Dream: California through the Progressive Era*. New York: Oxford University Press, 1985.

———. *Material Dreams: Southern California through the 1920s*. New York: Oxford University Press, 1990.

Stoloff, Sam. "Fatty Arbuckle and the Black Sox: The Paranoid Style of American Popular Culture, 1919–1922." In *Headline Hollywood: A Century of Film Scandal*, edited by Adrienne L. McLean and David A. Cook, 52–82. New Brunswick NJ: Rutgers University Press, 2001.

Streib, Victor L. *The Fairer Death: Executing Women in Ohio*. Athens: Ohio University Press, 2006.

Trope, Michael Lance. *Once upon a Time in Los Angeles: The Trials of Earl Rogers*. Spokane: Arthur H. Clark, 2001.

Turner, Lana. *Lana: The Lady, the Legend, the Truth*. New York: E. P. Dutton, 1982.

Vev, Peter. *Transforming the Screen, 1950–1959*. Berkeley: University of California Press, 2003.

Waldrep, Christopher. "Law and Society: Structuring Legal Revolutions, 1870–1920." *Journal of the Gilded Age and Progressive Era* 5, no. 4 (October 2006). http://www.historycooperative.org/cgi-bin/justtop.cgi?act=justtop&url=http://www.historycooperative.org/journals/jga/5.4/waldrep.html (accessed September 26, 2008).

———. *Roots of Disorder: Race and Criminal Justice in the American South, 1817–1870*. Champaign: University of Illinois Press, 1998.

Wandersee, Winifred D. *Women's Work and Family Values, 1920–1940*. Cambridge MA: Harvard University Press, 1981.

Ware, Susan. *Holding Their Own: American Women in the 1930s*. Boston: Twayne, 1982.

Wayne, Jane Ellen. *Lana: The Life and Loves of Lana Turner*. New York: St. Martin's Press, 1996.

Webster, Scott W. "'Lizzie Borden Took an Axe': Representations of American Culture in Plays about the Lizzie Borden Murders and Trial." *Proteus* 13, no. 1 (1996): 39–47.

Weinberg, Arthur, and Lila Weinberg, eds. *Clarence Darrow: Verdicts Out of Court*. Chicago: Quadrangle Books, 1963.

Welter, Barbara. "The Cult of True Womanhood: 1820–1860." In *Our American Sisters: Women in American Life and Thought*, edited by Jean E. Friedman and William G. Shade, 96–123. Boston: Allyn and Bacon, 1973.

Wishman, Seymour. *Confessions of a Criminal Lawyer*. New York: Palisades Press, 1981.

Wolf, Marvin J., and Katherine Mader. *Fallen Angels: Chronicle of L.A. Crime and Mystery*. New York: Facts on File, 1986.

———. "Louise Peete: Dr. Jekyll and Mrs. Hyde." In *Women Who Kill*, edited by Richard Glyn Jones, 343–55. New York: Carroll and Graf, 2002.

INDEX

Abarta, Lastencia, 13, 39–47, 54, 186, 189, 192
accidental killings, 13, 41, 46, 84, 117, 118
Actual Detective Stories, 9
Adams, Elmer, 123, 124
Adron, Allan, 153, 155, 157–58
Aggler, William Tell, 87
Allen, Walter, 176
Anderson, Clinton H., 163, 164, 168, 171, 179–80, 184–85
appeals, grounds for, 4–5, 34–35, 36, 61–62, 122, 129–30, 134
Appel, Horace H., 67, 71
Appel, Joe, 86
attorneys, 5, 7, 9–10, 51, 82, 160, 190, 191, 198
Atubil, Joseph F., 28
audience response, 46, 51, 87, 95–96, 149, 151, 168
Aument, Oda, 87
automobiles and sexual revolution, 82

Babcock, Otis D., 140, 142
Bailey, Marie Leonard, 13, 83–86, 110, 189
Baker, L. R., 155
Bara, Theda, 82
Barker, Bonnie, 189
Barrow, Clyde, 189
Barton, W. W., 47
"Bat Man" case, 108
battered woman defense, 4, 13,

121–22, 160, 177–78, 187–88, 193–94, 202n75
Baum, Peter, 159
Beecher, Henry Ward, 7
Beerstecher, Charles J., 38
Beirne, William B., 147–48
Bertoglio, Stella, 171
Biescar, Ruth, 117, 118
bigamy in Gibbons case, 73, 74
Birth of a Nation, 113
Biscailuz, Eugene W., 90–91, 101
Blackmail, 114
blackout by defendant, 13, 22, 50, 42, 85, 117–18
Blanda, Erma, 13, 192
Blau, Louis C., 167–68
The Bliss of Mrs. Bottom, 109
Blodgett, Julian, 167
Bonnell, John Sutherland, 174, 185
Borden, Lizzie, 11–12
Borders, Ray, 168, 171
Bosley, Henry, 86
Bove, Abele, 56–57
Bow, Clara, 82
Bradley, Belle, 126
Bradley, Joseph H., 43–44, 125–26
Brieglab, Gustav A., 94–95
Bright, William, 123
Broken Blossoms, 113–14
Brown, Charles, 128
Brown, William J., 123, 124, 128
Burch, Allie Gale, 96
Burch, Arthur C., 89, 90, 91, 94, 98–99, 100–101, 104–5, 111

In the Law in the American West series:

Christian G. Fritz
Federal Justice in California:
The Court of Ogden Hoffman, 1851–1891

Gordon Morris Bakken
Practicing Law in Frontier California

Shelley Bookspan
A Germ of Goodness:
The California State Prison System, 1851–1944

M. Catherine Miller
Flooding the Courtrooms:
Law and Water in the Far West

Blue Clark
Lone Wolf v. Hitchcock:
Treaty Rights and Indian Law
at the End of the Nineteenth Century

Mark R. Scherer
Imperfect Victories: The Legal Tenacity
of the Omaha Tribe, 1945–1995

Clare V. McKanna Jr.
The Trial of "Indian Joe":
Race and Justice
in the Nineteenth-Century West

James W. Hewitt
Slipping Backward: A History of
the Nebraska Supreme Court

Mark R. Ellis
Law and Order in Buffalo Bill's Country:
Legal Culture and Community on
the Great Plains, 1867–1910

John R. Wunder and Joann M. Ross
The Nebraska-Kansas Act of 1854

Gordon Morris Bakken and Brenda Farrington
*Women Who Kill Men: California Courts,
Gender, and the Press*

To order or obtain more information on these or
other University of Nebraska Press titles,
visit www.nebraskapress.unl.edu.